ISBN 978-1-330-64977-0
PIBN 10087394

1 MONTH OF
FREE
READING

at
www.ForgottenBooks.com

By purchasing this book you are eligible for one month membership to ForgottenBooks.com, giving you unlimited access to our entire collection of over 700,000 titles via our web site and mobile apps.

To claim your free month visit:

www.forgottenbooks.com/free87394

English
Français
Deutsche
Italiano
Español
Português

www.forgottenbooks.com

Mythology Photography **Fiction**
Fishing Christianity **Art** Cooking
Essays Buddhism Freemasonry
Medicine **Biology** Music **Ancient
Egypt** Evolution Carpentry Physics
Dance Geology **Mathematics** Fitness
Shakespeare **Folklore** Yoga Marketing
Confidence Immortality Biographies
Poetry **Psychology** Witchcraft
Electronics Chemistry History **Law**
Accounting **Philosophy** Anthropology
Alchemy Drama Quantum Mechanics
Atheism Sexual Health **Ancient History**
Entrepreneurship Languages Sport
Paleontology Needlework Islam
Metaphysics Investment Archaeology
Parenting Statistics Criminology
Motivational

SECOND EDITION

AMERICANISM

By

GEORGE B. LOCKWOOD

\

With a compilation, by John T. Adams,
of utterances on Americanism by great
Americans.

1921
THE NATIONAL REPUBLICAN PUBLISHING CO.,
WASHINGTON

35628

INTRODUCTORY

The American people have short memories. That is but natural. As history is measured, the United States is but a youth, and, as befits normal youth, self-sufficient and self-reliant, we have had little desire or need of dwelling upon the past. America has been busy dreaming and thinking of the morrow, with its duties and opportunities; busy exploring, settling and developing a new continent; engaged in construction rather than reflection. As a nation, we inherited no racial enmities or religious antipathies which made it natural to keep alive the memories of ancient grudges or necessary to appeal to ancient fears in order to maintain our national unity.

This was not accidental. "There is a divinity which shapes our ends" and orders the destinies of nations. It was necessary to our establishment as a nation, to the sturdy, healthy development of our institutions that we be free to work out our problems, uninfluenced and unfettered by old prejudices and hatreds. It was necessary that our fathers wholly discard the institutions and practices of European civilization, grown fetid, and model America's government along wholly new and wholesome lines.

But now we are developed physically; our frontiers have disappeared. We are developed politically; our institutions are firmly established and our national unity and solidarity tested and proved. America has reached maturity, that age when its future is served better by caution than by daring, and the interests and welfare of its citizens promoted better by holding fast to that which has proved true and enduring than by experimenting with the novel and untried.

At various times in our national life there have come testing periods when, standing at the parting of the ways, the people have been called upon to choose between keeping the faith of their fathers and following the call of visionaries and the self-seeking ambitious. America has just passed through such a crisis. It was providential that, in the hour when our citizenry were called upon to make their decision, there were stalwart Americans who fearlessly and vigorously protested against repudiating the advice of those who laid the foundations of this republic, who were neither ashamed nor afraid to preach America and Americanism first, who admonished their countrymen that American institutions could be preserved only by undivided devotion to the same principles which operated to upbuild these institutions and give them strength and stability, and who, above all else, warned Americans against accepting the doctrine of internationalism in the delusion they were acquiring a "new freedom." To substitute internationalism for American nationalism and style it "new freedom" is on all fours with substituting free love for the institution of marriage and calling it the new virtue. There are some things which are fundamental and absolute.

One of the most potent and most fearless advocates of straight old-fashioned Americanism during that crisis was The National Republican, under the editorship of George B. Lockwood. Upon the establishment of its offices in Washington in January, 1918,— a year before President Wilson's political tour of Europe,—The National Republican announced as one of its editorial policies,— "championship of stalwart, unwavering Americanism * * * which is for America first, last and all the time and would sacrifice no just interest of the American people in behalf of any visionary scheme of internationalism." On February 9, 1918, there appeared the editorial, "What Are We Fighting for in This War?"; June 22, 1918, the editorial, "The Aims of America Need No Explanation or Apology"; July 13, 1918, the editorial, "Settling the Terms of Peace"; all of which are reprinted in this volume. These, and many other contemporary editorials and articles in its news columns, entitle The National Republican to the credit and honor of being the first publication of national circulation, and, perhaps, the first publication of any kind in the United States to take an unequivocal stand against the menace of internationalism and to maintain that stand aggressively until the fight for Americanism was won.

For a time, The National Republican stood alone, among publications of national circulation, in its position. To The National Republican, with a circulation rising from 200,000 when the fight against the Wilson internationalism began to nearly a half million before the close of the campaign of 1920, more than to any other one influence, must be given the credit of arousing the masses and leaders of its party to a realization of the calamitous possibilities of such a program. In view of what transpired during the life of the Congress elected in November, 1918, the value of this, its service in behalf of Americanism, was incalculable.

So far as the records show, The National Republican's editorial of July 13, 1918, "Settling the Terms of Peace," was the first utterance by a publication of national circulation in opposition to the United States' being a party to any treaty of peace which would include certain terms and conditions which President Wilson had indicated (even at that early date, four months before the signing of the armistice) he would write into the treaty. This is the first utterance of record that there must be "certain reservations," safeguarding American rights and privileges, to such a treaty as the White House had intimated and for which it was, even before the war was won or certain of being won, conducting a nation-wide propaganda. This also was the first utterance to point out the sinister possibilities of the Wilsonian doctrine of "self-determination," the inclusion of which in the treaty has kept all Europe and the Near East in an armed ferment and bloody wars ever since the treaty was signed.

Attention should be called to another editorial, "A Decisive Peace—That Is What Is Desired by the American People," published a month before the armistice. It was a protest against the "peace by negotiation" obsession of the Wilson administration, a demand that Germany be decisively defeated on the field of battle, her armies crushed, her surrender unconditional and our soldiers brought home "rather than to start a long peace parley with the world still an armed camp." Public opinion of America and Europe today is agreed that the crowning mistake of the allies was failure to do that very thing.

These editorials are cited because they were pioneers. They were written before public opinion was crystallized, at a time when nearly every public expression was antagonistic to or skeptical of the sentiments they expressed. Moreover, they were written and published at a time when every fair means and foul was being used by the Wilson administration to muzzle free speech and put in irons the freedom of the press. Few and courageous were the publications during those days which dared stand their ground and defy the official blackjacking, intimidation and vengeful prosecution that was the lot of those who insisted that free speech and a free press were inalienable American rights that could not be suspended to serve the purposes of plotting partisanship or to furnish a wider field for the publicity efforts of a few fawning satellites who, "drest with a little brief authority," sought to make a rubber stamp of every medium of public expression.

The general public has had only intimations of that most disgraceful chapter of America's war history. Only the publishing world realizes its full shame; of how the vast powers granted by the Congress to the administration, to enable it to win the war and save free institutions, were twisted and prostituted into a weapon to suppress the institutions of free speech and free press, lose the war by a compromising peace and perpetuate a partisan administration which, maddened by a lust for world power, was plotting to substitute internationalism for American nationalism and was craftily planning to force the United States to agree to a treaty which would renounce American doctrines and American institutions and dissolve them in the pool of an international league which, officered by its proposer and author and his retinue, should rule the world. Publications which refused to carry this propaganda, or had the temerity to criticize it, were threatened with loss of their mailing privileges, with being classified as treasonable and prosecuted, with being denied paper, fuel and light with which to operate their enterprises. Here and there these threats were put in execution to strike terror to those who showed signs of independence. It was in such a period and under such conditions that The National Republican began its fight for the preservation of American institutions and keeping faith with those fundamental principles which made possible these institutions. Surely it took courage and high sense of patriotism thus to put its destiny to the touch.

Nor did The National Republican swerve from the policy thus fearlessly launched or slacken its vigor. The collection of editorials in this volume, covering the critical period of the Peace Conference in Paris, the treaty debates in the United States Senate and the "solemn referendum" of the presidential campaign of 1920, is as complete, logical and forceful a presentation of the reasons which determined the American Senate and the American people to reject the Paris treaty as has been compiled. They were written during the heat of the great controversy between Americanism and internationalism, when public opinion was still molten and so they caught and reflected the flaming spirit of the American people during that critical period. Yet, viewed in cold perspective, they ring true; events have marshalled and are marshalling in support of them instead of to their confusion and confutation.

The worth of this volume is greatly enhanced by the inclusion of quotations upon the subject of Americanism from the speeches and writings of America's greatest statesmen, orators and authors, from the earliest days of our republic down to the present day. This is by far the most complete collection of "Americanisms" yet made, and for it the readers are indebted to Hon. John T. Adams, of Dubuque, Iowa. Mr. Adams is a student of American history and an authority on the subject, and possesses one of the finest private American historical libraries in the country. His collaboration in the issuance of this book on Americanism is especially apropos because during the period covered by the editorials contained in this volume, he was an ardent supporter and wise counsellor of The National Republican in its militant support of American institutions and traditions.

These editorials by Mr. Lockwood and compilation of "Americanisms" by Mr. Adams are published "lest we forget." They call the people's attention to the landmarks of national safety and sanity. They emphasize by iteration and reiteration the fundamental principles of this government, enunciated by the statesmen who founded it and espoused by every statesman since who has contributed aught of value toward the development of the nation, the unity of its people and the stability and perpetuity of its institutions. America has reached the age when she should take counsel of her memory and keep ever in mind the advice of those who wrought in thought and deed and sacrifice to bring her to her high station, safeguard her liberties and make her ideals and institutions enduring throughout mortal time.

The fight for the preservation of American independence, ideals and institutions is not over. Already an organized effort is being put forth to galvanize the Wilson internationalism into life and to apotheosize its author. Sedulously and systematically the motives underlying the opposition to the Versailles treaty and covenant are being misrepresented. The history of the proceedings which terminated in the repudiation of President Wilson's international policies at the polls in 1920 is being mis-written by partisan press agents of the leadership repudiated so overwhelmingly by the American electorate. It seems well that at such a time the facts and arguments arrayed in opposition to this program of de-nationalization, so admirably set forth in this volume, should be put forth in permanent form.

J. BENNETT GORDON.

AMERICANISM
A Neglected Solution of World Problems

Americanism is not merely loyalty to a land or fealty to a flag. It is that, but it is more than that. Americanism, in the deepest sense of the term, is devotion to ideas and ideals of which our republic is distinctively the exemplar and exponent. The American republic came into being as an expression of new principles and purposes in government. Americanism is something more than Europeanism transplanted to a new continent. The American Revolution was fought, not merely to secure release from British control, but to free America from European influence and entanglement. This thought was expressed often by the founders of the nation; by Washington, whose Farewell Address is an admonition to America to keep herself disentangled from the European political system; by Jefferson, whose zeal for an American quarantine against the fundamental European conceptions of government was so great that he expressed the wish that the Atlantic Ocean were a sea of fire; by Monroe, who in his announcement of the doctrine that Europe must not use the Americas as a basis for the operations of the European system, only gave expression to a thought that was common to all the sages, soldiers, statesmen who "brought forth upon this continent a new nation." These men constituted the greatest galaxy of greatness that ever blazed in the horizon of a nation's life.

The European conception of government is that the citizen is a creature of the state; the American conception, that the state is the creature of the citizen. European institutions were gradually being liberalized before the American Revolution, it is true; but the struggle for larger individual freedom was against the intellectual and political inheritance of centuries,—"the rotten survivals of by-gone circumstances." The progress was slow from the condition in which the serf belonged to the land, the land to the noble, and the noble to the king. But in this new land the citizen wrested the soil from the savage, and by his own strength made conquest of the wilderness. A state which assumed to govern without his consent was so far out of harmony with American environment that its continuance, or that of any government based upon such a conception of the relation of the government to the individual, was impossible. The Revolution came to pass not from the immediate causes assigned by the revolting colonists, but because the time had come for Americans to throw off the misfit garments of a Europeanism they had outgrown.

So we find the Declaration of Independence declaring that governments exist for the preservation of the unalienable rights of men; that governments derive their just powers from the consent of the governed; that when a government ceases to serve the public welfare, it is the right of the people to overthrow it "and to institute new government, laying its foundations on such principles, and organizing its power in such form, as to them shall seem most likely to effect their safety and happiness."

American institutional development is not merely a chapter in European political history; it is a new chapter in world history. The influence of European political conceptions and ideals upon American civilization, has been less marked during the last century and a half than the influence of American declaration and example upon European civilization, reflected not merely in the rapid spread of the republican form of government, but in the popularizing of political institutions in nations which have clung to monarchical forms of government.

The greatness of the men who founded the American republic was evidenced not more by the boldness and ability with which they announced to the world the new principle upon which they based their determination to cut free from Europe, or the courage and capacity with which independence was achieved by arms and diplomacy, than in the wisdom, which seems inspired, with which they fashioned the institutions of their new government. At a time when the air was filled with the sophistries of demagogues and doctrinaires, prophets of the political millennium to be brought about merely by utopian systems of government; within a few years of the time when a revolution in one of the most enlightened of European nations was accompanied by the same orgy of murder and rapine which has blackened the record of Russia since the downfall of the old autocracy, they created a frame of government which the most eminent of modern English statesmen has called "the greatest work struck off at a given time by the hand and brain of man." As Lowell said, referring to the rejection of utopianism by the founding fathers:

> "Herein they were great,—
> "That they conceived a deeper rooted state. * * *
> "And more devoutly prized
> "Than all perfection theorized
> "The more imperfect, that had roots, and grew."

The system of representative republican government, with its checks and balances, its division of authority and responsibility, its safeguards against tyranny, either of the one or of the many; its distribution of functions between national and state governments; its independent judiciary, with power to stand between the people and violation of their charter of liberties either by the legislative or executive branches of government; its practical plan for federation of the constituent commonwealths; this system is a monument to the political genius of the men who laid the foundations of our national governmental structure. So well has it stood the test of time that every suggestion of change in the system it has established should be subjected to the most careful scrutiny, in the knowledge that the men who framed our national Constitution have few prototypes in public life anywhere in the world today, and that their work, dealing as it did with fundamentals as old as the race, was not for the moment, but is justified today by the same considerations argued in its behalf in the days of Washington.

The American Declaration and the American Constitution were expressive of something more than academic doctrines as to human rights. The conception of government of which they were an expression made possible the great principle of federation which, vindicated in a great war, has kept this nation free from the constant menace of war which has been overhanging Europe during the entire life-time of our republic, and which, still rejected on the other side of the Atlantic, still keeps and will ever keep, the multiplied states of Europe armed to the teeth, except for the influence this nation may be able to exert.

The opportunity came to our representatives at the peace conference, when it was possible to begin a reconstruction of the world on a new basis of a peace of justice, to stand for the American policy, vindicated by the successful experience of a century and a half, as against the European policy, discredited by centuries of failure. It was the peculiar misfortune of America and of the world that at such a time we had as our representative one who, typical of a class all too numerous and influential, was by reason of origin, environment and the scholastic associations of a lifetime, steeped in European conceptions of government. To the phrases of the new freedom Europe has been returned to the old slavery of a system which has left its trail of bloodshed, tyranny, poverty and famine through the centuries.

In proportion as governments leave to individuals, to component states, to localities, the right of self control, it is possible for them to permanently rule over wide areas and diverse elements. In proportion as they are autocratic, paternal, standardized, they can maintain control only by force over widespread areas. That government which appeals to the interest of its people by service to the common welfare can be maintained without a military establishment larger than our insignificant standing army of peace time. The state which governs by fear must have the backing of bayonets. The state which undertakes the ownership and control of the people; the exaggerated state like Germany under the Kaiser or Russia under Lenine; which thrusts its nose and its hand into

3

the daily life of every citizen; which undertakes to become the universal policeman, provider and proprietor; such a state must govern by fear. Government by fear is, in varying degrees, the European conception of government. Its vital principle is force. That principle caused the World war, as it caused the Balkan wars which were the curtain raisers for the general war. It has caused the wars which, almost without interruption, have been progressing in the eastern hemisphere. It compelled Europe to arm to the teeth for the great struggle which marked the climax of this theory of government in world history. And that principle, through the failure of an American President to stand for a distinctive American policy, is the cornerstone of the league of nations. To what extent have we been officially and unofficially refashioning our own government and civilization on the European model during the past few years?

Americans hear much from our apostles of European kultur, culture, or by whatever name you wish to call it, of the origin of our political conceptions and institutions in European history, but it is not often written that Great Britain's system of a federated empire is founded upon the philosophy of Alexander Hamilton. In so far as modern British government has succeeded, it is due to the use of that principle; in so far as it has failed, it is due to a denial of that principle. If Ireland had been given years ago the autonomy of an American state, if the political leaders of the United Kingdom had applied the principle of federation rather than of subjugation to Ireland, it seems probable that there would be little more disposition to rebel against British authority in Ireland than there is in the Dominion of Canada.

The American principle of federation, made possible through limitations of governmental power, is expressed in the national motto: "Out of many, one." Out of many states, one Union; out of many races, religions, nationalities, one people. Through that principle a continental domain is governed; more remarkable still, through it, homogeneity of the very elements which in Europe are at continual war with one another is achieved. Europe is a crazy quilt of nationalities, necessarily conflicting, because in most cases insufficient in territory, resources or population to be economically independent. Naturally enough the World war started in the Balkans, where "self determination of peoples" had been carried to the limit in the creation of small nations reaching out from sheer necessity for the land and materials of their neighbors, and played, one against another, by greater powers each anxious to exploit these dependent governments having the shadow, rather than the substance, of independent nationality. The principle of federation, as applied to the Balkan states, would in itself have prevented the European war, for it was through the struggle between Austria and Russia for dominance in Servia that the war began. Yet America carried to the peace conference a policy of "self determination of peoples," based upon European governmental conceptions, which, far from fusing the smaller nations whose dependence invites the intriguing and conflict of the powers, created some sixteen new nations, some sixteen new causes of war.

This spirit of separatism, originating in the thought that government is a mere instrumentality of force to be used by those who can control it against those who cannot, has not only caused some fifty governments to arm against one another, but it is reflected in class cleavage within these governments themselves. Politics is a mere arrayal of class against class, religion against religion, race against race, element against element, locality against locality. It is to this spirit of class cleavage, distinctively European, that bolshevism is appealing, with its promise of division of the fruits of despoliation.

Assuming that it was America's place to lead in Europe's reconstruction,—and that was the theory of President Wilson,—how much more effective in the interests of world peace than the multiplication of petty powers, would have been the creation of a United States of Europe, federating the Balkan states, the sixteen new governments, and others which might wish to attach themselves to the new world power, in a United States of Europe, permitting each constituent power to retain its own system of local government, but uniting all in an economic and political union that would give to this new nation the status of an independent and self sufficient power. If the peace conference had adopted such a policy it would have followed the one course calculated to promote the peace of central Europe, the prosperity of western Europe and prevent the spread of bolshevism into the western world. To such a power the mandatories rejected by the United States could have been assigned; to such a power, with its stability guaranteed by the other European powers, credit could safely have been extended, and with all causes of dispute over boundary lines, access to the seacoast, and similar problems of disunion eliminated, the new state might have become a working model of the success of the federated system the rest of Europe would in time have been glad to follow.

America failed at the peace conference because Americanism was abandoned. The greatest opportunity that ever came to American leadership was missed. The Canadian representative in the assembly of the league who declared that the European war represented the failure of European diplomacy, and that fifty thousand youths from the Dominion slept under the sod of Europe because of it, told a startling truth which should have come long before from the lips of an American President. The protest of Canada against Article X as an expression of the policy of government by force rather than of justice, is one which should long ago have been made by an American representative in the peace conference. The protest of the Argentine delegate at Geneva against making the league of nations a mere instrumentality for serving the purposes of victorious European powers is one it should not have been necessary to come from South America.

America failed at the peace conference because of the abandonment of Americanism by the man who misrepresented the United States in a failure so monumental that it constitutes one of the greatest calamities in history. To President Harding comes the opportunity to make the best of a most difficult situation, and to substitute, in so far as it is now possible, the spirit of Americanism for that of traditional Europeanism, in the war settlement and the world's reconstruction.
—December 18, 1920.

So, likewise, a passionate attachment of one nation for another produces a variety of evils. Sympathy for the favorite nation, facilitating the illusion of an imaginary common interest in cases where no real common interest exists, and infusing into one the enmities of the other, betrays the former into a participation in the quarrels and wars of the latter without adequate inducement or justification. It leads also to concessions to the favorite nation of privileges denied to others, which is apt doubly to injure the nation making the concession, by unnecessarily parting with what ought to have been retained, and by exciting jealousy, ill will, and a disposition to retaliate in the parties from whom equal privileges are withheld; and it gives to ambitious, corrupted or deluded citizens (who devote themselves to the favorite nation) facility to betray or sacrifice the interests of their own country without odium, sometimes even with popularity; gilding with the appearances of a virtuous sense of obligation, a commendable deference for public opinion, or a laudable zeal for public good, the base or foolish compliance of ambition, corruption or infatuation.—George Washington.

Let those gentlemen who consider themselves quite too respectable and decent to mingle in our elections, remember that God Almighty will hold them responsible for the manner in which they discharge their duty as voters. That right and privilege is not given to them for their benefit, or to be used at their pleasure, but for my benefit, for your benefit, and for the benefit of the thirty millions of people in the United States. If one sees an unworthy man go to the polls and take possession of the government, and he will not prevent it, if there be such a thing as future responsibility—as we all believe—that man will have something to answer for upon that final day when all of us must account for our acts.— Thomas Corwin.

WHAT ARE WE FIGHTING FOR IN THIS WAR?

Tremendous injury has been done to the American cause in this war by mis-statements of American justification for participation in it. Both by seditious agitators and by vainglorious politicians and press agents we have been told that we are in the war to force certain academic, political and economic theories on the rest of the world by force of arms, as Mahomet thrust his religion on Asia by the sword.

No government worthy of being considered civilized would send its sons to the firing line to vindicate the mere political or economic opinions of any man, party or faction. The only cause for which any nation has any moral right to go to war is the necessary defense of the people's fundamental rights of person and property against foreign or domestic aggression. Any nation worthy of the people's protection must protect its people. It must make not only their own country, but the world in general safe for them, so long as they are proceeding within their rights under treaties and international law.

We are in this war for one cause, and one cause only, and that is to make the world safe for America and Americans: to make the whole world understand that the nation which gratuitously insults and assaults our flag, or those entitled to its protection, must suffer the consequences which in a century and a third of American history always befell those who attacked every American by attacking every American's flag. We are in a war of national defense, and not of international propaganda: the claims set up to the contrary are mere matters of opinion, unauthorized by any public decision, unjustified by public opinion, and vastly harmful to the American cause.

To insure, hereafter, that respect for American rights always firmly enforced by this government prior to that abandonment of national duty and responsibility in Mexico which gave Europe mistakenly to understand that anyone could spit on the American flag who cared to do so and would find us "too proud to fight," we must fight the central empires to a decisive conclusion. No mere agreement to respect these rights hereafter would now be sufficient. We must make our adversaries understand that the American eagle still has a beak and talons. We must not only force Germany to recognition of our national rights, but pull the fangs which she repeatedly sunk into us while we were neutrals.

We are not animated by racial or dynastic hatred, by trade rivalry or territorial greed. We are out for the plain, old-fashioned cause of American safety on sea and land which sent Decatur against the Barbary pirates. We do not aspire to historic immortality as arbiters of the world's destiny; our job is to work out our own high destiny, and a big enough job it is. We are not in the war to establish world-wide socialism, communism, free trade or internationalism; we are in the war to beat and disarm the bully we are fighting and to make it impossible for this or any other thug hereafter to swish a club around our ears with the command to stand and deliver.

If we could only dam the flood of drivel that has been let loose in this country to drown out good old-fashioned American patriotism, and clear the whole atmosphere by a plain statement of what every sincere American understands we are really in the war for, the effect would be electrical. The people have shown their devotion to the republic; they will continue to do so; but if appealed to in the name of national, rather than of international and academic ideals which are bothering the brains only of the word artists and millennium makers and which no civilized government would send its soldiers to fight and die for, the unified and stimulated efforts of Americans will be irresistible.

This motto is enough: Our cause is our flag!
—February 9, 1918.

Storms, in the political atmosphere, may occasionally happen, by the encroachments of usurpers, the corruption or intrigues of demagogues, or in the inspiring agonies of faction, or by the sudden fury of popular frenzy; but, with the restraints and salutary influences of the allies before described, these storms will purify as healthfully as they often do in the physical world, and cause the tree of liberty, instead of falling, to strike its roots deeper. In this struggle the enlightened and moral possess also a power, auxiliary and strong, in the spirit of the age, which is not only with them, but onward, in everything to ameliorate or improve.

When the struggle assumes the form of a contest with power, in all its subtlety, or with undermining and corrupting wealth, as it sometimes may, rather than with turbulence, sedition or open aggression by the needy and desperate, it will be indispensable to employ still greater diligence; to cherish earnestness of purpose, resoluteness in conduct, to apply hard and constant blows to real abuses, rather than milk-and-water remedies, and encourage not only bold, free and original thinking, but determined action.—Levi Woodbury.

The stability of this government and the unity of this nation depend solely on the cordial support and earnest loyalty of the people.—Ulysses S. Grant.

THE AIMS OF AMERICA NEED NO EXPLANATION OR APOLOGY

Despite all the conspicuous pronouncements to the contrary, altruism in American international relations is not a recent invention. From the days of Washington this republic has maintained an altruistic attitude toward the rest of the world. So patent is this fact to any friendly student of American history that it is unnecessary to explain it to anyone not unfriendly, in his heart, to the United States of America. It is true that we have been misrepresented by prejudiced critics abroad and prejudiced critics, possessed by the spirit of European provincialism and only nominally Americans, here at home. There is only one incident in our history which can with any degree of justice be called a departure from our consistent policy of disinterested friendship for all the world. That is the Mexican war, which was precipitated by sectional politicians who represented not the people of any portion of the republic, but the old special property interest of human slavery which long since ceased to be a dominant factor in American politics. This war was, however, an outgrowth of the rebellion of Texas against an intolerant tyranny, and viewed in the light of years, it cannot be said that the occupation of our Pacific slope by Americans was a blow to civilization. The outcome was altruistic so far as the republic is concerned, and it was a service of immeasurable value to those states whose status would be that of Lower rather than of American California if the Mexican war had not been fought.

Barring this possible exception we have fought no selfish war, we have done no selfish thing. On the contrary we have done a great many things, expressive of the spirit of the American people, which prevents the belief on the part of anyone disposed to be fair with the American nation, that we have not been altruistic in our attitude toward our neighbors and the world in general. Vastly the strongest of all nations in the western hemisphere, it has been within our power at all times to take anything we wanted. We have used our power only to prevent land grabbing European nations, to whom we are told we must now explain our altruism, from seizing territory in the hemisphere. Immediately following the Civil war, when we had an army and navy strong enough to defeat any nation, we ordered France out of Mexico instead of going in, as many urged we should, to displace one invader with another.

AMERICANISM

Our attitude in China prevented the European nations to whom we are now explaining that we have turned over a new leaf and are now unselfish, from seizing territory after the expedition of the allies to Pekin following the Boxer uprising. Only the meanest and most prejudiced critics of the United States assume that our record in the Spanish-American war fails to support this theory of American altruism. We did a thing without parallel in history when we withdrew from Cuba, and when we established in Porto Rico and the Philippines a government which blessed, rather than bled, the people of these dependencies, flung by fate into our hands to their own infinite betterment. Hostile critics of the United States talk about our "taking Panama." We did nothing of the kind. We had no selfish purpose in Panama. We were putting through there a vast project not more beneficial to the United States than to the rest of the world, and most of all to Colombia, whose politicians attempted to blackmail the United States and inflict injury upon Panama while holding up the consummation of this great altruistic project, paid for by the people of the United States.

If our history as a nation had not been marked by altruism, no profession of unselfish purposes now would weigh against the record. To friends of the United States, it is unnecessary to explain that we have no designs of territorial aggression in this war. To the peoples of the United States, who understand that no one in this country has any such thought of such a thing, such professions are totally unnecessary protestations of suddenly acquired national virtue.

We are in this war to make the world safe for this republic; to preserve our rights and our self respect as a nation; to prove that we are neither too proud nor too cowardly to take up arms in defense of the flag for which the soldiers of Washington, of Lincoln and of McKinley shed their blood. It is unnecessary to explain the altruism of our aims either to our allies or our enemies. Only one thing counts now, and that the weight of our military resources cast into the scale against the power which has insulted and assaulted the republic.

—June 22, 1918.

There is a sort of courage, which, I frankly confess it, I do not possess,—a boldness to which I dare not aspire, a valour which I cannot covet. I cannot lay myself down in the way of the welfare and happiness of my country. That, I cannot—I have not the courage to do. I cannot interpose the power with which I may be invested—a power conferred, not for my personal benefit, nor for my aggrandizement, but for my country's good—to check her onward march to greatness and glory. I have not courage enough, I am too cowardly for that.—Henry Clay.

10

SETTLING THE TERMS OF PEACE

The Constitution of the United States does not vest the chief executive with the exclusive function of determining terms of peace in any war declared by Congress, and which can only be terminated by Congress in the ratification of a treaty of peace. This matter, therefore, is one upon which every citizen of the republic has a right to think and to speak. ··

That responsibility for the determination of declarations of war and treaties of peace does not rest in any one quarter is indicated by President Wilson himself when he lays down as one of the conditions of peace, the destruction of every arbitrary power that can separately, secretly or of its own choice disturb the peace of the world, or if it cannot be destroyed that such power be at least greatly contracted. Undoubtedly the power of the Kaiser to declare war without consulting the German people or other branches of the German government had much to do with precipitating the present war. The lesson is that everywhere throughout the world power exercised in the name of government should be subjected to checks and limitations. No branch of the government should be permitted to fall into contempt. It should be understood that those who seek to degrade Congress, for instance, to a state of impotence, are not true friends of genuine democracy. It should be understood that those who, like Senator Owen, would take from the Supreme Court the power to place its decree between Congress or the executive and the violation of any of the fundamental guarantees or principles of the Constitution, are trying to save the world for an autocracy quite as dangerous as that which flourishes in Germany, Austria and Turkey.

With President Wilson's declaration that hereafter nations should be governed in their relationships by the common law of civilized society, and that there should be established after the war some organization of peace which will make binding upon the world the decisions of some definite tribunal of justice, free and enlightened people everywhere will agree. Upon the details of such an arrangement there may be wide differences of opinion. A league of some nations to compel other nations to be guided by their principles of justice might become as subversive of its original purpose as the Holy Alliance. A league of all nations consenting to certain settled principles of international justice, with power to enforce the decisions of a tribunal in which all nations shall be represented, might be a solution of this problem of world justice

11

and world peace. As in our Constitution, however, there would have to be certain reservations, such as the recognition of the Monroe Doctrine, and the right of this republic, for instance, to regulate its own economic relations in conformity with long established American policies.

The second condition of peace laid down by President Wilson reads:

"The settlement of every question, whether of territory, of sovereignty, of economic arrangement, or of political relationship, upon the basis of the free acceptance of that settlement by the people immediately concerned and not upon the basis of the material interest or advantage of any other nation or people which may desire a different settlement for the sake of its own exterior influence or mastery."

As a generality this will meet approval, but there will be considerable difficulty in practically applying the principle in the settlement of issues which figure in the present war, and of some which existed before the war in nations not originally involved in the struggle. The settlement of all territorial and economic and political questions at the end of this war to the mutual satisfaction of France and Germany would be some job, even for a master mind like that of Colonel Edwin M. House, of Texas. The settlement of the question of economic relationship between rival commercial powers, heretofore left to the decision of the nation which makes the laws affecting trade relations, would present some difficulties. For instance, it might be a bit difficult to enact a tariff law for the United States which would get the approval of a referendum in Europe. It might be difficult to pass an immigration law in the United States which would secure free acceptance in China and Japan. Under such a system Great Britain might be stripped of her colonies, in most instances with detrimental effect to the people of these dependencies. Russia under the plan of local self determination would dissolve into a mass of petty principalities.

It is impossible to believe that a settlement of the war can be arrived at which will be satisfactory to everybody concerned. The first condition of a just settlement is the defeat of the central empires and their allies. Until that end is accomplished it is idle to talk definitely of peace terms. The United States will not be the only nation at the council table; on the contrary it will be one of many nations; doubtless the most influential of all, but with no final voice upon the matters that will be there determined. The American people seek no selfish advantage as to the result of their participation in this war; neither do they seek the sacrifice of their own interests and their own welfare in the peace bargaining; desiring to attain no selfish end, they do not intend, for instance, to be sacrificed to the selfish demands of any foreign power which may be looking to the exploitation of American markets as a means of recouping itself for the losses incident to a war for world mastery, military and economic.

The thing to be thought of now is fighting the war to a victorious finish. Thereafter the people who have borne the burdens and made the sacrifices of war may be depended upon to assert themselves in the day of settlement. As Lincoln said at Indianapolis on his way to take up the Presidency, the future rests not with Presidents, or politicians, or office seekers, but with the people of the republic, who have at heart no purpose other than that of making the world safe for this republic, and making the republic safe for its people and for the world.
--July 13, 1918.

Wherever the standard of freedom and independence has been or shall be unfurled, there will her (America's) heart, her benedictions and her prayers be. But she goes not abroad in search of monsters to destroy. She is the well-wisher to the freedom and independence of all. She is the champion and vindicator only of her own. She will recommend the general cause, by the countenance of her voice and the benignant sympathy of her example. She well knows that by once enlisting under other banners than her own, were they even the banners of foreign independence, she would involve herself, beyond the power of extrication, in all the wars of interest and intrigue, of individual avarice, envy and ambition, which assume the colors and usurp the standard of freedom. The fundamental maxims of her policy would insensibly change from liberty to force. The frontlet upon her brow would no longer beam with the ineffable splendor of freedom and independence but in its stead would soon be substituted an imperial diadem, flashing in false and tarnished lustre the murky radiance of dominion and power. She might become the dictatress of the world; she would be no longer the ruler of her own spirit.—John Quincy Adams.

The first object of a free people is the preservation of their liberty, and liberty is only to be preserved by maintaining constitutional restraints and just divisions of political power. Nothing is more deceptive or more dangerous than the pretence of a desire to simplify government.

The simplest governments are despotisms; the next simplest, limited monarchies; but all republics, all governments of law, must impose numerous limitations and qualifications of authority, and give many positive and many qualified rights. In other words, they must be subject to rule and regulation. This is the very essence of free political institutions.

  This is the nature of constitutional liberty, and this is OUR liberty, if we will rightly understand and preserve it. Every free government is necessarily complicated, because all such governments establish restraints, as well on the power of government itself as on that of individuals. If we will abolish the distinction of branches, and have but one branch; if we will abolish jury trials, and leave all to the judge; if we shall then ordain that the legislator shall be that judge; and if we place the executive power in the same hands, we may readily simplify government. We may easily bring it to the simplest of all possible forms, a pure despotism. But a separation of departments, so far as practicable, and the preservation of clear lines of distinction between them, is the fundamental idea in the creation of all our constitutions; and, doubtless, the continuance of regulated liberty depends on maintaining these boundaries.—Daniel Webster.

In the American state, the legislature is not supreme, but has limits to its authority prescribed by a written document known as the Constitution; and if the legislature happens to pass a law which violates the Constitution, then whenever a specified case happens to arise in which this statute is involved, it can be brought before the court, and the decision of the court, if adverse to the statute, annuls it, and renders it of no effect. The importance of this feature of civil government in the United States can hardly be overrated. It marks a momentous advance in civilization, and it is especially interesting as being peculiarly American. Almost everything else in our fundamental institutions was brought by our forefathers in a more or less highly developed condition from England; but the development of the written constitution, with the consequent relation of the courts to the law-making power, has gone on entirely on American soil.—John Fiske.

"Separated by a wide ocean from the nations of Europe and from the political interests which entangle them together, with productions and wants which render our commerce and friendship useful to them and theirs to us, it can not be the interest of any to assail us, nor ours to disturb them. We should be most unwise, indeed, were we to cast away the singular blessings of the position in which nature has placed us, the opportunity she has endowed us with of pursuing, at a distance from foreign contentions, the paths of industry, peace and happiness, of cultivating general friendship, and of bringing collisions of interest to the umpirage of reason than of force."—Thomas Jefferson.

Public sentiment is everything. With public sentiment nothing can fail; without it nothing can succeed. Consequently he who molds public sentiment goes deeper than he who enacts statutes or pronounces decisions. He makes statutes and decisions possible or impossible to be executed.—Abraham Lincoln.

AMERICAN INSTITUTIONS ARE WORTH FIGHTING
TO PRESERVE

September seventeenth, perhaps the most important anniversary in the calendar of American patriotism, passes by each year almost without notice. It is the date of the adoption of the American Constitution by the Philadelphia convention over which George Washington presided, twelve years after the adoption of the Declaration of Independence. The adoption of the Declaration was a great event; the achievement of national independence in a struggle of eight years against the mightiest nation of the time an even greater one; but greatest of all achievements of our Revolutionary forefathers was the adoption of a frame of government, "the greatest work," as Gladstone said, "ever struck off at a given time by the hand and brain of man," which has so well stood the test of time that under it there has been developed upon this continent the freest and mightiest people of all time.

So much is said in deprecation of our form of government by demagogues and doctrinaires, so little in its defense, that the supreme merit of our national Constitution is not generally understood even by the American people. The framers of the Constitution did not throw together a plan of government in haphazard fashion. It represented the most conscientious research into every governmental experiment in history by the greatest group of publicists that ever appeared in one group in the life of a nation.

In these later days critics of the American Constitution have appeared who complain that it does not provide a pure democracy. The framers of our Constitution knew, from the study of history, the dangers of pure democracy, a form of government which, even in little Greece, banished wise men for being called just, and courageous men for speaking the truth. They knew that unrestrained rule by a majority was just as much of an autocracy as unrestrained rule by a monarch. They devised the great plan of checks and balances, of responsibilities and restraints, of divided prerogative and supervision, which has given us that liberty safeguarded by law that is the glory of our civilization.

We are pointed, too, in these days, to the virtues of the exaggerated state under which the citizen is the creature, rather than the master, of government. This form of state is not progressive, but reactionary. It had an early example in Sparta, and under it developed nothing but slave spirits and stoic deeds. The modern example is Prussianism, which the whole world has had to rise up and fight because it has substituted the soulless state for the individual conscience.

Of the perils of mere majority rule, without the restraint of law we have the horrible example of Russia under the bolshevik socialists. The word bolsheviki means the majority. Without constitutional restraints this majority, not of the Russian people, but of the faction temporarily in control of the Russian government, has proceeded upon the theory that only the class in power has any rights that need to be respected. Therefore we have had murder and rapine on a scale unprecedented in history, and the net result is a people reduced to such depths of misery as the world has never before conceived.

With so much agitation against our form of government being carried on by demagogues and doctrinaires possessed by European conceptions of government, and with no adequate appreciation of what Americanism means, it is the duty of the American people to study for themselves the merits of their own peculiar form of government. While there is so much talk of saving the world for democracy, there are many Americans who believe that the adoption by Europe of the federated republican form of government, possibly by the division of the continent into two or three governmental groups, would be a better solution of the situation there than many of the schemes which have been proposed.
—September 21, 1918.

Where, then, shall we go to find an agency that can uphold and renovate declining public virtue? Where should we go but there, where all republican virtue begins and must end; where the Promethean fire is ever to be rekindled until it shall finally expire; where motives are formed and passions disciplined? To the domestic fireside and humble school, where the American citizen is trained. Instruct him there, that it will not be enough that he can claim for his country Lacedaemonian heroism, but that more than Spartan valor and more than Roman magnificence is required of her. * * * that their country has appointed only one altar and one sacrifice for all her sons, and that ambition and avarice must be slain on that altar, for it is consecrated to humanity.—William H. Seward.

"To stand in firm and cautious independence of all entanglements in the European system, has been a cardinal point of their policy under every administration of their government, from the peace of 1783 to this day."—John Quincy Adams, 1820.

A DECISIVE PEACE

That Is What Is Desired by the American People

Were Germany to indicate acceptance of the terms of peace proposed by President Wilson, withdraw her armies to the borders of Germany and, while strengthening her powers of resistance by the reorganization of an army now trembling under the blows of a triumphant enemy, transfer the war from the field of battle to the council table, the most dangerous phase of the war would have been entered.

A still undefeated Germany would thus be enabled to play one of the enemy powers against another with the justified hope of creating discord that would enable the central powers to emerge from the present war, if not victorious, then armed for a resumption of the conflict either upon disagreement at the peace conference, or by attacking her divided enemies one by one after peace, on paper, has been concluded.

Not out of any desire to crush or humiliate the German people, but out of a determination to make this great struggle eventuate in permanent relief from the menace of militarism, the war should come to a decisive conclusion. Our adversaries should either confess defeat by an unconditional military surrender which would invite the generosity of her foes, accompanied by a dissolution of her vast armies, or defeat should be inflicted upon them in actual conflict.

There is unity of military command in the armies of the nations united in the task of defeating Germany, but we do not know that there is complete unity of command among the statesmen of the several powers joined in this great enterprise. The victories gained on the field at the loss of so much blood and treasure may be lost in a premature peace conference.

We can, of course, get out of the war without achieving a conclusive issue of the struggle. We could have kept out of the war in the beginning with the same result, and without loss of blood and treasure. We have struck blows at Germany, we have inflicted injuries not easily forgotten, and if we now take the issue out of the hands of our soldiers and sailors and put it in the hands of diplomats, all that our armies have fought for, all that our people have been burdened for, may be lost.

The people of this country went to war somewhat reluctantly. Having gone to war they do not desire to cease fighting until some-

17

thing has been settled, and settled for all time. They do not want to take the chance, at a moment when victory seems in sight, of permitting the enemy an opportunity to reform its lines, to rest and refit and prepare for new aggressions. This might mean an indefinite prolongation of the war. That Germany is ready to make terms means only that her whole campaign of force is about to collapse. Why not let it collapse, dissolving the enemy armies and bringing our soldiers home, rather than to start a long peace parley with the world still an armed camp? Why not let it be demonstrated to the world, once for all, that there is force enough in the world to defeat force when employed for the world's oppression and subjugation? And if we did not intend to do this, why did we go to war at all?
—October 12, 1918.

There is no disposition to disturb the colonial possessions, as they may now exist, of any of the European powers; but it is against the establishment of new European colonies upon this continent that the principle is directed. * * * Europe would be indignant at any American attempt to plant a colony on any part of her shores, and her justice must perceive, in the rule contended for, only perfect reciprocity.

While we do not desire to interfere in Europe with the political system of the allied powers, we should regard as dangerous to our peace and safety any attempt, on their part, to extend their system to any portion of this hemisphere. The political systems of the two continents are essentially different. Each has an exclusive right to judge for itself what is best suited to its own condition and most likely to promote its happiness; but neither has a right to enforce upon the other the establishment of its peculiar system.
—Henry Clay.

It is obvious that all the powers of Europe will be continually manoeuvring with us, to work us into their real or imaginary balances of power. They will all wish to make of us a make-weight candle, when they are weighing out their pounds. Indeed, it is not surprising; for we shall very often, if not always, be able to turn the scale. But I think it ought to be our rule not to meddle; and that of all the powers of Europe, not to desire us, or perhaps, even to permit us, to interfere, if they can help it.—John Adams, 1782.

Determined as we are to avoid, if possible, wasting the energies of our people in war and destruction, we shall avoid implicating ourselves with the powers of Europe, even in support of principles which we mean to pursue. They have so many other interests different from ours, that we must avoid being entangled in them.
—Thomas Jefferson.

AMERICA'S SEPARATE DESTINY

The American people have no desire to trade the Monroe Doctrine for the right to meddle in the affairs of Europe, and thereby to become parties to the controversies growing out of traditional territorial, trade and dynastic rivalries.

The American people prefer to have the American republic fulfill its own peculiar and separate destiny than to have it enter into any world-wide partnership with any other nation or group of nations, except for the sole and single purpose of preserving the world's peace by the substitution of arbitration for war in the settlement of international disputes.

There is no such thing, so Washington said, as disinterested friendship between nations. The enemies of today are the friends of tomorrow; the friends of today, the enemies of yesterday.

The sentimental ties, cemented by the blood of common ideals and common heroism, which unite us with the nations allied with us in the great war now drawing to a close, will never be forgotten. They afford no good reason for abandoning the splendid isolation which is the sure protection of this republic from the embroilments of other powers.

The American people did not go to war for any selfish purpose, but neither did they go for an opportunity to enter into any world-wide system of communism under which we are to divide up our wealth with the world's poverty, surrender our ideals and interests to those of other lands, or sacrifice the peculiar advantages of our situation.

—November 16, 1918.

In the discharge of my official duty I shall endeavor to be guided by a just and unstrained construction of the Constitution, a careful observance of the distinction between the powers granted to the federal government and those reserved to the states or to the people, and by a cautious appreciation of those functions which by the Constitution and laws have been assigned to the executive branch of the government.

But he who takes the oath today to preserve, protect, and defend the Constitution of the United States only assumes the solemn obligation which every patriotic citizen—on the farm, in the workshop, in the busy marts of trade, and everywhere—should share with him. The Constitution which prescribes his oath, my countrymen, is yours; the government you have chosen him to administer for a time is yours; the suffrage which executes the will of freemen is yours; the laws and the entire scheme of our civil rule, from the town meeting to the state capitals and the national capital, is yours. Every voter, as surely as your chief magistrate, under the same high sanction, though in a different sphere, exercises a public trust. Nor is this all. Every citizen owes to the country a vigilant watch and close scrutiny of its public servants and a fair and reasonable estimate of their fidelity and usefulness. Thus is the people's will impressed upon the whole framework of our civil polity—municipal, state and federal; and this is the price of our liberty and the inspiration of our faith in the republic.— Grover Cleveland.

In order that this republic may become fully independent it must become not merely politically, but also industrially independent; for, broadly considered, political freedom is not so much an end as a means; it is not a goal, but a starting point. In the presence of false industrial and economic systems political freedom can not avail. After inducing the mass of the people to indulge in high aspiration, to believe in the principles of our immortal Declaration that "all men are created equal," to understand that here they are living under no system of caste, that the people constitute the government, and that all opportunities are open to the least among them, it is vain to say that they must be content to live in conditions of misery identical with those which surround the subjects of despotic governments who have never drank in the spirit of liberty. We must not say to our people, "Aspire, be proud, be independent—and live in squalor."
To be independent in the true and full sense a nation must become self-sustaining. Its work must be done by its own people on its own soil. In the means of livelihood of its citizens it must be independent of all the world. It should not leave them subject to the shifting, uncertain and antagonistic policies of foreign governments. A great people should possess themselves of all the arts and industries of civilization.—Senator John P. Jones, of Nevada, in U. S. Senate Sept. 10, 1890.

I hope the United States of America will be able to keep disengaged from the labyrinth of European policies and wars. It should be the policy of the United States to administer to their wants without being engaged in their quarrels.—George Washington, 1788.

A great free people owes it to itself and to mankind not to sink into helplessness before the powers of evil.—Theodore Roosevelt.

EXECUTIVE LEGISLATION VIOLATES
THE CONSTITUTION

The American people are deeply stirred by the presentation of the fundamental issue of autocracy. This was the issue upon which the verdict of November 5th was rendered. Since that time it has been intensified. Today it stirs to the depths the Democratic as well as the Republican party. Something larger than any ordinary party issue has aroused the people of the United States. The deeply underlying cause of the existing excitement has not been definitely stated in public. To this paper the cause seems clear.

The people of this country have been accustomed to determine public questions by a process defined in the American Constitution, in accordance with the principles of representative republicanism. It has been customary here to decide great public questions on the basis of expressed public opinion. This expression has been given at the polls, in the election of duly constituted legislative authority.

The American Constitution anticipates both commercial treaties in time of peace and political treaties as conclusions of war. It provides methods by which the adjustment of such matters may be made. Treaties concluding war are handled as the exercise of war power, on the assumption that issues determined by war must be settled therein. These issues, so far as the United States is concerned, are outlined in our declarations of war, and cannot properly go beyond these except by legislative consent. The framing of treaties of peace was not expected by the framers of our Constitution to include world legislation affecting the whole economic and political structure of nations. This is clearly shown by the fact that legislative powers in this government are confided to a particular branch of the government apart from the executive.

President Wilson has chosen to regard the formulation of the treaty of peace as an opportunity for world legislation: legislation binding upon the United States and upon the rest of the world, both as to domestic and international policies. He has in his personally determined fourteen points declared a program of legislation by an international conference to which he has asked the assent of no one but himself, and which has never been submitted for sanction to the real legislative branch of our government. This departure from the spirit of our Constitution might be considered only technical except that the President has chosen to completely ignore the coordinate treaty making branch of government, with the advice and consent of which all international covenants, under the Constitution, must be made. He has violated both precedents and clear constitutional implications by leaving the Senate entirely out of consideration in connection with the selection of his peace commission.

The very creation of an international legislative body to determine questions of both domestic and international concern, and entering the realm of economics and sociology as well as police power, constitutes an exercise of the treaty making power which requires the assent of the Senate. A new kind of peace treaty is proposed: one in which a program of legislation affecting vitally the domestic concerns of the United States is included. But legislative power in the United States belongs to Congress, and not the executive. There is no constitutional warrant for the assumption of legislative powers by the executive. Under our form of government legislative functions are by the people temporarily confided to a definite representative body, chosen by the people in accordance with their views upon the issues these representatives advocate. This is the essence of American civil liberty. Without it there is taxation without representation: the thing against which the Revolution was fought. There is legislation by the executive power: the essence of that autocracy against which the Constitution undertakes to safeguard the people.

It is grossly improper for a President of the United States to appoint a peace commission which represents only himself personally; which denies representation not only to a coordinate treaty making body but to the opposition party of the country, representing, as shown by recent election returns, more than half the people in it. But the assumption by the executive that he may, through such representatives, undertake legislative powers which may, for instance, prevent national self determination in such matters as our domestic fiscal policy, or our attitude toward the secession of any portion of the nation, is a clear violation of the Constitution the President is sworn to support.

The constitutional functions of our representatives at a peace conference extend only to the determination of matters at issue in the war, and the submission of the agreement effected to the Senate of the United States for confirmation. The adoption of any form of international government, or legislation with reference to any question affecting the domestic policies of the United States is clearly beyond the constitutional power of any but the legislative branch of our government. Such legislation could clearly be neither initiated in nor adopted by the executive branch of government, and even the representatives to such an international parliament could be selected only by the American people direct, or by their legislative representatives in the Congress of the United States.

The question of an international parliament is clearly one for legislative determination. It is for the people, either directly or through their duly constituted legislative representatives, to say what functions they are willing to yield to a world's congress such as it is proposed to constitute at Paris under the name of peace conference. Such a conference may be desirable; that is for the American people to determine, since they must bear the burdens and accept the consequences, whether good or bad, of such an arrangement. The problem, therefore, is not one of the wisdom or unwisdom of such an international legislative body, but of the authority possessed by the executive alone to enter into it without the consent of the governed within the nation by whose constitution and laws he is bound. The problems confronting such a world congress would be of such infinite range and complexity that no thoughtful person believes they could be settled off hand. Their settlement, beyond the disposition of the questions between the victors and the vanquished, should not be based merely upon armed force, but upon the deliberate consideration and debate of the matters at issue by the peoples affected in the selection of their representatives, and by these representatives in council assembled.

The issue raised, therefore, is essentially one between autocracy and representative republicanism. The people have been deeply stirred because they feel instinctively the existence of such an issue, which we believe has here been in specific terms defined. —December 7, 1918.

I ask each of you to remember that he cannot shove the blame on others entirely, if things go wrong. This is a government by the people, and the people are to blame ultimately if they are misrepresented, just exactly as much as if their worst passions, their worst desires are represented; for in the one case it is their supineness that is represented exactly as in the other case it is their vice. Let each man make his weight felt in supporting a truly American policy, a policy which decrees that we shall be free and shall hold our own in the face of other nations.—Theodore Roosevelt.

The framers of the Constitution did not believe that any man or any body of men could safely be intrusted with unlimited power. They thought, and all experience justified them in thinking that human nature could not support the temptation which unlimited power always brings. They had deeply ingrained the belief of the English-speaking people that the power of the king should be strictly limited. They felt that this great principle applied with equal force to ten thousand or ten million kings—in other words to a popular majority of numbers. They established a representative democracy and a thoroughly popular government, but they thought that the "right divine of kings to govern wrong" was as false a maxim when applied to many men called voters as when applied to one who happened to wear a crown.—Henry Cabot Lodge.

Columbia should have been the name of the western hemisphere—the republican half of the world—the hemisphere without a king on the ground—the reserved world, where God sent the trodden spirits of men to be revived; to find, where all things were primitive, man's primitive rights.

Royal prerogatives are plants that require a walled garden and to be defended from the wild, free growths that crowd and climb upon them. Pomp and laced garments are incongruous in the brush. Danger and hardships are commoners. The man in front is the captain—the royal commission to the contrary notwithstanding. The platoon and volley firing by the word would not do—the open order, one man to a tree, firing at his own will and at a particular savage, was better. Out of this and like calls to do things upon his own initiative the free American was born. He thought he might get along with kings and imperial parliaments if they were benevolent, and did and allowed what he wished, but they were forever doing their own pleasure, as the way of absolutism always is. And he found it necessary first to remonstrate and then to resist.—President Benjamin Harrison.

The history of human conduct does not warrant that exalted opinion of human virtue which would make it wise in a nation to commit interests of so delicate and momentous a kind as those which concern its intercourse with the rest of the world, to the sole disposal of a magistrate created and circumstanced as would be a President of the United States. It must, indeed, be clear, to a demonstration, that the joint possession of the power in question by the President and Senate would afford a greater prospect of security than the separate possession of it by either of them.—Alexander Hamilton.

Only those are fit to live who do not fear to die, and none are fit to die who have shrunk from the joy of life and the beauty of life. Both life and death are parts of the same great adventure. Honor, highest honor, to those who fearlessly face death for a good cause. No life is so honorable or so fruitful as such a death. Unless men are willing to fight and die for great ideals, including love of country, ideals will vanish.—Theodore Roosevelt.

The nation which indulges toward another an habitual hatred, or an habitual fondness, is in some degree a slave.—George Washington.

A FUNDAMENTAL ISSUE

The argument is made that the Senate's part in the formulation of treaties is confined to the process of ratification or rejection. The statement is not true. Treaties must be ratified under the Constitution by a two-thirds vote of the Senate, but separate and apart from this is the provision that treaties must be made "by and with the consent of the Senate." "Advice and consent" imply initiative as well as mere ratification. It is grossly unfair to the Senate, moreover, to thrust before it a treaty ready made, affecting in its terms in a tremendous way the future of the country, and then say to it that it must either ratify the compact or take the responsibility for overthrowing the peace arrangements. This advantage is fully realized by those who are insisting that the Senate should not be consulted in advance about the terms of the peace treaty. The arrangements made mean that the Senate will never have opportunity to exercise material influence upon the terms of the treaty. Those who cannot comprehend the fundamental wrong of this procedure merely lack in an understanding of the processes of free government on the American pattern. In this matter the masses of the people seem to comprehend the situation more clearly than many alleged leaders.
—December 14, 1918.

Let the passion for America cast out the passion for Europe. Here let there be what the earth waits for,—exalted manhood. What this country longs for is personalities, grand persons, to counteract its materialities. For it is the rule of the universe that corn shall serve man, and not man corn.

They who find America insipid,—they for whom London and Paris have spoiled their own homes,—can be spared to return to those cities. I not only see a career at home for more genius than we have, but for more than there is in the world.—Ralph Waldo Emerson.

The Senate of the United States must remain an important part of a thoroughly independent, coordinate branch of the government, neither arrogating to itself functions not devolved upon it under the Constitution, nor, upon the other hand, subtracting from its legitimate powers. Its legislative duties are vast, while its duties

25

with respect to treaties and appointments to the public service are of very great moment. A servile Senate was not contemplated by its founders. The Senate is today as jealous as ever of its proper dignities and its just powers and as worthy as ever of the popular respect and confidence. * * *

The Senate, it is sometimes said, is not always responsive to the popular will. Such assumption is erroneous, judging by the record of legislation accomplished. The will of the people finds utterance in the public law in due course; not that will which is the unreasoning passionate expression of the moment, but that will which is the fruit of deliberate, intelligent reflection.

The Senate of the United States was designed by our fathers to be a deliberate chamber in the fullest and best sense—a chamber where the passions of the hour might be arrested and where the better judgment of the people would find ultimate expression. Those who in their unreflecting moments would sweep it away would overturn one of the strongest safeguards of our political fabric.—Charles W. Fairbanks.

Let the American youth never forget that they possess a noble inheritance, bought by the toils and sufferings and blood of their ancestors, and capable if wisely improved and faithfully guarded, of transmitting to their latest posterity all the substantial blessings of life, the peaceful enjoyment of liberty, property, religion and independence. The structure has been erected by architects of consummate skill and fidelity; its foundations are solid; its compartments are beautiful as well as useful; its arrangements are full of wisdom and order; and its defenses are impregnable from without. It has been reared for immortality, if the work of man may justly aspire to such a title. It may, nevertheless, perish in an hour by the folly or corruption or negligence of its only keepers, the people. Republics are created by the virtue, public spirit and intelligence of the citizens. They fall when the wise are banished from the public councils, because they dare to be honest; and the profligate are rewarded, because they flatter the people in order to betray them.—Justice Story.

The will of the people is the law of the land. * * * The great body of the people have a single interest, that of having their government wisely, faithfully and honestly administered. They have little care for mere individuals, except as the individual may serve them best, and best represent the principles which are dear to them in governmental policy.—William McKinley.

Our diplomatic relations connect us on terms of equality and honest friendship with the chief powers of the world, while we avoid entangling participation in their intrigues, their passions and their wars.—George Bancroft.

ON THE QUESTION OF ENDORSING POLICIES
NOT YET DISCLOSED

The people of the United States are anxious beyond the power of expression that this war shall prove to be the war to end wars.

They have no idea that a just peace can be guaranteed by any arrangement which does not provide for the reduction of armaments.

They therefore believe in the abolition both of militarism and navalism.

Their idea of world freedom is not the guardianship of the world by one power, or two powers, or a selected group of powers, believing as they do that such guardianship is only another name for domination.

The people of this country do not favor any league of nations which does not relieve the world of the necessity of maintaining great armaments, understanding that with any one or two or three powers in a position to dominate the world, treaties are liable at any moment to become scraps of paper.

If armaments are to be maintained, then this country must be left free to protect itself as circumstances may require, not remanded by our own choice or the choice of others to any secondary position as an independent power.

If great navies are to be maintained then this nation must have a navy equal to that of any other power in the world. There is no more suggestion of belligerency in such a program than there is in the theory that some other power should have a first navy. Such a navy must be maintained not as a means of getting into trouble, but of keeping out of trouble, and as the means of making unnecessary the maintenance of huge land forces.

The mere adoption by a peace conference of a string of glittering generalities declaring the mutual good intentions of everybody concerned will not constitute a guarantee of the world's peace. That must be accompanied, as an evidence of good faith, by the actual reduction of all armaments, and the failure to reduce these armaments is proof of mental reservations on the part of the signatory powers.

The creation of many new and untried governments in Europe only adds to the probability of conflicts in the other hemisphere which do not directly concern this republic. If we are to take responsibility in this connection, it means, of course, not the assurance of peace, but a vastly increased danger of war. To involve this country in the European political situation permanently, and at the same time to relegate this republic to any secondary position in the matter of sea power, would be to commit an incredible act of folly.

To be controlled in this situation either by partiality for or prejudice against any particular nation is equally un-American. The treaty of peace is one thing; the permanent settlement of the future relationship of nations is another. Nothing was ever said truer than the declaration of Washington that there is no such thing as disinterested friendship among nations. Very properly every nation in the world is looking out for its own interests. This is the duty of American statesmanship, for if our representatives do not protect the interests of the United States no one else is going to attend to this job.

Two courses lie before the United States; the maintenance of its own independent national existence and the fulfillment of its own special national destiny, or entrance into a world-wide combination or corporation. If we enter the corporation, let us be sure that its effects, if not its purposes, are not less altruistic than our own and that it does not merely substitute consolidated for independent force as a factor in world affairs; second, let us not too readily abandon business at the old stand in order to become minority stockholders in a political company wherein our own interests may be subjected to the control of some other stockholder or combination of stockholders. The worst enemies of the United States today are the mental blanks who are demanding that the American people, either directly or through their legislative representatives, shall express no opinions or convictions upon these problems, vitally affecting the future of the republic, but shall leave it all to the White House and Colonel House.
—December 28, 1918.

As nature hath separated her from Europe, and hath established her alone (as a sovereign) on a great continent, far removed from the Old World and all its embroiled interests, it is contrary to the nature of her existence, and consequently to her interest, that she should have any connections of politics with Europe other than merely commercial.—Thomas Pownall, formerly a colonial governor, in 1781.

Let us as men who value freedom use our utmost care to support liberty, the only bulwark against lawless power which in all ages has sacrificed to its wild lust and boundless ambition the blood of the best men that ever lived.—Alexander Hamilton.

KEEPING US OUT OF WAR: THEN AND NOW

In 1916 the American people were told that they were being "kept out of war," despite the fact that the policies then being pursued made it inevitable that they would become involved in war. The only end served by the cry was to promote the political fortunes of those who employed it, and prevent the country from adopting a program of preparedness for the war every thinking man realized was just ahead.

Now the "he keeps us out of war" slogan is again abroad in the land. It is being employed by the same politicians for the same purposes, and it is duping the same gullible people, whose ardent love of peace makes them pathetically subject to any program proposed on the theory that it means the ending of war, even if, as a matter of fact, it only makes certain the involving of this country in dangers and responsibilities that mean an increased menace of war rather than an insurance of peace.

The people are being told by the same propagandists who put over on the public the campaign cry of 1916, that if this country will involve itself in the creation of a super-state which is to control the relations of nations, it will mean an insurance of the world's peace. It would doubtless contribute to some extent to peace in Europe, but so far as this country is concerned, it will serve only to complicate American with European affairs to such an extent that whatever menaces the peace of the older continents will threaten that of the United States.

An interesting commentary upon the sincerity of this outcry that "he will keep us out of war" is the recommendation of the Secretary of the Navy that we shall build the world's largest navy, and that of the Secretary of War that by the purchase of all the cantonment sites we shall make provision for the world's largest army. These officials understand that the task of assuming responsibility for the world's peace means that this country must undertake military and naval preparations heretofore unknown beyond the borders of the continent from whose feuds and rivalries and embroilments we have heretofore been fortunately separated. The recommendations of these two officials, involving vast expenditures, give far better evidence of what we are drifting into than all the highflown phrases of the same demagogues and doctrinaires who befuddled and befooled the country in the last national campaign with the assurance that we had been "kept out of war."

AMERICANISM

Fooling the people in 1916 was the fault of the politicians. But if the same people are fooled by the same politicians in the same way now it can be only the people's fault. It is evidently intended that we shall be kept out of war now in the same way and to the same extent and from the same motives and with the same result which followed the great confidence game of the last national campaign, when the politicians in power were taking credit for keeping this country out of a conflict they knew then we would inevitably be swept into, and which they now say was at that time a struggle in behalf of civilization from which no nation could honorably withhold participation.
—January 4, 1919.

To safeguard America first,
To stabilize America first,
To prosper America first,
To think America first,
To exalt America first,
To live for and revere America first.
Call it the selfishness of nationality if you will. I think it an inspiration to patriotic devotion.

We may do more than prove exemplars to the world of enduring representative democracy where the constitution and its liberties are unshaken. We may go on securely to the destined fulfillment and make a strong and generous nation's contribution to human progress, forceful in example, generous in contribution, helpful in all suffering and fearless in all conflicts.

Let the internationalist dream and the bolshevist destroy. God pity him "for whom no minstrel raptures swell." In the spirit of the republic we proclaim Americanism and acclaim America.— Warren G. Harding, January 8, 1920.

The people are the rightful masters of both Congress and the courts,—not to overthrow the Constitution, but to overthrow the men who pervert it. Legislation and adjudication must follow and conform to the progress of society. Is it unreasonable to expect that some man, possessed of the loftiest genius coupled with ambition sufficient to push it to the utmost stretch, will at some time spring up among us? And when such a one does, it will require the people to be united with each other, attached to the government and laws, and generally intelligent, to successfully frustrate his designs.—Abraham Lincoln.

The moral character of the United States is of more importance than any alliance.—John Adams.

AMERICA HAS SET AN EXAMPLE TO THE WORLD

The difficulty encountered by some of our statesmen in approaching the problems of world reconstruction after the great war, is that they have never attained an adequate comprehension of what Americanism means.

We have heard much recently of the "self determination of peoples," and one high in authority has spoken of "the readily discernible lines of historic demarcation." The big thing demonstrated in this American nation is that national allegiance has nothing, necessarily, to do with racial origin. Our national homogeneity is a convincing denial of the necessity of considering government a mere system of segregating peoples, or uniting merely in form, rather than in fact, diverse groups based upon racial, religious or class allegiance.

Our national motto, "Out of many, one," may be interpreted as meaning not merely one nation out of many states, but one national allegiance out of many racial and religious stocks, many occupational and geographical interests. The European system has tended to accentuate the barriers separating groups of men; the American system has broken them down, and we have taught the world that men, as men, may be brought together politically on the mere ground of common devotion to identical ideals of liberty and common conceptions of common self-interest, entirely without regard to where they come from or what they believe other than upon fundamental political questions.

We have drawn to this country representatives of every European racial and national stock. Despite all the talk about our lack of homogeneity, the unity of spirit which has been created from this mass is the marvel of all history. The American is not essentially different in Maine from the American of Oregon; the American of Kansas is so much like the American of Texas that if one were lost in either state he would have difficulty in determining his location from the sort of people with whom he came in contact.

In Europe, on the contrary, a journey of a few miles brings differences in dialect, in tongue, in dress and in traditions which demonstrate the stubbornness with which lines of demarcation have been maintained. There are greater differences in dialect in adjoining counties in England than can be found in the journey across the width of a continent here. And this is not because we are all descended from the same racial stock. On the contrary we have absorbed in this country during the past third of a century

31

twenty million immigrants; they and their children and grand children constitute half our population.

What has happened in Europe is that modern invention has so reduced distance that it is no longer possible peaceably and comfortably to maintain so many divergent and in many instances conflicting types of civilization. Europe is trying to live six in a room, and the over-crowding brings too many points of difference into conflict.

Talk of pacifying Europe by a mere formal league of this European patch-work civilization, made even more complicated and impossible by the addition of a few more governments established on this European idea of racial self determination, will, of course, end in talk. Where there is a war of ideas and ideals and customs and languages and traditions and dynasties and religions, there can be no peace through the formulation of some utopian scheme of combination under which these very differences are to be preserved, and, indeed, encouraged.

The greatest contribution that could be made to the peace of Europe and of the world would be a new grouping of states under a decreased number of central sovereignties, rather than an increase in the number of governments. If Europe were to follow the example of the North American continent, and set up three or four federated nations, each state preserving its local government, but committing national affairs to a central government, under some such constitution as that of the United States, then indeed we might hope for permanent peace. We have talked a great deal of saving the world for democracy. Why we have not sufficiently believed in our own form of government, which has created homogeniety out of infinite variety, is not clear except upon the hypothesis that some Americans do not understand or appreciate Americanism.

So long as the idea is upheld in the world that there can be no political merger between people of varying racial and religious stocks, we are going to have continuing conflict between the prejudices of these groups. There are persons in the United States who are attempting to introduce into this country the European political system whereby government becomes a mere balancing of class conscious groups, each seeking its own advantage at the expense of all the rest; a sort of perpetual civil war. These men are not Americans but European provincials who have not yet risen to the full stature of American citizenship.

Let Europe show some disposition to make those sacrifices to human unity which have been made in this country by scores of millions of men who have proved by their ready amalgamation into the body of American citizenship that these multiplied racial antagonisms are the artificial creation of men and interests, served by their maintenance, before we indulge in the fond delusion that we are to have permanent peace on earth, good will to men through

some scheme of union which, upon careful examination, is found to consist only of glittering generalities. The world is getting too small to permit every little racial group or cult to have its own government, and such an arrangement will prove to be a menace, not a contribution, to the peace of the world.
—January 4, 1919.

Cultivate free commerce and honest friendship with all nations, but make entangling alliances with none. Our best wishes on all occasions, our good offices when required, will be afforded to promote the domestic peace and foreign tranquility of all nations with whom we have any intercourse. Any intervention in their affairs further than this is contrary to our principles.—Andrew Jackson.

Two ideas there are which, above all others, elevate and dignify a race,—the idea of God and country. How imperishable is the idea of country! How does it live within and ennoble the heart in spite of persecution and trials, difficulties and dangers? After two thousand years of wandering, it makes the Jew a sharer in the glory of the prophets, the law-givers, the warriors and poets who lived in the morning of time. How does it toughen every fibre of an Englishman's frame, and imbue the spirit of a Frenchman with Napoleonic enthusiasm? How does the German carry with him even the "old house-furniture of the Rhine," surround himself with the sweet and tender associations of "Fatherland;" and wheresoever he may be, the great names of German history shine like stars in the heaven above him! And the Irishman, though the political existence of his country is merged in a kingdom whose rule he may abhor, yet still do the chords of his heart vibrate responsive to the tones of the harp of Erin, and the lowly shamrock is dearer to his soul than the face-crowning laurel, the love-breathing myrtle, or storm-daring pine.

What is our country? Not alone the land and the sea, the lakes and rivers, and valleys and mountains; not alone the people, their customs and laws; not alone the memories of the past, the hopes of the future; it is something more than all these combined. It is a divine abstraction. You cannot tell what it is, but let its flag rustle above your head, you feel its living presence in your hearts. They tell us that our country must die; that the sun and the stars will look down upon the great republic no more; that already the black eagles of despotism are casting lots for the garments of our national glory. It shall not be! Not yet, not yet shall the nations lay the bleeding corpse of our country in the tomb! If they could, angels would roll the stone from the mouth of the sepulchre! It would burst the cerements of the grave and come forth a living presence, "redeemed, regenerated, disenthralled." Not yet, not

AMERICANISM

yet shall the republic die! The heavens are not darkened, the stones are not rent. It shall live,—it shall live, the embodiment of the power and majesty of the people. Baptized anew, it shall stand a thousand years to come, the colossus of the nations,—its feet upon the continents, its sceptre over the seas, its forehead among the stars.—Newton Booth.

What then is the American, this new man? He is neither an European or the descendant of an European, hence that strange mixture of blood, which you will find in no other country. I could point out to you a family whose grandfather was an Englishman, whose wife was Dutch, whose son married a French woman, and whose present four sons have now four wives of different nations. He is an American who, leaving behind him all his ancient prejudices and manners, receives new ones from the new mode of life he has embraced, the new government he obeys, and the new rank he holds. He becomes an American by being received in the broad lap of our great Alma Mater.

Here individuals of all nations are melted into a new race of men, whose labors and posterity will one day cause great changes in the world. Americans are the western pilgrims, who are carrying along with them that great mass of arts, sciences, vigor and industry which began long since in the East; they will finish the great circle. The Americans were once scattered all over Europe; here they are incorporated into one of the finest systems of population which has ever appeared, and which will hereafter become distinct by the power of the different climates they inhabit.

The American ought therefore to love this country much better than that wherein either he or his forefathers were born. Here the rewards of his industry follow with equal steps the progress of his labor; his labor is founded on the basis of nature, self-interest; can it want a stronger allurement? Wives and children, who before in vain demanded of him a morsel of bread, now fat and frolicsome, gladly help their father to clear those fields whence exuberant crops are to arise to feed and to clothe them all; without any part being claimed, either by a despotic prince, a rich abbot, or a mighty lord. Here religion demands but little of him; a small voluntary salary to the minister, and gratitude to God; can he refuse these? The American is a new man, who acts upon new principles; he must therefore entertain new ideas, and form new opinions. From involuntary idleness, servile dependence, penury and useless labor, he has passed to toils of a very different nature, rewarded by ample subsistence.—This is an American.— J. H. St. John de Crevecoeur.

America has a hemisphere to itself. It must have its separate system of interests, which must not be subordinated to those of Europe—Thomas Jefferson.

THEODORE ROOSEVELT

At the moment when his heroic spirit, his matchless mind, his dauntless courage, his flawless Americanism were needed most by a nation groping for leadership in an hour of great decision, Theodore Roosevelt has laid his body beside that of his soldier son in France in the last sleep. But not before he had spoken words of counsel to his countrymen which will live after him to shape and determine the issues of a national emergency perhaps the gravest yet faced by the American people.

Alone among American Presidents it was reserved to Theodore Roosevelt to perform larger service to the American people following his retirement from the Presidency and in the final months of his life than during his executive incumbency. His was the voice which, in the months before the war, sounded forth the warning of impending national danger and the call to national preparedness. His was the voice which, when the war came, summoned the American people to unity of sentiment and of endeavor in behalf of the national cause, where, in every former national war emergency, leaders of the party opposition had failed in unreserved support of their country's cause. Upon the altar of his country he offered himself, only to be rejected; and then he gave his four sons to make in the service of their country a proud record of heroic sacrifice. The war over and the victory won, the voice of our last soldier President was heard reaffirming, in an hour when departures from American tradition and precedent and spirit seemed imminent, the sentiments of our first soldier President in behalf of AN INDEPENDENT NATIONAL EXISTENCE FOR THE UNITED STATES OF AMERICA, free from the domination or interference or preponderant influence of any alien nation or group of nations.

Contemporaneous opinion does not finally fix the place of any man in history. Some men whose fame fills the world for an hour are forgotten by succeeding generations. Only to the extent that the names of men are linked heroically with eternal principles are they gratefully remembered. The time server dies with the time he serves, the demagogue must take all his pay as he goes. It is asked of the men who aspired to greatness in the past of a nation: Wherein did their service contribute to the permanent well being of the republic? What principle did they stand for that lives and serves the nation? It is not enough that men should have commanding ability or lofty position or persuasive oratory or inspiring personality; the test applied to fame by Time to men's reputations is: Were they champions of truth or of error, of right or of wrong, of practical wisdom or sophistical theory, of good or evil to the nation and the people? Judged by that inexorable standard Theodore Roosevelt's fame will live beyond that of any other American leader of his day and generation; for his creed of single-track Americanism will tomorrow, as it was in an earlier era, be the faith of the American people.

Theodore Roosevelt's career was one of almost continuous battle from the days of his youth to the moment of his death. Born to wealth which invited him to a life of ease and repose, his dauntless spirit called him to the arena of conflict, and there he bore a warrior's part in the arena of municipal, of state, of national and of international politics. That he was ambitious, that he was not invariably just in his judgments, that he was not always wise or temperate or fair in his utterances or his actions, that he made many mistakes in a career crowded with action, that there were times in his career when many, even a majority of the American people did not feel justified in following his leadership, is true. But there never has been a moment when Colonel Roosevelt was not first and foremost a lover and servant and warrior of his country. In the light of that unquestioned fact the hatreds and prejudices and grievances of the past will be forgotten, and Americans without regard to party or race or creed will join in doing honor to this great national and world leader, whose wonderful career now becomes part of the rich inheritance of Americanism.
—January 11, 1919.

Have you not learned that not stocks or bonds or stately houses or lands or products of mill or field are our country? It is a spiritual thought that is in our minds. It is the flag and what it stands for; it is the fireside and the home; it is the high thoughts that are in the heart, born of the inspiration which comes of the story of the fathers, the martyrs to liberty; it is the graveyard into which our grateful country has gathered the dust of those who died. Here in these things is that thing we love and call our country rather than anything that can be touched or handled. Let me hold the thought—that we owe a duty to our country in peace as well as in war.—Benjamin Harrison.

May our children and our children's children for a thousand generations continue to enjoy the benefits conferred upon us by a united country and have cause yet to rejoice under these glorious institutions bequeathed to us by Washington and his compeers.—Abraham Lincoln.

The power of treaties is vested jointly in the President and in the Senate, which is a branch of the legislature.—James Madison.

THE POSITION OF THE REPUBLICAN PARTY ON THE NEW INTERNATIONALISM

No one leader or element of the Republican party has the power to determine the policies of the Republican party. The Republican party is not a one party or a one element affair. It readily leaves that distinction to another great political organization, which does its thinking entirely under one hat. The Republican party is and always has been a party of independence and tolerance; of individual rights. The doctrines of the party are declared in the national and state and local platforms of the party; they are not oracularly handed down from on high.

The Republican party seems to be united in the belief that President Wilson owes to the country a clearer outline of his plans for the internationalism he proposes than have yet been given the people. Intelligent discussion of schemes of international rearrangement not yet disclosed is impossible. It is certain only that no one can intelligently approve a program he really knows nothing about, and no one knows anything clearly about what President Wilson has in mind. Eloquent generalities in favor of the true, the good and the beautiful, while commendable in themselves, do not constitute a program, and the people have discovered that sometimes disagreeable things are put over to the music of agreeable phrases.

* * * * *

An effort is being made to put the Republican party in the light of opposing any movement looking to the removal from the world of the menace of war,—of militarism and navalism. It is the same effort, made by the same men, that succeeded in putting over on the American people the biggest confidence game of modern times in the political campaign of 1916. Then the people were told that the policies of President Wilson, the policies of unpreparedness and note writing, would keep us out of war. They were told this at a time when no one knew so well as the politicians who coined the phrase that this was absolutely untrue. The claim made by many Republican leaders that the policies of the administration, instead of keeping us out of war, would inevitably drive us into war, unprepared for it, fell upon deaf ears. Because the policies of the administration were said to be insurance against war, millions of well-meaning voters, anxious for peace, believed they would guarantee peace. The result is well known.

AMERICANISM

If the program, whatever it may be, President Wilson is vaguely talking about, meant in its practical effect what his champions say it does, then, of course, every well meaning person would be for it; the introduction of peace on earth, good will to men, the exaltation of humanity into a millennial state of perfection and the removal of all the wrongs and errors that have inflicted mankind since the days of Adam. Is it not entirely safe to suggest, however, in view of the outcome of the 1916 campaign, that the mere statement that a certain program is calculated to produce these beneficent results, does not in itself prove that it will do so? In 1916 we were going to be kept out of war, and those who were against the administration were the advance agents of bloodshed; but in 1917 we were at war. Now we are being told that President Wilson's plans mean that this country will forever be removed from the shadow of war. But if any conclusion can intelligently be drawn from the various proposals of the Wilson program of internationalism, it is that our risk of becoming involved in war will be tremendously increased thereby, and that, instead of being kept out of war, we will be kept constantly in the shadow of war by becoming partners in responsibility for the peace of nations at a time when there is more trouble in sight than ever before in the world's history.

* * * * *

While the people do not know, and have no means of knowing, since the advocates of the new internationalism disagree among themselves as to what it is all about, just what benefits and perils and responsibilities may come to them as the result of incorporating the United States into a union for world regulation, they are vaguely apprehensive that what is now proposed is a radical departure from the American policy, operative here from the days of Washington; a departure which will make every home apprehensive of mobilization every time a quarrel breaks out in Russia, in the Balkans, in the Near East or in the Orient. The people of the United States know that for a century and a third they were untouched by the international disputes which continually kept the peoples of the Old World anxious, which necessitated vast standing armies, and maintained a continual game of intrigue in which peoples were pawns. They know they were drawn into the European war only because of its unprecedented, world-wide significance. The American people believe that this terrible struggle has settled one thing for a century or more to come, and that is that no one nation can hereafter safely set out to attain world-wide dominion. They believe that in the peace conference there should be mutual and progressive limitation of armaments, a settlement of an international modus vivendi and the declaration of certain fundamentals of international law and practice. The American people believe that the powers should exchange either individual or collective covenants providing for the arbitration of international disputes. They do not favor, however, the abdication of American sovereignty in favor of the sway of an international military and naval force, directed and commanded by powers without the United States.

Men dominated by common sense rather than by mere sickly sentimentality, men who are not deluded by mere mouth filling phrases expressive of utopian ideals, understand that partnership in a concert of European and Asiatic powers would be about as satisfactory a guarantee of peace as membership in a Balkan league. To deliberately involve ourselves in the consequence of every European dispute would be an act of fatal folly. It is enough that we should be responsible to the rest of the world for our own acts. That we should accept responsibility for the acts of governments with the control of which we have nothing to do, and the control of which is, indeed, constantly shifting from within, would be to accept responsibility without exercising real authority.

* * * * *

Lurking in the background of all this program of international partnership, is a vaguely defined but fairly well understood plan of international communism, involving the merging of American with world-wide economic interests. It is to be a partnership in which we, for the most part, if we rightly interpret the prospectuses, are to furnish the assets and the other partners the liabilities. It is one in which the American people are to make the sacrifices and the rest of the world reap the benefits. It is, of course, possible to work up considerable enthusiasm for such a project abroad. The scheme is the natural outcome of the Democratic-Socialistic doctrine of free trade which denies that American prosperity should be made an object in American legislation. The removal of economic barriers and the establishment of a condition of trade equality among nations means, in effect, that the American producer must be put on the same level as the foreign producer; and this, at last, means that the American mechanic and farmer must go to the level of the coolie in a breech clout, the peon in a coffee sack and the peasant in rags, since it is impossible, from an economic standpoint, to level ninety-four per cent of the world up to the standard of the remaining six per cent rather than to reverse this process.

* * * * *

The American people went into the war for no selfish purpose. We are asking no trade or territorial advantages, and we have asked no indemnities of our beaten foes up to this time. That we did not go to war for any selfish purpose, however, does not necessarily demonstrate that we fought for the opportunity to rob ourselves of our special advantages of situation, our resources, our wealth, our institutions and the standards of our civilization. The people have borne the burdens of war loyally, uncomplainingly, cheerfully. That these sacrifices of theirs should be made an occasion for further and greater sacrifices, vitally affecting the future material welfare and moral greatness of this republic, attained through the exercise of the right to work out our own special and peculiar national destiny, is unthinkable.

* * * * *

A moment's reflection must convince anyone that many of those who throw off glib phrases about the new internationalism either do not believe or do not comprehend what they are talking about. While President Wilson discourses upon permanent world-wide peace, his Secretary of War asks for the purchase of cantonment sites foreshadowing the largest army in the world, while his Secretary of the Navy proposes appropriations for the largest navy in the world. While British statesmen announce their acceptance of the plan of a league of nations, they say at the same time that this should be accompanied by British retention of dominant sea power. In these proposals we see the very wide difference between theorizing about a thing and putting that thing into operation. Of course, if great armaments are to be maintained, either naval or military, the talk about guaranteeing the peace of the world by international agreement rather than by national force is an idle dream; the coupling of the two plans reduces the scheme to the grossest absurdity.

* * * * *

The practical effect of the conversations which have been going on since the signing of the armistice give some suggestion of what is likely to happen in the future. We are maintaining a large army in Europe. We are maintaining a fighting force in Russia. We do not know today what demands may be made tomorrow upon the more than two million soldiers who remain under arms. The war was practically over nearly three months ago. Little or no progress has been made toward a peace settlement. President Wilson is in Europe engaged in preliminary conversations while many of the most pressing domestic problems in all American history await at home the attention of constructive statesmanship. War expenditures, with the war over, continue at a greater rate than while the war was on. The federal government continues expenditures on a vast scale which involve the piling up of huge additional tax burdens on the backs of the American people, and largely increased governmental toll upon trade and industry, confronting the serious problems of peace time, becomes necessary. The situation in Europe is more complicated today than it was a week after the armistice was signed. Is it a spectacle which invites the American people to the perpetuation of the conditions in which we find ourselves involved? The formal conclusion of war awaits the determination of a large number of matters with which the war had nothing to do, and which are so much a subject of controversy that their determination by discussion and compromise may be delayed for many months. Meanwhile we approach, practically unprepared, the serious problems of peace, with the menace of depression and unemployment which these involve, unless wise counsels prevail in national legislation and administration. Does not all this suggest that we are taking on a little too much territory, and argue strongly against the permanent continuance of the policy of trying to police and control the universe, even in behalf of the lofty ideals so soulfully professed?

* * * * *

Upon this proposition the Republican party is united: that the people of this country have had all too little part in the deliberations which have succeeded the signing of the armistice. The people never were asked whether or not they were fighting for the particular economic and political and sociological schemes we are now told, by apparent inspiration, constituted our cause in this war. Congress has not been consulted,—not even the coordinate treaty making power of the government, the United States Senate. Here is the chief source of the confusion of counsel which now prevails; there has been no attempt to consult those legally charged with the duty of advising and consenting when international agreements are considered. After all the American people are seriously concerned in this subject; those who think, as well as those who merely record and throw back the ideas that are handed down to them by the rubber stamp statesmanship and journalism of the country, have some right to be considered and consulted in this matter, vitally affecting the whole body of the people,—not merely one party or one person. What opportunity has been given to the legislative representatives of the American people to be heard, either privately or publicly, upon the questions involved in the conclusion of peace and more particularly in the proposed new internationalism? The fact that no such opportunity has been given, and that, indeed, the advice of the Senate has been treated with ill-concealed contempt by the administration's partisans, should awaken those possessed by a spirit of true Americanism, to a realizing sense of the change it is sought to bring over the fundamental character of American government.

* * * * *

If ever there was, in the history of this country, a time for serious thinking on the part of every American citizen, rather than the ready acceptance of every polished phrase and glittering generality handed out from high places, that time is now. The destiny of this republic is at stake. A false step taken now can never be retraced. It is the duty of every citizen to think about these matters, so vitally affecting the future of his country, and to express courageously his own views rather than to parrot the phrases of politicians who may be deceived by the glamor that sometimes surrounds high places and often deludes those who occupy them. There are those who believe that in the working out of the domestic problems of the American people is a task

large enough to try to the uttermost the capacity of American leadership, and that in pursuing the rainbow of the new fangled internationalism we may lead old-fashioned American nationalism into the bottomless pit.
—January 18, 1919.

That our government should have been maintained in its original form, from its establishment until now, is not much to be wondered at. It had many props to support it through that period, which now are decayed and crumbled away. Through that period it was felt by all to be an undecided experiment; now it is understood to be a successful one. Then, all that sought celebrity and fame and distinction expected to find them in the success of that experiment. * * * But this field of glory is harvested, and the crop is already appropriated. New reapers will arise, and they too will seek a field. It is to deny what the history of the world tells us is true, to suppose that men of ambition and talents will not continue to spring up amongst us. And when they do, they will as naturally seek the gratification of their ruling passion as others have done before them. The question then is: Can that gratification be found in supporting and maintaining an edifice that has been erected by others? Most certainly it cannot. Many great and good men, sufficiently qualified for any task they should undertake, may ever be found whose ambition would aspire to nothing beyond a seat in Congress, a gubernatorial or a presidential chair; but such belong not to the family of the lion, or the tribe of the eagle. What! think you these places would satisfy an Alexander? Caesar or a Napoleon? Never! Towering genius disdains a beaten path. It seeks regions hitherto unexplored. It sees no distinction in adding story to story upon the monuments of fame erected to the memory of others. It denies that it is glory enough to serve under any chief. It scorns to tread in the footsteps of any predecessor, however illustrious. It thirsts and burns for distinction; and if possible, it will have it, whether at the expense of emancipating slaves or enslaving freemen. Is it unreasonable, then, to expect that some man possessed of the loftiest genius, coupled with ambition sufficient to push it to its utmost stretch, will at some time spring up among us? And when such an one does, it will require the people to be united with each other, attached to the government and laws, and generally intelligent, to successfully frustrate his design.—Abraham Lincoln.

We here highly resolve that government of the people, by the people, for the people, shall not perish from the earth. * * * From these honored dead we take increased devotion to that cause for which they gave the last full measure of devotion.—Abraham Lincoln.

WHY DO THEY OPPOSE DEBATE
AND DELIBERATION?

Can anyone give a good reason why a plan for world reconstruction involving the destiny of the American people and of the world should not be a subject of debate and deliberation in the United States of America?

Why is it insisted by proponents of the plans evolved at Paris, for the most part in secret, not by representatives of the peoples affected, democratically chosen, but by government functionaries exercising war powers, that the hastily constructed and as yet little understood compact, forever binding, shall be accepted without discussion and without the amount of consideration ordinarily given in this country to any important single question of domestic legislation?

Why is it insisted that this particular plan for a society of nations, comprising as a matter of fact only a few of the nations, concerning the implications of which men equally intelligent disagree, shall be adopted hurriedly, merely on the say so of its advocates that the result of the organization will be so and so? For instance, that it will keep us out of war, as the Democratic platform of 1916 did?

Why, in the settlement of the details of a league of nations, are not the people or the legislative bodies of the several nations given opportunity to choose the representatives who are to work out the new world frame of government? Did George Washington and four or five men of his selection undertake to write a complete constitution for the liberated American colonies and then insist upon the adoption of the plan in toto? No such procedure was even thought of. The duly constituted legislative bodies of the several states elected their representatives, and these representatives framed a constitution which was then submitted to the several colonial assemblies, without insistence that it be rammed through in a few days or weeks. Such a course would have been considered the height of autocratic effrontery.

The peace conference at Paris should, of course, have first settled the terms of peace with the central powers, and insisted upon their enforcement. It should then have settled such problems growing out of and directly related to the war as could have been adjudicated without extended deliberation. It should have decided upon the general form and purpose of a league of nations, and have accorded

AMERICANISM

to the legislative bodies of the governments concerned the right to
select representatives authorized to undertake world legislation.
This is true if we have saved the world for democracy, or even
lived up to the conceptions of democracy prevalent in the United
States of America for nearly a century and a half before we
entered the war. President Wilson declares that hereafter the
world is to be ruled by the "plain people" rather than by "select
classes," and yet in the method of formulating the league of nations plan now presented there has been complete exclusion not
merely of the people, but of the representatives of the people duly
chosen for the purpose of legislating in their behalf. We have
presented for our consideration the system of legislating by executive ukase.

The league of nations plan as agreed upon at Paris has elements
of good and of evil, of safety and of danger. The claim that it is
without merit and the claim that it is a divinely inspired charter
of world reconstruction that is going to bring on the kingdom of
heaven, as Prof. Herron puts it, and that it should be swallowed
hook, line and sinker without giving it the least original consideration, even in the body charged with the duty of ratifying or
rejecting international agreements in this country,—these two
claims are equally unwarranted and unpatriotic. The argument
that this compact, which is not a peace treaty but a world constitution, must be ratified as rapidly as a billion dollars is appropriated by a subservient Congress, in order that President Wilson may
catch the next boat back to Paris, attaches too little importance to
the fate of the American people and of the world, and too much
importance to sailing dates. Up to this time the legislative representatives of the American people have been completely ignored
in the proceedings at Paris. Now a tremendous claque begins the
cry that Congress must supinely succumb to the demands of the
vast publicity organization of the national administration and the
sundry influences joined with it in this movement to effect world
reconstruction in as short a time as is ordinarily devoted to boiling
an egg, and content itself with doing the rubber stamp act again.
We are told that if Congress should fail to asquiesce, the administration will appeal over the heads of the people's representatives
to the people themselves. Well, there was a little appealing of
this kind done in November last, with a result well remembered,
—a popular majority of a million and a half votes against the
appealer.
—February 22, 1919.

Let us go on to extend the area of our usefulness, until the
light of the stars on our banner shall shine upon five hundred millions of free and happy people."—Abraham Lincoln.

44

THE HERITAGE OF WASHINGTON

Fortunate is America in the character of the man whose valor and genius won for this nation its independence, and whose wisdom, patience and patriotism evolved, in large measure, the institutions which perpetuated for the American people the liberty and opportunity our Revolutionary forefathers fought to achieve.

The world was full of visionary schemes of social, political and industrial regeneration at the moment the American colonies won their independence. But Washington, Madison, Jefferson, Franklin, Hamilton, Adams, Jay and the other giants of the Revolutionary period, founded a government based not upon imagination, doomed to disaster at the first shock of adversity, but upon human nature as revealed in human history. They studied the record of every government in history, ancient and modern, and, after long debate and deliberation formulated a frame of government of which Gladstone said that it was "the greatest work ever struck off at a given time by the hand and brain of man."

In France the overthrow of tyranny was followed by a debauch of lawlessness in which the heritage of patriotic sacrifice was wasted. But here was founded the great republic which in the succeeding years has been the world's best example of free government, this government of ordered liberty, the hope and the inspiration of democracy throughout the world.

Never before in American history were the wise counsels of Washington's Farewell Address more immediately applicable to national affairs than they are today. As we read them again, we are struck with the lofty patriotism, the sound sense and the far-reaching vision which inspired them. They are the chart and compass by which the old ship of state should be navigated in this hour of storm and stress.

Washington declared that the safety of America was best defended by its isolation from the interests and concerns of Europe. He saw and declared the fact that there is no such thing as disinterested friendship between nations; therefore international alliances were undesirable, since the first clash of interest would dissolve them. He declared that Europe had her rivalries, hatreds and attachments, based upon a political and social order from which we fortunately had been liberated, in which we might not wisely or safely involve ourselves. And Washington was put to the test in this matter in a situation much like the present. France had been our ally during the Revolution, and turned to us confi-

45

dently for help in her conflict with England, after France had overthrown her own tyrant and grappled with the nation so recently our oppressor. The national hatred of England, the national sympathy for France, was appealed to by the visionaries and demagogues of that day in the effort to involve the United States in European entanglements. It was in the light of these recent events that Washington wrote his historic appeal in behalf of an America minding her own business and fulfilling her own destiny.

In that appeal Washington was not unmindful of the necessity of providing for the national defense. He urged us "to take care always to keep ourselves, by suitable establishments, in a respectable defensive posture." These are the words neither of a jingo nor a pacifist, but of the wisest and most unselfish soldier, statesman and diplomat the world has yet produced.
—February 22, 1919.

In order that this republic may become fully independent it must become not merely politically, but also industrially independent; for, broadly considered, political freedom is not so much an end as a means; it is not a goal, but a starting point. In the presence of false industrial and economic systems political freedom can not avail. After inducing the mass of the people to indulge in high aspiration, to believe in the principles of our immortal Declaration that "all men are created equal," to understand that here they are living under no system of caste, that the people constitute the government, and that all opportunities are open to the least among them, it is vain to say that they must be content to live in conditions of misery identical with those which surround the subjects of despotic governments who have never drank in the spirit of liberty. We must not say to our people, "Aspire, be proud, be independent—and live in squalor."

To be independent in the true and full sense a nation must become self-sustaining. Its work must be done by its own people on its own soil. In the means of livelihood of its citizens it must be independent of all the world. It should not leave them subject to the shifting, uncertain and antaongistic policies of foreign governments. A great people should possess themselves of all the arts and industries of civilization.—Senator John P. Jones, of Nevada, in U. S. Senate Sept. 10, 1890.

It has been the policy of the United States since the foundation of the government to cultivate relations of peace and amity with all the nations of the world, and this accords with my conception of our duty now.

We have cherished the policy of non-interference with the affairs of foreign governments, wisely inaugurated by Washington * * * content to leave undisturbed with them the settlement of their own domestic concerns.—William McKinley.

WHY NOT A NATIONAL BILL OF RIGHTS IN THE PROPOSED WORLD CONSTITUTION?

The sudden ending of the great war left in existence the most powerful league of nations the world has ever known. It was composed of a score of nations united by a great common cause, and fighting for common ends fully understood. It was within the power of that league of nations, in the determination of the terms of peace stipulated for the ending of the war, to settle at the council table every problem affecting and affected by the war, and thereby to give the world assurance that these problems, at least, would not again menace its peace.

But the Paris peace conference, largely because of the influence of President Wilson, has failed to do the natural and essential things incident to a peace council. It has scarcely touched its hand to the work of adjusting the economic, territorial and military problems presented at the war's ending; today these problems are more serious, the peace of the world is therefore now more in jeopardy, than it was the day the armistice was signed. Through the insistence of President Wilson the peace conference has left undone the things it ought to have done; the time of the conference has been expended in developing a scheme of world government, a task which belonged, not to a peace conference, composed of men whose commissions are based upon military exigency, but to a legislative body representative of the peoples affected. The peace conference had a clear commission to settle the problems immediately growing out of the war; it had no commission whatever to write a new constitution for the world, though it might properly have called into being an international legislative body charged with this duty.

The people of this country favor a court of nations for the arbitration of international disputes and the reduction of armaments. They notice, in connection with President Wilson's league scheme, that it is considered entirely consistent with the plan that one of the constituent nations is to maintain the mastery of the seas through the ownership of the world's most powerful navy. The people are not sure, therefore, that even in exchange for the surrender of national sovereignty apparently involved, we are to be insured against war, or the rule of force. But if we are to become members of a world league, the people of this country undoubtedly favor the inclusion in the world constitution of certain reserved powers of American nationality. Such reserved rights for the individual and the state governments were found essential to the acceptance of the American Constitution. These are found set forth in the first ten amendments, and are known as the "bill of rights" of the Constitution. They include provisions for freedom of speech and the press, the right to bear arms, right of trial by jury, etc. There are certain national rights which opponents of the league of nations scheme as proposed believe are menaced under its provisions, but which its friends say are not by any reasonable interpretation threatened.

Then let there be included in this constitution of the league of nations, a bill of national rights something like this:

"Nothing in this constitution shall be interpreted:

"To supplant the Monroe Doctrine;

"To substitute international for national sovereignty;

"To impair or destroy the rights of American citizens at home or abroad;

"To limit the right of the American people to determine for themselves their own domestic policies, particularly those bearing upon the tariff and immigration;

"To involve the United States in any war without the specific approval of the American Congress;

"To abrogate any guarantee of the American Constitution;

"To impose any liability for policing or financing of any foreign government or territory, not authorized by the American Congress;

"To prevent the United States from maintaining as large a navy as any other power;

"To prevent the American government from withdrawing from the proposed league of nations, by giving reasonable notice of intention, whenever the league operates to the serious impairment of just American rights and interests."

If there are no hidden dangers in the proposed constitution of the league of nations, what possible objection can there be to the clear setting forth, within the document, of the things the American people would not surrender except through deception?

The seed, not of peace, but of war, is in any governmental compact which leaves unsettled differences which may become irreconcilable. The greatest war ever waged in the world, prior to the present war, was the American Civil war. It was fought, necessarily, because the American Constitution failed to settle two fundamental questions: human slavery, and the right of secession. With this precedent in view, foolish indeed would be the policy of accepting the proposed constitution of a league of nations without settling, so far as is possible, every question which in the future might, if left undetermined, present to this country the alternatives of war, unequally waged, or the sacrifice of American fundamentals.

—March 1, 1919.

SEEDS OF INTERNATIONAL CONFLICT
LEFT IN THE GROUND

The creation of a new fabric of international government will not save the world from the danger of conflict unless there be, at the very beginning a meeting of minds upon fundamental questions liable to become subjects of dispute. The United States Constitution, although it was a compact which created a single nation of people speaking one tongue and having common traditions, and on the whole, common interests, did not keep the American people out of war, because it failed to settle what was the most perplexing national problem at the time the compact was made, and became more and more difficult as time went on. The question of the right of a state to secede and of the right of the system of human slavery to continue was not settled in the Constitution, and it had, at last, to be settled by the sword in the greatest war in history up to the time of the beginning of the present World war.

It is very clear that the Paris peace conference has side-stepped almost every problem growing out of the war. It has not even settled the terms of peace. It has not attempted to fix new boundaries. It has made no decision upon the question of reduced armaments. It has done nothing toward settling what, so far as this country is concerned, is likely to become the most menacing of problems,—that of the rights of the yellow race and the relationship of Japan to China and the Orient in general. Every day that has been permitted to go by since the signing of the armistice has made the settlement of these vital questions more difficult. Nothing, absolutely nothing, has been settled; all that has been done is to propose a form of world government in which this nation is to have one vote out of nine, at the beginning, in the settlement not only of European and Asiatic problems, but of the problems of this hemisphere.

Before the American people bind themselves to accept decisions upon matters of peculiar American concern by a body dominated by European and Asiatic powers, there should be some understandings not yet reached. It is not understood in the United Kingdom that the formation of this league is to prevent Great Britain from maintaining an army of one million and a navy able to dominate the seas. Coincident with the submission of this plan guaranteed to keep us out of war, we are told that we must

have a vast navy and army. Not only is it the right, but it is manifestly the duty of the American people to discuss the vital problem now before them. The whole people must live with the consequences of this proposed compact. They should have some opportunity to deliberate upon it and decide upon its terms, and those who oppose such deliberation and decision must be prompted by ulterior motives.
—March 1, 1919.

It is natural for man to indulge in the illusions of hope. We are apt to shut our eyes against a painful truth, and listen to the song of that siren till she transforms us into beasts. Is this the part of wise men, engaged in a great and arduous struggle for liberty? Are we disposed to be of the number of those who, having eyes, see not, and having ears, hear not, the things which so nearly concern their temporal salvation? For my part, whatever anguish of spirit it may cost, I am willing to know the whole truth; to know the worst, and to provide for it. I have but one lamp by which my feet are guided; and that is the lamp of experience. I know of no way of judging of the future but by the past.
—Patrick Henry.

Washington clearly discriminated between alliances that would entangle and those that would not, and between alliances that were permanent and those that were temporary. Justly construed, Washington's utterances are as wise today as when they were made, and are no more applicable to the United States than to any other nation. It must be the policy of every state to avoid alliances that entangle, while temporary and limited are better than general and permanent alliances because friends and partners should be chosen in view of actually existing exigencies rather than in reliance upon doubtful forecasts of the uncertain future.
—Richard Olney, 1900.

Before the expiration of his last Presidential term, he (Washington) gave us his paternal advice, which, if duly attended to. will forever preserve to us the inheritance of freedom. Let us pursue this advice, and never depart from it; it is addressed to us all; it is addressed to every American. "Let just and amicable feelings, devoid of all partialities and antipathies, regulate your conduct with all nations; guard against the interference of foreign nations in your internal concerns." In this advice, our Washington still lives; in this bequest the father of our country, to the whole American people, our Washington will forever live, in the hearts and minds of all patriots over the whole globe; and his venerable name will descend with unfading glory, down the perpetual succession of time, through ages of ages.—Joseph Blyth, 1800.

SHALL WE BE DELIVERED TO AN
INTERNATIONAL AUTOCRACY?

What the American people want is the world-wide rule of justice. What the Smuts-Wilson league of nations scheme provides is the world-wide sway of force.

What the American people asked and expected, following that prompt decision of the immediate issues of the war which, to the world's peril, has been denied it, was a charter of international law, interpreted by a court of nations, "composed," as Colonel Roosevelt said, "of representatives from each nation, these representatives being sworn to act as judges in each case, and not in a representative capacity."

What they are offered is a world parliament, bound by no guarantees of fundamental reserved national rights; a world autocracy governed by a majority on the basis of interest; that majority being alien in interest and spirit to this republic.

A spokesman of the administration (Senator Hitchcock) says that this pact creates "a powerful legislative, executive and judicial body." It does. Alexander Hamilton said that the combination of all, or any two of these powers in one body was "the essence of tyranny." Montesquieu said that such a combination was "destructive of liberty." This scheme embodies the socialist theory of the state; government by an autocracy claiming the right to exercise unlimited authority over those subject to its jurisdiction as compared with the republican idea of government by the majority, restrained by checks and balances guaranteeing deliberative decision, and limited by the reserved rights of the individual,—or in this case of the nation member of this proposed world state.

Put forward in the name of peace, it pledges us to enter every war which alien decision may make ours.

Put forward in the name of justice, it binds us on penalty of armed invasion to the acceptance of every arbitrary decision, right or wrong, of the trustees and masters of mankind constituting this combination of king, congress and court to which has been affixed the alluring title of "League of Nations," which may through the growth of its now vaguely defined powers become the plague of nations.

It destroys the greatest political corporation in the world to merge it with every bankrupt governmental concern on earth in

51

an international company wherein we are to enjoy the well known privileges of a minority stock holder in a company controlled by one's competitors.

Of all the conflicting claims and ambitions, designs and deserts of nations, the seeds of future conflict, it settles none, nor does it require nations to lay down their arms.

It tramples the Declaration of Independence, it destroys the American Constitution. It is nothing that it claims to be; it is all that it claims not to be.

The American people ask for the rule of right. This scheme enthrones the rule of might.

We have won "a war for democracy" only to be asked to deliver this republic into the control of an international autocracy. —March 8, 1919.

We find ourselves in the peaceful possession of the fairest portion of the earth as regards extent of territory, fertility of soil, and salubrity of climate. We find ourselves under the government of a system of political institutions conducing more essentially to the ends of civil and religious liberty than any of which the history of former times tells us. We, when mounting the stage of existence, found ourselves the legal inheritors of these fundamental blessings. We toiled not in the acquirement or establishment of them; they are a legacy bequeathed to us by a once hardy, brave and patriotic but now lamented and departed race of ancestors. Theirs was the task (and nobly they performed it) to possess themselves, and through themselves us, of this goodly land, and to uprear upon its hills and its valleys a political edifice of liberty and equal rights. It is ours only to transmit these—the former unprofaned by the foot of an invader, the latter undecayed by the lapse of time and untorn by usurpation—to the latest generation that fate shall permit the world to know. This task, gratitude to our fathers, justice to ourselves, duty to posterity, and love for our species in general all imperatively require us faithfully to perform.—Abraham Lincoln.

The nations of America are equally sovereign and independent with those of Europe. They possess the same rights, independent of all foreign interposition, to make war, to conclude peace, and to regulate their internal affairs. The people of the United States cannot, therefore, view with indifference attempts of European powers to interfere with the independent action of the nations on this continent.

The American system of government is entirely different from that of Europe. * * * We must ever maintain the principle that the people of this continent alone have the right to decide their own destiny.—James K. Polk.

THE NEED OF THE WORLD

The fundamental wrong in the plan for a league of nations now proposed is that it establishes, not a world court but a world government.

It establishes, not the sway of justice, but the reign of force.

It creates, not a body of international law, to govern the relations of nations, and a court to construe that law in each instance of dispute, but a world legislature, or executive world autocracy.

The people of the world want disarmament as the only certain guarantee of world peace; mutual disarmament; this proposed constitution of a league of nations does not provide it; it merely binds the American people to the acceptance of whatever decisions may be made upon this matter by a world legislature,—no matter what that decision may be.

The people of the world want wars to end; but this constitution of a league of nations settles none of the many problems which now menace the world's peace. On the contrary, it leaves them all unsettled, but binds the American people to the acceptance of any settlement that may be made, in a world legislature dominated by alien interests, regardless of whether or not American interests and ideals, or the welfare of Americans in general, are sacrificed in that settlement.

The American people are willing to dip their flag to justice, but not to force, regardless of whether that force is behind a righteous or an unrighteous cause.

The Paris peace conference should settle the terms of peace with the central powers, should settle the questions growing immediately out of the present war, should propose a code of international law and a world court, composed of men of such legal ability and standing that, nominated by each of the nations, signers of the compact, they would be ratified by all the rest, to interpret that code of general principles in its application to every international dispute. To the enforcement of the decrees of such a court every nation should pledge itself.

The supernational government, as proposed in the league of nations, represents only the sway of numbers, not the reign of wisdom or of right. The court of nations would represent the rule of justice. The proposed league of nations is founded upon the socialistic idea of the sway of brute force, regardless of equity. It would, if adopted, mark, not the ending, but the beginning of perpetual warfare with the people of this country obligated to partici-

pate in every war as well as to surrender the national independence achieved by Washington and preserved by Lincoln.
—March 8, 1919.

Unhappy Europe! The judgment of God rests hard upon thee! Thy sufferings would deserve an angel's pity if an angel's tears could wash away thy crimes! The Eastern Continent seems trembling on the brink of some great catastrophe. Convulsions shake and terrors alarm it. Ancient systems are failing; works reared by ages are crumbling into atoms. Let us humbly implore Heaven that the wide-spreading desolation may never reach the shores of our native land, but let us devoutly make up our minds to do our duty in events that may happen to us. Let us cherish genuine patriotism. In that, there is a sort of inspiration that gives strength and energy almost more than human. When the mind is attached to a great object, it grows to the magnitude of its undertaking. A true patriot, with his eye and his heart on the honor and happiness of his country, hath an elevation of soul that lifts him above the rank of ordinary men. To common occurrences he is indifferent. Personal considerations dwindle into nothing in comparison with his high sense of public duty. In all the vicissitudes of fortune, he leans with pleasure on the protection of Providence and on the dignity and composure of his own mind. While his country enjoys peace, he rejoices and is thankful; and, if it be in the counsel of Heaven to send the storm and the tempest, his bosom proudly swells against the rage that assaults it. Above fear, above danger, he feels that the last end which can happen to any man never comes too soon if he falls in defense of the laws and liberties of his country.—Daniel Webster.

This lovely land, this glorious liberty, these benign institutions, the dear purchase of our fathers, are ours; ours to enjoy, ours to preserve, ours to transmit. Generations past and generations to come hold us responsible for this sacred trust. Our fathers, from behind, admonish us, with their anxious paternal voices; posterity calls out to us, from the bosom of the future; the world turns hither its solicitous eyes; all, all conjure us to act wisely and faithfully, in the relation which we sustain.

If we cherish the virtues and the principles of our fathers Heaven will assist us to carry on the work of human liberty and human happiness. Auspicious omens cheer us. Great examples are before us. Our own firmament now shines brightly upon our path. Washington is in the clear, upper sky. These other stars have now joined the American constellation; they circle round their center, and the heavens beam with new light. Beneath this illumination let us walk the course of life, and at its close devoutly commend our beloved country, the common parent of us all, to the Divine benignity.—Daniel Webster.

THE ALTERNATIVE TO THE LORD CECIL-WILSON LEAGUE

The statement that those who oppose the Lord Cecil-Wilson plan for a league of nations thereby give evidence of their opposition to international action with a view to minimizing the danger of war, is false and unpatriotic.

The assumption that those who favor the Lord Cecil-Wilson plan for a league of nations, which President Wilson says the American people must accept without change, are more anxious than others to keep this country out of war is just as unfair and as unpatriotic as the cry, in 1916, that "a vote for Hughes means war, a vote for Wilson means peace,"—a cry, be it remembered, in which President Wilson himself led.

War never had as few friends or apologists in the United States as it has today, and with good reason. The American people knew something of the horrors of the battlefield, but they never dreamed of the horrors of war administration of civil affairs as exemplified by the present administration. They never knew what use could be made of a condition of war to fasten upon the country, as war measures, ventures in state socialism; how far an administration could go in restricting freedom of speech and of the press; in coercion and confiscation; in the domination of public opinion through propaganda and control of the channels of information; in aggressions of the executive upon the legislative branch of government; in extravagance and inefficiency and waste. The sort of administration the Democratic party has furnished the country in the last two years has at least done one thing: It has made hell popular as compared with the civilian conditions accompanying war as waged by a Democratic administration.

Those who oppose the Lord Cecil-Wilson plan for a league of nations do so on the ground that while it may decrease the number of wars on other continents, it will increase the number of wars in which we of America will become involved. They oppose an international arrangement which forfeits the right of this republic to determine for itself what wars it will and will not enter, and involves the necessity of furnishing men and money to fight battles in which the American people have no direct, national interest.

The alternative to a league of nations is a court of nations; to a super-state the alternative is a world supreme court, with a fixed code of fundamental international law for the guidance of the nations. It is the sway of justice the American people desire, not the erection of a world parliament to make decisions by majorities, based upon interest rather than equity, and in which we are to hold but a minority membership. The nations which have fought the present war to a victorious conclusion are competent to write that code of international law and to create a world court for its application to individual cases of conflict. Beyond this, but two things are needed; a voluntary pledge by the associated powers, an enforced pledge by the rest, properly guaranteed, for submission to a supreme law which does not invade the domestic rights of any nation, or sacrifice its sovereignty in any essential respect; second, progressive disarmament, begun at once,—a thing not definitely provided for in the proposed league of nations covenant, but without which any so-called peace program becomes the merest farce.

This is the alternative,—but what chance is there for the American people to present it? What attention is paid, or has been paid, either to the people or their legislative representatives? We are told that whatever is done in Paris, without consulting more than one man in the United States, must be accepted here, because peace will not be permitted until the scheme proposed is swallowed in its entirety regardless of its content or its consequences.

That the American people and the American Senate, charged with joint responsibility in the formulation of treaties, have been permitted to bear no part in the proceedings at Paris, is no fault of either the people or the Senate. Their very existence has been ignored. Who is to blame for this? Does the determination to put through a plan to Europeanize America in accordance with the program of the socialist International mean the saving of the world for democracy or the deliverance of this country to autocracy? If the people and the constitutional authorities of the United States are ignored in the creation of a world parliament, what may we expect as to the part they will play in the operation of the world state, should it be established?
—March 15, 1919.

$$\boxed{\;\square\!\!\supset 0 \subset\!\!\square\;}$$

I thank God that America abounds in men who are superior to temptation, whom nothing can divert from a steady pursuit of the interest of their country, who are at once its ornament and safeguard. And sure I am I should not incur your displeasure if I paid a respect so justly due to their much honored characters in this place; but, when I name an Adams, such a numerous host of fellow-patriots rush up to my mind that I fear it would take up too much of your time should I attempt to call over the illustrious roll; but your grateful hearts will point you to the men; and their revered names, in all succeeding times, shall grace the annals of America.—John Hancock.

WILSON VETOES PEACE

In a Paris cablegram dated March 17, and published in the United States two days later, Frank H. Simonds, the most reliable of all American correspondents now in Europe, and not unfriendly to President Wilson, makes the astounding statement that when President Wilson returned to Paris, he found that an agreement had been unanimously made by all representatives at the peace conference, including his associates on the American delegation, to perfect a preliminary peace with Germany on March 21st. This preliminary peace was to include military, naval, economic and geographic terms. It was intended by the conference to be in substance the final peace treaty, exclusive of the league of nations constitution. There had been no difference of opinion in the peace conference in arriving at this conclusion, Mr. Simonds says, and there was no feeling on the part of the American delegates that this action was intended to defeat the league of nations by indirection or to evade the question even temporarily. The sole idea was to end the war, stop the growing unrest in Europe, enable the belligerent countries to demobilize their armies and get back to work at the earliest moment possible without awaiting the discussion and decision of features of the proposed world constitution.

Upon the arrival of President Wilson, Mr. Simonds says, he abruptly and imperatively vetoed the program, overruling the entire membership of the peace conference. He issued a denial of the statement authorized by M. Pichon that such an agreement had been reached and asserted that it would not be permitted. By so doing he assumed responsibility for continuing a state of war for at least two months, possibly longer, and to that extent delayed the return of American troops to the United States and the cessation of the vast expenditure incident to keeping a huge American army in Europe. The preliminary peace treaty will be postponed until April, and President Wilson will not, if he can prevent it, permit peace to be declared finally before the American Senate is forced to accept a final peace treaty into which the Cecil-Wilson league of nations plan is so interwoven that it will be impossible to separate the two.

It is evident that in so doing President Wilson made the peace and safety of Europe secondary to his desire for a triumph in his proposed battle with the American Senate, this in turn, according to Norman E. Mack, of the Democratic national committee, to be made the basis of a third term candidacy for the Presidency. In

other words, President Wilson fears that the Cecil-Wilson scheme will not secure the approval of the American people on its own merits. He fears to permit it to stand alone. He is determined that the American people shall have no hand in the framing of the new world constitution, and he proposes to offer them the alternative of swallowing the scheme as he brings it home, or permitting the continuance of a state of war. It is scarcely necessary to make comment upon such a situation, but if the old spirit of Americanism is not dead, it will find expression.
—March 22, 1919.

Sir, I agree to this Constitution, with all its faults, if they are such, because I think a general government necessary for us, and there is no form of government but what may be a blessing to the people, if well administered; and I believe, further, that this is likely to be well administered for a course of years, and can only end in despotism, as other forms have done before it, when the people shall become so corrupted as to need despotic government, being incapable of any other. I doubt, too, whether any other convention we can obtain, may be able to make a better constitution. For when you assemble a number of men, to have the advantage of their joint wisdom, you inevitably assemble with those men all their prejudices, their passions, their errors of opinion, their local interests, and their selfish views. From such an assembly can a perfect production be expected? It therefore astonishes me, sir, to find this system approaching so near to perfection as it does; and I think it will astonish our enemies, who are waiting with confidence to hear that our counsels are confounded, like those of the builders of Babel, and that our states are on the point of separation, only to meet, hereafter, for the purpose of cutting one another's throats.—Benjamin Franklin.

The genius of our institutions, the needs of our people in their home life, and the attention which is demanded for the settlement and development of the resources of our vast territory, dictate the scrupulous avoidance of any departure from that foreign policy commended by the history, the traditions, and the prosperity of our republic. It is the policy of independence, favored by our position and defended by our known love of justice and by our own power. It is the policy of peace suitable to our interests. It is the policy of neutrality, rejecting any share in foreign broils and ambitions upon other continents and repelling their intrusion here. It is the policy of Monroe, and of Washington, and Jefferson— "Peace, commerce, and honest friendship with all nations; entangling alliance with none."—Grover Cleveland.

DEMOCRATIC DETERMINATION OF A
WORLD CONSTITUTION

Speaking at a Democratic party rally in New York, Secretary of the Navy Daniels, declared that Congress had committed itself to the Cecil-Wilson plan for a league of nations when, in 1916, it passed a resolution inviting all the great governments of' the world to send representatives to a conference, to be held at the close of the war, which should "be charged with the duty of formulating a plan for a court of arbitration or other tribunal, to which disputed questions between nations shall be referred for adjudication and peaceful settlement."

Not only does this plan not coincide with the Cecil-Wilson scheme for a league of nations, but its distance from it brings into clear view the defects of the plan President Wilson, without the advice or consent of the Senate or the American people, insists upon putting over, without discussion or decision upon its merits.

First, this resolution contemplated the settlement, by the nations involved, of the issues growing out of the war, before entering upon negotiations for the creation of a tribunal of arbitration.

Second, it contemplated the formulation of the permanent plan, by more than one man acting on behalf of this country, without the consent and against the advice of the branch of government constitutionally charged with joint responsibility in the framing of international obligations. Not enough emphasis has been placed upon the undemocratic and unrepublican procedure of President Wilson in connection with the formulation of the league of nations plan. The initiation of a peace treaty is constitutionally his responsibility, though an understanding of and sympathy with the letter and spirit of the Constitution would require that even in this matter President Wilson should follow the example of his predecessors and not only consult the Senate, but appoint representatives of that body upon the peace commission. On the contrary, President Wilson chose the personnel of this delegation entirely from among his own personal following, and on the same principle that a celebrated Shakesperean actor is said to have always picked his cast, —to form a background of mediocrity upon which genius would shine the more brilliantly.

But the creation of a league of nations is clearly a legislative function, and it is utterly out of harmony with the spirit of American institutions or with democracy itself for one man to take upon

59

himself, without legislative sanction, the sole duty and responsibility of writing the constitution of such a league. Just as the various state assemblies chose the delegates to the American constitutional convention, so should Congress, or the people even more directly, choose the representatives of the United States in a body charged with world legislation. Mere executive domination of such a body is, of course, the height of autocratic usurpation. It is not clear that in the new world congress that is proposed, the representatives of the nations will not be chosen by their several executives; indeed, the procedure in the present peace conference, which has converted itself on its own motion into a constitutional convention for the entire world, would seem to contemplate that our representatives in the world legislature thus to be created shall represent, not the people, not the national Congress, not the government, but the executive only; it is natural, of course, for Secretary Daniels to assume that when the word "government" is used, the executive and his appointed ministers only are referred to.

Third, the Cecil-Wilson plan for a league of nations does not comply with the expressed will of Congress as set forth in the resolution of 1916; on the contrary, it violates it. The proceedings at Paris do not contemplate what Congress suggested, namely, a court or other tribunal of arbitration, but it provides a world government combining in one body, after the fashion of autocracy, legislative, executive and judicial powers. This world government is to settle the affairs of nations by combined force, rather than by equity. It imposes upon the United States obligations and responsibilities, involves it in sacrifices and perils no one dreamed of suggesting prior to the time President Wilson began to assume, acting in the capacity of government of the United States, that it was up to us to assume the trusteeship for Asia, Europe, Africa and the islands of the sea, and for these alien continents to share trusteeship over the American people.

The people of this country would be glad to have the intent of this congressional resolution of 1916, as quoted by Secretary Daniels, followed out to the letter. They would like to see the belligerent powers settle the questions arising out of the war, that they may not be left in the ground as the seed of future conflict. They would like to see a world conference called, composed of representatives of the nations of the world, with a view to writing a just code of international law and establishing a tribunal to interpret it, and to provide for progressive disarmament and peaceful means of enforcing the decrees of the world court. But they want this plan evolved as the result of debate and deliberation in a world convention composed of representatives duly chosen by the peoples and congresses of the various nations of the world, not merely of diplomatic and military puppets of potentates and powers, selected without the advice or consent of the peoples or their

constitutional legislative representatives. That a world constitution should be the mere by-product of a peace conference acquiring its authority only from military exigency, is a fine commentary upon the doctrine that we have been saving the world for democracy. No procedure so grossly violative of the fundamentals of democracy has been undertaken since the time when a few grand monarchs assumed the responsibility of governing the affairs of the world in their own persons. That it should gain the acquiescence of any considerable number of people in this country proves that the worst horror of war is not in the list of killed and wounded. It is in that departure, under the stress of war, from the mental attitude and procedure consistent with free institutions which those who acquire war powers are likely to consider warrant for a continuance of that autocracy even free peoples loyally endure while the need exists.
—March 22, 1919.

It is a good thing for all Americans, and it is an especially good thing for young Americans to remember the men who have given their lives in war and peace to the service of their fellow countrymen and to keep in mind the feats of daring and personal valor done by some of the champions of the nation in the various crises of her history. Thrift, industry, obedience to law, and intellectual cultivation are essential qualities in the make up of any successful people; but no people can be really great unless they possess also the heroic virtues which are as needful in time of peace as in time of war, and as important in civil as in military life. * * *

America will cease to be a great nation whenever her young men cease to possess energy, daring and endurance, as well as the wish and the power to fight the nation's foes. No citizen of a state should wrong any man; but it is not enough merely to refrain from infringing on the rights of others; he must also be able and willing to stand up for his own rights, and those of his country against all comers, and he must be ready at any time to do his full share in resisting either malice domestic or foreign levy.

Patriotism should be an integral part of our every feeling at all times, for it is merely another name for those qualities of soul which makes a man in peace or in war, by day or by night think of his duty to his fellows, and of his duty to the nation through which their and his liftiest aspirations must find their fitting expressions.—Theodore Roosevelt.

The rapid extension of our settlements over our territories heretofore unoccupied, the addition of new states to our confederacy, the expansion of free principles, and our rising greatness as a nation are attracting the attention of the powers of Europe, and lately the doctrine has been broached in some of them of a "balance of power" on this continent to check our advancement. The United States, sincerely desirous of preserving relations of good understanding with all nations, can not in silence permit any European interference on the North American continent, and should any such interference be attempted will be ready to resist it at any and all hazards.

It is well known to the American people and to all nations that this government has never interfered with the relations subsisting between other governments. * * * We have not sought their territories by conquest; we have not mingled with parties in their domestic struggles; and believing our own form of government to be the best, we have never attempted to propagate it by intrigues, by diplomacy, or by force. We may claim on this continent a like exemption from European interference. The nations of America are equally sovereign and independent with those of Europe. They possess the same rights, independent of all foreign interposition, to make war, to conclude peace, and to regulate their internal affairs. The people of the United States cannot, therefore, view with indifference attempts of European powers to interfere with the independent action of the nations on this continent. The American system of government is entirely different from that of Europe. Jealousy among the different sovereigns of Europe, lest any one of them might become too powerful for the rest, has caused them anxiously to desire the establishment of what they term the "balance of power." It can not be permitted to have any application on the North American continent, and especially to the United States. We must ever maintain the principle that the people of this continent alone have the right to decide their own destiny.

In the existing circumstances of the world the present is deemed a proper occasion to reiterate and reaffirm the principle avowed by Mr. Monroe and to state my cordial concurrence in its wisdom and sound policy. The reassertion of this principle, especially, in reference to North America, is at this day but the promulgation of a policy which no European power should cherish the disposition to resist. Existing rights of every European nation should be respected, but it is due alike to our safety and our interests that the efficient protection of our laws should be extended over our whole territorial limits and that it should be distinctly announced to the world as our settled policy that no future European colony or dominion shall with our consent be planted or established on any part of the North American continent.—James K. Polk.

Interest in public affairs, national, state and city, should be ever present and active and not abated from one year's end to the other.—William McKinley.

SHALL OUR AMERICA BE EUROPEANIZED?

It will soon be four hundred years since the Pilgrim Fathers braved the perils of a wintry sea to find civil and religious liberty in a new land, a land of hardship and of peril, but a land of freedom.

They turned their backs upon a Europe covered with "the rotten survivals of bygone circumstances," preferring the freedom of a far wilderness to the slavery of citizenship in the Old World. They, and those who, from similar motives and with similar hopes and aspirations, came after them, laid broad and deep the foundations of a new social and political order.

Finally there was reared upon these foundations "the young republic of the west." It became the world's one great working model of deliberative democracy, where liberty safeguarded by law developed the civilization we call American.

Long regarded as "the American experiment," this new nation, "dedicated to the proposition that all men are created equal," this "government of the people, for the people, by the people," at length became the richest and strongest as well as the freest of earth.

When European civilization faced a crisis brought upon it by the continuance, through centuries, of hatreds and rivalries based upon racial and dynastic and commercial conflict, as well as by the clash of conflicting ideals, it was America whose duty and opportunity it became to enter the conflict and crush the aspiration of a great military power to become a new Rome and bestride the world like a Colossus.

Surely such a history should thrill any American with the thought of his citizenship, and cause him to hesitate before surrendering any of the things which have made Americans Liberty's "peculiar people."

But it is true that for years there has been in this country a formidable movement for the Europeanization of America.

It has been carried on by a variety of elements; by those of recent alien origin who have been unable to forget their allegiance to some European fatherland, to give up some centuries-old tradition of believing their own particular culture better than that of other peoples or that of their adopted country; by the people who think it a sign of superiority to affect the belief that anything foreign is better than the home brand, whether that be clothing or culture, a class typified by the New England professor whose press agent announced a few years ago that he was the only American possessing culture in the European sense of the term; by economists and politicians who have imported their text books and their programs from Europe; by toady journalists and publicists who have thought American institutions and ideals too "smelly" of the woods and fields, and have become European colonials in spirit; by persons of too little faith in genuine democracy and think tone would be given to our social and political order by titles and decorations; by people who have inherited the instincts either of peasantry or of aristocracy and believe both labor and leisure should constitute a basis of permanent caste, with every man "knowing his place;" by the agents and spies and press agents and lobbyists of alien and international commercial and political and financial interests, working under camouflage through all sorts of publications and organizations and never in the open with a revealed motive; by people who, being too lazy or too lacking in confidence to think for themselves, want a super-man to do the job for them and for others as a sort of American Kaiser, the embarrassments of legislative bodies being eliminated.

We have our aliens in spirit among the professors and among the protetariat. Some have imported their ideas and some have brought them along with them in the steerage. We have our parlor aliens who think it vulgar to be American; and our cellar aliens who still reek with the scent and the sentiment of the European purlieus; they are wings of the same army, however, and the wings flap together.

The work of Americanization in this country should begin at the top rather than at the bottom.

The recently arrived alien, speaking a foreign tongue, is not to be blamed if he fails to grasp the meaning of America and Americanism. This is especially true because in the dozen years prior to the war such people heard little talk and read little in the newspapers or magazines in behalf of American ideals, or American institutions, or American achievements; the seamy side of Americanism, rather than the face of the fabric in which is woven its real story and its real message, was constantly held up before them by the yellow press, the yellow politician, the parlor and the cellar socialist.

The class we need to educate in this country, a class for which there is no particular excuse, is composed of those who have enjoyed to the full the advantages and opportunities this country offers but who have so totally missed the point of it all in their devotion to European conceptions of things, that they have talked of this country as only a vulgar plutocracy which needs to have a "new freedom" conferred upon it, a new freedom consisting of the jargon of European socialist and free trade pamphleteers, a phraseology which, when translated into a program, consists, as we have learned by experience, of mere sound and fury, signifying nothing.

It is not surprising as we face, at the Paris peace conference, problems which fundamentally affect Americanism as ingrained Americans understand it, we suffer the effects of years of agitation by this cult of American infidelity. If the Europeanism of caste and class be, as they affect to believe, better than Americanism, why attempt to preserve the distinctive features of Americanism which our forefathers believed were safe only because a broad ocean rolled between us and entanglement with the affairs of princes and proletarians in a world as unlike our own, in many essentials, as the planet of Saturn? Why not throw in our lot with a hemisphere in which patriotism attaches more to a class or a caste than to a country or a people? Why not transfer this system of caste and class to America? Why not, as Lowell said, turn the prow of the Mayflower back

"Toward Europe, entering her blood-red eclipse?"
—March 29, 1919.

EXTRACTS FROM JEFFERSON'S WRITINGS

We have a perfect horror of everything like connecting ourselves with the politics of Europe.—To Wm. Short, 1801.

Commerce with all nations, alliance with none, should be our motto.—To T. Lomax, March, 1799.

We wish not to meddle with the internal affairs of any country, nor with the general affairs of Europe.—To C. W. F. Dumas, 1793.

The fundamental principle of our government is never to entangle us with the broils of Europe.—To M. Coray, 1823.

I know that it is a maxim with us, and I think it a wise one, not to entangle ourselves with the affairs of Europe.—1787.

Better keep together as we are, haul off from Europe as soon as we can, and from all attachments to any portions of it.—To John Taylor, 1798.

All entanglements with that quarter of the globe (Europe) should be avoided if we mean that peace and justice shall be the polar stars of the American societies.—To J. Correa, 1820.

I join you in a sense of the necessity of restoring freedom of the ocean. But I doubt, with you, whether the United States ought to join in an armed confederacy for that purpose; or rather, I am satisfied they ought not.—To George Logan, 1801.

Our nation has wisely avoided entangling itself in the system of European interests; has taken no side between its rival powers, attached itself to none of its ever-changing confederacies.—Reply to address of Baltimore Baptists, 1808.

I have ever deemed it fundamental for the United States never to take active part in the quarrels of Europe. Their political interests are entirely distinct from ours. Their mutual jealousies, their balance of power, their complicated alliances, their forms and principles of government, are all foreign to us. They are nations of eternal war.—To President Monroe, 1823.

It ought to be the very first object of our pursuits, to have nothing to do with the European interests and politics. Let them be free or slaves at will, navigators or agricultural, swallowed into one government or divided into a thousand, we have nothing to fear from them in any form.—To George Logan, March, 1801.

About to enter, fellow citizens, on the exercise of duties which comprehend everything dear and valuable to you, it is proper you should understand what I deem the essential principles of this government, and consequently, those which ought to shape its administration. I will compress them in the narrowest compass they will bear. Equal and exact justice to all men of whatever state or persuasion, religious or political; peace, commerce, and honest friendship with all nations, entangling alliances with none; the support of the state governments in all their rights, as the most competent administrations for our domestic concerns, and the surest bulwarks against anti-republican tendencies; the preservation of the general government in its whole constitutional vigor, as the sheet-anchor of our peace at home and safety abroad; a jealous care of the right of election by the people; economy in the public expense, that labor may be lightly burdened; encouragement of agriculture, and of commerce as its handmaid; the diffusion of information, and arraignment of all abuses at the bar of public reason; freedom of religion, freedom of the press, and freedom of person. These principles form the bright constellation which has gone before us, and guided our steps through an age of revolution and reformation. The wisdom of our sages and blood of our heroes have been devoted to their attainment; they should be the creed of our political faith; the text of civic instruction; the touchstone by which to try the services of those we trust; and should we wander from them in moments of error and alarm, let us hasten to retrace our steps and to regain the road which alone leads to peace, liberty and safety.—From Jefferson's first inaugural address.

The institution of government, to be lawful, must be pacific, that is, founded upon the consent, and by the agreement of those who are governed; each nation is exclusively the judge of the government best suited to itself, and no other nation can justly interfere by force to impose a different government upon it. The first of these principles may be designated as the principle of liberty—the second as the principle of national independence. They are both principles of peace and of good will to men.—John Quincy Adams, 1823.

DOES MR. WILSON SEEK TO THWART PEOPLE'S DESIRE FOR WORLD PEACE?

The theory is advanced, in the light of the recent announcement of President Wilson's third term candidacy, that Mr. Wilson may not be so anxious for the formation of a league of nations, as for putting his adversaries in a hole by framing up a plan the Senate could not conscientiously accept, and then going to the country with the plea that he had been thwarted in an attempt to keep the country out of war once more, through permanent international arrangement.

While this paper is not fully prepared to accept this theory, it is evident that if President Wilson were determined upon preventing the consummation of an international arrangement for safeguarding the world's peace, he could not adopt a course more cunningly calculated to further such an end.

Ninety-five percent of the people of the United States favor some form of international arrangement which will constitute as near absolute insurance against war as it is humanly possible to attain. As to principle, there is unity of sentiment; as to the means by which this purpose is to be achieved, there are divergent views.

As a whole-hearted advocate of joint action of the nations to prevent war, the natural course of President Wilson would have been to coordinate and unify public opinion in the United States, the nation he represents at the peace table, and the nation which, because of the disinterested character established by American diplomacy in our century and third of national life, and because of the unique and determinative part America has played in the war, has been in position to exercise so tremendous an influence upon the negotiations proceeding at Paris.

What President Wilson has done has been calculated, if not intended, to divide rather than unify public sentiment in the United States. He has taken the position that he, and he alone, among all the hundred millions of people who go to make up the United States, is entitled to think, speak or act upon this problem, so vital in its influence upon the destiny of this republic and of the world. He has assumed an attitude, not merely of indifference, but of defiance, toward that branch of the national legislature, representative of the people, charged with joint responsibility in the making of treaties. Far from acting, as the Constitution prescribes, with the advice and consent of that body, his effort has been to exclude the Senate from any degree of participation in the formulation either of the treaty of peace or the evolution of a world constitution. He has openly joined battle with the Senate in this matter, although he knows that the ratification of the treaty by the Senate is essential to its adoption. He has insisted that no peace treaty should be submitted which does not contain within it his plan for a world constitution so inextricably interwoven that the separation of the treaty and the constitution would be impossible.

President Wilson knows that the people of this country are as anxious for peace today as they were in 1916 when he proclaimed to the country the doctrine that the election of Hughes meant war and his re-election meant peace. He is again playing upon and with this sentiment. He is endeavoring to make it appear that only through the adoption of his particular plan is it possible to have either immediate or permanent peace. He is attaching his particular scheme for a league of nations, which millions of Americans believe involves a sacrifice of our national independence and the permanent peril of war, as a rider to the peace treaty. He is saying to the American Senate and the American people: "You must swallow this treaty as it stands, without change or amendment, on peril of assuming responsibility for preventing any sort of league or court or tribunal of nations."

Is this a constructive, or a destructive, position? Is it a democratic or an autocratic procedure? Is it calculated to promote, or to destroy, the prospect of a permanent arrangement for the safeguarding of the world's peace. Are we, by President Wilson's course, losing or gaining friends among the nations of the world, and thereby are we decreasing or increasing the danger of future wars? Are we helping or hindering Europe in the restoration of peace and order by taking the responsibility, through President Wilson, of delaying for months the settlement of the questions growing out of the war, and which are now flaming forth in fighting in several quarters in Europe?

Has President Wilson no friends in the United States who comprehend the situation, are courageous enough to tell him the truth, and influential enough to induce him to adopt a course which will promote, rather than prevent, the realization of the American people's hope for a righteous and an enduring peace? The people of this country are not so easily deceived as is evidently imagined. They are beginning to understand that the real friends of an international peace covenant consistent with American traditions and American welfare are those who wish this matter determined in American fashion, by the coordination and unification of American public opinion, and not the one man who sets himself up as master and dictator of the situation, refuses to permit the consideration of any plan but his own particular proposal, who throws the gauntlet into the faces of those who question the wisdom or safety of some features of his particular plan.

If there should fail to come out of this war an international agreement for disarmament, the ending of war, and the judicial determination of international disputes, the responsibility will rest upon the wilful one who offers to the American people the alternative of no plan for peace at all, or the particular plan he has brought home from Europe, with the admonition to "take it or leave it alone." A plan which millions of Americans believe to be a remedy worse than the disease it is advertised to cure.

Therefore, if it be in the mind of President Wilson to make a campaign issue of his course, it would be well for him to drop the methods of autocracy and adopt those of representative democracy. The American people are in the habit of settling vital national issues for themselves, and not to have their laws and treaties handed down to them from on high. They are willing to accept the leadership, but not the domineering mastery of their President. The issues presented by the effort to exclude the people and their constitutionally chosen representatives from participation in the fashioning of what may prove to be the most important state document in history, is in this free land, greater than the issue involved in the covenant itself.
—March 29, 1919.

An incident, from which we may derive occasion for important reflections, was the attempt of the Pilgrims at Plymouth to establish among them that community of goods and of labor, which fanciful politicians, from the days of Plato to those of Rousseau, have recommended as the fundamental law of a perfect republic. This theory results, it must be acknowledged, from principles of reasoning most flattering to the human character. If industry, frugality and disinterested integrity were alike the virtues of all, there would apparently be more of the social spirit in making all property a common stock, and giving to each individual a proportional title to the wealth of the whole. Such is the basis upon which Plato provides, in his republic, the division of property. Such is the system upon which Rousseau pronounces the first man who enclosed a field with a fence, and said, this is mine, a traitor to the human species.

A wiser and more useful philosophy, however, directs us to consider man according to the nature in which he was formed; subject to infirmities, which no wisdom can remedy; to weaknesses, which no institution can strengthen; to vices, which no legislation can correct. Hence it becomes obvious that separate property is the natural and indisputable right of separate exertion; that community of goods without community of toil is oppressive and unjust; that it counteracts the laws of nature, which prescribe that he only who sows the seed shall reap the harvest; that it discourages all energy, by destroying its rewards, and makes the most virtuous and active members of society' the slaves and drudges of the worst. Such was the issue of this experiment among our forefathers, and the same event demonstrated the error of the system in the elder settlement of Virginia.

Let us cherish that spirit of harmony which prompted our forefathers to make the attempt, under circumstances more favorable to its success than, perhaps, ever occurred upon earth. Let us no less admire the candor with which they relinquish it, upon discovering its irremediable inefficacy. To found principles of government upon too advantageous an estimate of the human character, is an error of inexperience, the source of which is so amiable that it is impossible to censure it with severity. We have seen the same mistake committed in our own age, and upon a larger theater. Happily for our ancestors, their situation allowed them to repair it before its effects had proved destructive.—John Quincy Adams.

So through the night rode Paul Revere;
And so through the night went his cry of alarm
To every Middlesex village and farm—
A cry of defiance and not of fear,
A voice in the darkness, a knock at the door,
And a word that shall echo forevermore!
For, borne on the night-wind of the Past,
Through all our history, to the last,
In the hour of darkness and peril and need,
The people will waken and listen to hear
The hurrying hoof-beats of that steed,
And the midnight message of Paul Revere.
                                    Henry W. Longfellow.

I ask each of you to remember that he cannot shove the blame on others entirely, if things go wrong. This is a government by the people, and the people are to blame ultimately if they are misrepresented, just exactly as much as if their worst passions, their worst desires are represented; for in the one case it is their supineness that is represented exactly as in the other case it is their vice. Let each man make his weight felt in supporting a truly American policy, a policy which decrees that we shall be free and shall hold our own in the face of other nations.—Theodore Roosevelt.

Shall we regard with indifference the great inheritance which cost our sires their blood because we find in their gift an admixture of imperfection and evil? Surely there is good enough, in the contemplation of which every patriotic heart may say "God bless my own, my native land."—James A. Garfield.

SHALL AMERICA BE EUROPEANIZED, OR EUROPE AMERICANIZED?

The fundamental error of some men conspicuous in national and world leadership at this time is that, with an inadequate comprehension and appreciation of the true meaning and message of Americanism, they have undertaken to Europeanize America rather than to Americanize Europe.

The great American example, no longer an experiment, points the way to permanent world peace through sane nationalism rather than internationalism; through the federalization of states on the representative principle, into larger groups as the first step toward that parliament of man which the poets have dreamed of, but which cannot be brought to pass except through the removal of ancient obstacles now being multiplied and exaggerated rather than minimized.

The motto of the republic, "Out of many, one," gives expression to the message of Americanism which even some conspicuous Americans do not seem to comprehend. Out of many states, one nation; out of many races, religions, tribes and tongues, one people.

America has taken all the conflicting strains of Europe and has combined them into the American blend. It has produced homogeneity out of a mass which in Europe remains heterogeneous, to that continent's constant peril. America has pointed the world the way to the true internationalism,—the subordination of racial and religious and class and caste lines to the national ideal, the common sense ideal of common interest and common safety and common progress.

Travel from the Atlantic to the Pacific and from the Lakes to the Gulf and one will find in this country a population which on the whole looks alike, talks alike and thinks alike. What has been achieved here is little less than a miracle, when it is remembered that our sources of population run into every quarter of the globe, and particularly into every community in Europe. It has been demonstrated by the readiness with which people slough off their age-old prejudices and characteristics, and mingle with the general current of American civilization, that the barriers erected between peoples and localities and classes in Europe are artificially maintained.

Travel a few hours in Europe and one will come face to face with a half dozen complete and many partial differentiations of peoples; differences extending even to physical and mental characteristics. Europe is separatist in the extreme sense. This tendency is manifest even within nations. There are such differences in dialect among the peasants even of little England, that the inhabitants of some counties with difficulty understand the inhabitants of other counties. Scotland, Wales, Ireland,—these tell a story of stubborn clinging to ancient tongue, custom, tradition· and prejudice.

This separateness, this aloofness of Europe, extends to the whole social and political order. Political formations are stratified, —and ossified. The peasantry, the middle class, the aristocracy, the proletariat, the bourgeoisie, the junker,—these are terms which reflect the intra-nation tendency toward separateness, and as these numerous nations, with their racial and dynastic and territorial and trade rivalries and hatreds, have long glared at each other across their borders, and meanwhile trained armies and navies for the business they knew was coming, so these separate classes have been in a state either of armed neutrality or of civil war.

Europe has had, not too little, but too much self determination of peoples. Where this hiving system has been most thorough,— in the Balkans,—the trouble started. Servia, Montenegro, Albania, Bulgaria, Roumania, Greece and Turkey in Europe carried on the curtain raisers for the great war. These wars were fought with a savagery beyond our comprehension, and when the governments involved were too poor to buy modern armament, the fight was carried on with primitive weapons until populations had been decimated. There was a fundamental reason for this, independent of the historic causes. No one of these countries is big enough, or strong enough, or well governed enough, to possess economic independence. Sovereign politically, they have been unable to find at home the soil, or the resources, or the play for enterprise and labor, necessary to an independent national existence.

The processes of modern civilization have so tremendously decreased distance that Europe has become like a crowded tenement; each family more or less a nuisance to its strongly individualized neighbor. The system Europe attempts to maintain,—that of a country, a flag, a language and a civilization for each tribe or tong, has collapsed. National boundaries have expanded to the bursting point under the pressure for independent national existence. Germany, armed to the teeth, wanted more territory and especially more markets obtainable only over the dead bodies of prostrate neighbors,—and so the war began.

A century and a third ago the United States of America achieved political independence; cut loose from Europe and Europe's rivalries and hatreds,—just as much a menace to peace today as they were when Washington and Jefferson declared the determination of the new republic to avoid alien entanglements. Political freedom attained, the fathers of the republic set out to achieve the economic independence of the nation, through protective legislation, fostering domestic manufacturing and agricultural interests, through the development of a merchant marine, and the creation of a home market for American production, with ample American production for that home market. Only twice in our earlier history was there resort to the methods of Europeanism in the United States,—both times by the same elements in American life,—the war upon Mexico with its consequent acquisition of territory, and the Civil war, with the effort to place local above national interests, and reproduce on American soil this system of self determined sectionalism.

Why do not those ambitious for the erection of a super-state ask Europe to follow the great American example and try it on? Why not the United States of Europe before the fate of this country is thrown in with that of the rest of the world, and a universal sovereignty is attempted? Can we by treaty remove the danger of war which lurks constantly in this European system, and, while this continent, north of the Mexican border, has enjoyed ten times as many years of peace as of war, has given the nations of Europe ten times as many years of war as of peace?

The people of America want peace. The road to peace does not lie through the devious pathways of European intrigue or the shambles of European conflict. The people of this country insist upon such a settlement of the war, such an arrangement for the adjudication of international disputes hereafter, that this nation may never again be thrown into the vortex of European conflict. This will come about, however, not through making ourselves a part of the European system, or underwriting the peace of Europe, at the sacrifice of our own peace, under that war-breeding system. The people of this republic want America to remain American.

—April 5, 1919.

During the administration of President Monroe this doctrine of the Farewell Address was first considered in all its aspects and with a view to all its practical consequences. The Farewell Address, while it took America out of the field of European politics, was silent as to the part Europe might be permitted to play in America. Doubtless it was thought the latest addition to the family of nations should not make haste to prescribe rules for the guidance of its older members, and the expediency and propriety of serving the powers of Europe with notice of a complete and distinctive American policy excluding them from interference with American political affairs might well seem dubious to a generation to whom the French alliance, with its manifold advantages to the cause of American independence, was fresh in mind. * * * The

Monroe administration, however, did not content itself with formulating a correct rule for the regulation of the relations between Europe and America. It aimed at also securing the practical benefits to result from the application of the rule. Hence the message just quoted declared that the American continents were fully occupied and were not the subjects for future colonization by European powers. To this spirit and this purpose, also, are to be attributed the passages of the same message which treat any infringement of the rule against interference in American affairs on the part of the powers of Europe as an act of unfriendliness to the United States. It was realized that it was futile to lay down such a rule unless its observance could be enforced. It was manifest that the United States was the only power in this hemisphere capable of enforcing it. It was therefore courageously declared not merely that Europe ought not to interfere in American affairs, but that any European power doing so would be regarded as antagonizing the interests and inviting the opposition of the United States.— Richard Olney, 1895.

This is now the United States—that colossus of power, that colossus of liberty, that colossus of the spirit of nations, which invites all men from the four corners of the globe to come hither, and find here a refuge from oppression; here to find inexhaustible resources for the development of industry and enterprise; here to add each an item from his intelligence, his virtue, his strength— to add the atom of his own individual capacity to the vast total of the untiring enterprise and industry of the people of the United States. This is the point at which we now stand; and I repeat that it is to no trivial question of the past, it is to no exhausted passions of the past, that we of this day are confined. Our flight is into other elements. Our duty is for other objects. It is, gentlemen, in the confidence of our strength; for force is, of itself, the irrepressible instinct of action.
He who is strong, who feels coursing in his veins the blood of maturity and vigor, needs action and must have action. It is the very necessity and condition of existence.
I say, then, we are strong in our territorial extent; strong in the vast natural resources of our country; strong in the vigorous men and in the fair women who inhabit it; strong in those glorious institutions which our fathers of the Revolution transmitted to us; but above all, strong, stronger, strongest, in the irrepressible instinct of patriotic devotion to country which burns inextinguishably, like the vestal fire on its altars, in the heart of every American.—Caleb Cushing.

The first duty of an American citizen or of a citizen of any constitutional government, is obedience to the constitution and laws of his country.—Stephen A. Douglas.

LET THE WORLD CONSTITUTION BE CONSTITUTIONALLY WRITTEN

This paper protests again against the thoroughly undemocratic and unrepublican methods employed to put over on the people of this country a world constitution and a world parliament. These objections apply with equal force whether the constitution proposed be the mere beginning of a super-state, or whether it be the fully panoplied world autocracy outlined in the Cecil-Wilson covenant, with legislative, executive and judicial powers combined in one world parliament, in which this country was to have but a feeble minority voice.

The suspicion persists that there is an Ethiopian in the woodpile in any hand-me-down, made-in-Europe plan for a league of nations, in which the American people are not given the right of original suggestion; which represents, in the making, the usurpation of legislative powers by the executive branch of this and other governments, without giving to the people of this country, supposed to be a representative republic, any voice whatever in framing a world constitution, the most important document ever presented for their consideration.

The people of this country have been accustomed to bearing a hand in the framing of the laws which bind them. Their constitution was not handed down to them from on high; it was written by the representatives of the states, duly chosen for that particular purpose, and then referred for ratification to the representatives of the people in the several states. This hand-me-down method of writing constitutions and laws exemplified in the procedure of the Paris conference is familiar enough in Europe, where governments and not the people are the sources of authority, but it is an absolutely new experience here. That such a procedure is defended by anybody in the United States is evidence that "the wiles of foreign influence" and the seduction of alien ideals are at work in America to the possible undoing of the republic.

Why is it seriously proposed that the question of whether the people of this country shall underwrite the political and financial and commercial solvency of the rest of the world, and bind themselves to duties and responsibilities and burdens and possible sacrifices and dangers vaguely defined, shall be decided in a military council, assembled for the purpose of formulating terms of peace after a great war, a body totally unrepresentative in a legislative way?

Would it not be the natural and the legal procedure for this body to settle the issues of the war, leaving the establishment of a world constitutional convention, and the election of the members thereof, to the various governments of the world, in accordance with their usual procedure in such matters? For instance, should not the legislative representatives of the United States in such a body be chosen by the Congress of the United States, rather than by the executive merely? Is it not an act of the most supreme assurance, the most flagrant usurpation, for this peace conference to dodge all the problems properly falling within its jurisdiction, and turn instead to the task, never committed to it, of writing a constitution for a world government, throwing over on this proposed world government the vast and perilous unsettled business the Paris peace conference does not seem to have the courage or capacity to finish?

We say this question of usurpation of authority to write a world constitution and give the people of this republic no initiative in its formulation, this organized effort so apparent throughout the country to hush criticism, prevent discussion and hurry action; this manifest determination to deprive even the United States Senate of its constitutional part in the framing of treaties; this feverish, wholesale, strongly organized and heavily financed propaganda against deliberation and in favor of implicit consent to anything suggested by authority; all this ought to arouse in every American the firm determination that with so much at stake, the people and the Congress of the United States MUST have something to say in the framing of this document, rather than be content with the poor satisfaction of humbly suggesting minor amendments.

The Paris peace conference should long ago have settled problems arising out of the war. It should have settled them many weeks ago. It would have settled them long ago except for the stubborn persistence of certain men, acting entirely in a personal capacity, in neglecting the real work of the conference in order to take up a clearly usurped function of framing a world constitution. By this course the whole fabric of civilization, at least in Europe, has been endangered.

It is not too late to remedy this frightful error, originating in the spirit of autocracy, that spirit this war was fought to overthrow. Let the peace conference settle the war problems. Let the allied peoples and governments which have won the right to leadership in this work of building bulwarks for the defense of world peace, elect through their representative legislative bodies real representatives of the popular sentiment of these several nations. Let these men deliberately and intelligently debate and decide. with due deference to American public opinion, upon a proposed plan for the permanent preservation of the world's peace; whether or not they want an international court, interpreting a comprehensive code of international law, or a world legislature. Let discussion of this vitally important project be encouraged, rather than discouraged. This is democracy. This is republicanism. Any other course is autocracy, not to be accepted by any free people whose sense of responsibility has not been blunted by the aggressions of tyrannical usurpation.

There is a right way and a wrong way of going about this matter. We want no world constitution, full of vague generalities, advocated on the ground of good intentions on the idiotic theory that contracts should be signed first and considered afterward. We want no patch-work world constitution, with an amendment stuck on here and there to hide the blemishes and allay the suspicions of the people. We want an "open covenant, openly arrived at" in the old-fashioned American way, in which the people, through their duly chosen representatives, exercise initiative in formulating the proposed world constitution.

This, it seems to us, is the most fundamental issue involved in this whole matter. It is a question of representative government as against autocratic usurpation. It is a question of bringing to bear upon this question the power of deliberate public opinion in a country which has become accustomed to this method of settling questions vitally affecting the destiny of the American people, as this one does so peculiarly.

Let the thirty-nine senators who signed the new Declaration of Independence, and the other senators in sympathy with their position, take their stand here.

Get peace quickly; get a world constitution deliberately, and in the democratic-republican way.

If we are true to the traditions of this republic, and of free government in general, there is no other road for us, as Americans, to travel.

—April 12, 1919.

The Monroe Doctrine may be abandoned; we may forfeit it by taking our lot with nations that expand by following un-American ways; we may outgrow it, as we seem to be outgrowing other things we once valued; or it may forever stand as a guarantee of protection and safety in our enjoyment of free institutions; but in no event will this American principle ever be better defined, better defended or more bravely asserted than was done by Mr. Olney in this dispatch. * * * The doctrine upon which we stand is strong because its enforcement is important to our peace and safety as a nation, and is essential to the integrity of our free institutions and the tranquil maintenance of our distinctive form of government. It was intended to apply to every stage of our national life, and cannot become obsolete while our republic endures. If the balance of power is justly a cause for jealous anxiety among the governments of the Old World and a subject for our absolute non-interference, none the less is the observance of the Monroe Doctrine of vital concern to our people and their government. * * * Holding that an engagement to share in the obligation of enforcing neutrality in the remote valley of the Congo would be an alliance whose responsibilities we are not in a position to assume, I abstain from asking the sanction of the Senate to that general act. * * * This incident and the events leading up to it signally illustrate the impolicy of entangling alliances with foreign powers. * * * It has been the settled policy of the United States to concede to people of foreign countries the same freedom and independence in the management of their domestic affairs that we have always claimed for ourselves.—Grover Cleveland.

I have always, from my earliest youth, rejoiced in the felicity of my fellow-men; and have ever considered it as the indispensable duty of every member of society to promote, as far as in him lies, the prosperity of every individual, but more especially of the community to which he belongs, and also as a faithful subject of the state, to use his utmost endeavors to detect, and having detected, strenuously to oppose every traitorous plot which its enemies may devise for its destruction. Security to the persons and properties of the governed is so obviously the design and end of civil government that to attempt a logical proof of it would be like borrowing tapers at noonday to assist the sun in enlightening the world; and it cannot be either virtuous or honorable to attempt to support a government of which this is not the great and principal basis; and it is to the last degree vicious and infamous to attempt to support a government which manifestly tends to render the persons and properties of the governed insecure. Some boast of being friends to government; I am a friend to righteous government founded upon the principles of reason and justice, but I glory in publicly avowing my eternal enmity to tyranny.—John Hancock.

Liberty can be safe only when suffrage is illuminated by education. For a man to feel that every impulse for laudable ambition must be strangled at its birth, that like fabled Enceladus he has been rived by the thunder-bolt of power and crushed beneath the mountain of its strength, is more than this human nature of ours can endure. What wonder then that ever and anon, when freedom turns the weary side—the fires of devouring vengeance burst forth and shake the fabrics of the old world, till tyrants chatter on their gilded thrones in idiotic terror. At such moments, freedom may seem to have triumphed there, but when the fury of the tempest is past she lies bleeding—Samson-like—beneath the ruin she has wrought.—James A. Garfield.

WANTING NOTHING, WE TRADE
EVERYTHING TO GET IT

President Wilson's "dramatic victory" for the Monroe Doctrine in the Paris peace conference reminds one of the achievement of the country editor, who, in giving an account of his victory over a belligerent visitor, wrote:

"Fixing our hair in his hands and our nose securely between his teeth, we held on until help arrived."

The amendment adopted reads: "The covenant does not affect the validity of international engagements, such as treaties of arbitration, or regional understandings like the Monroe Doctrine, for securing the maintenance of peace."

The Monroe Doctrine is not an "engagement." It is the declared policy of the United States, never given the force of an agreement with any other nation. As the Monroe Doctrine is not an agreement, and is not made so by the proposed covenant, this declaration is like saying: "Nothing in this covenant shall be construed as invalidating the law against a man blowing his nose on a windy day." There is no such law, therefore it cannot be validated or invalidated by such a declaration.

What this amendment does validate, however, as the delegates from China pointed out, is the Lansing-Ishii secret agreement recognizing the "special interests" of Japan in China. The Japanese have persisted in the claim that the Monroe Doctrine, applied to Asia, means that Japan shall have commercial if not political suzerainty in China. Evidently our delegation at the peace conference assents to this preposterous theory. The complement of our claim, set up in the Monroe Doctrine, that Europe shall not establish new possessions in the United States and thus involve us in the European system from which until recently it was thought desirable to remain free, is that the United States shall not grab territory in this hemisphere. We have followed that policy, chronic libelers of American motive to the contrary notwithstanding. We are the protectors, not the oppressors, of the republics of the western hemisphere. Japan's interpretation of the Monroe Doctrine is the right to acquire, by governmental action, exclusive trade privileges in China, to operate and police China's railroads,—to prevent China from making treaties without her consent. This bears no more resemblance to the Monroe Doctrine than the Kaiser does to Patrick Henry.

AMERICANISM

The "dramatic victory" so reverently chronicled by the press agents was, therefore, not a victory for the Monroe Doctrine of a western hemisphere free from imperialistic aggression, but for the Lansing-Ishii doctrine of an Asia delivered into the hands of imperialistic aggression.

As was once said: "We want nothing at the peace conference." We seem to be trading off at this conference not only the independent sovereignty of the United States and our freedom from the European system, but the sovereignty of the republic of China, formed in emulation of the great American example. And trading it all off for the nothing we went over to Paris to get.
—April 19, 1919.

I have not allowed myself to look beyond the union, to see what might lie hidden in the dark recess behind. I have not coolly weighed the chances of preserving liberty when the bonds that unite us together shall be broken asunder. I have not accustomed myself to hang over the precipice of disunion, to see whether, with my short sight, I can fathom the depth of the abyss below; nor could I regard him as a safe counsellor in the affairs of this government, whose thoughts should be mainly bent on considering, not how the union may be best preserved, but how tolerable might be the condition of the people when it should be broken up and destroyed.

While the union lasts, we have high, exciting, gratifying prospects spread out before us, for us and our children. Beyond that I seek not to penetrate the veil. God grant that, in my day at least, that curtain may not rise! God grant that on my vision never may be opened what lies behind! When my eyes shall be turned to behold for the last time the sun in heaven, may I not see him shining on the broken and dishonoured fragments of a once glorious union. Let their last feeble and lingering glance rather behold the gorgeous ensign of the republic, now known and honoured throughout the earth, still full high advanced, its arms and trophies streaming in their original lustre, not a stripe erased or polluted, nor a single star obscured, bearing for its motto no such miserable interrogatory as "What is all this worth?" nor those other words of delusion and folly, "Liberty first and union afterwards;" but everywhere, spread all over in characters of living light, blazing on all its ample folds, as they float over the sea and over the land, and in every wind under the whole heavens, that other sentiment, dear to every true American heart,—Liberty and union, now and for ever, one and inseparable!—Daniel Webster.

Heroes did not make our liberties, they but reflected and illustrated them.—James A. Garfield.

THE KEYNOTE OF THE WORLD CONSTITUTION

The keynote of the peace conference, and of the world government for which it has prepared a constitution, is sounded in the delivery of the Chinese province of Shantung, with its forty million people, its ports, railways, and resources into the hands of Japan, the "title" of Germany thereto, identical in validity with Germany's title to Belgium, being thus confirmed. It is as if we had delivered Belgium, over her protest, to France, in confirmation of the German occupation. Thus is betrayed the "idealism" expressed in so many high-sounding pronunciamentos. Thus are the professions of the Fourteen points cast to the winds, as against, not an enemy, but a friend; not against a militaristic power, but in behalf of one, and against a sister republic.

Thus the Hay policy of the open door in China and of China's territorial integrity and national sovereignty is abandoned; thus the doctrine of the rights of weak peoples and of racial unity and self-determination are sacrificed to the old diplomacy of barter and intrigue and secret agreement. These things have gone on in the world before; but for the first time America will become a party to them. We are to participate in the sacrifice of the world's most populous republic, a friendly nation, to that system, if the proposals of our representatives at Paris, assuming we have any, be confirmed.

Moreover, by that decision, the friendship of America and of the strong, militant, efficient, shrewdly governed nation which fronts us in the Pacific basin is endangered. America has come out of the war with the prejudice against Japan, as a nation, eliminated. We have fought side by side with Japan in a war to eliminate from the world the sort of thing now proposed in China. We have seen Japan perform bravely and effectively her part in that great struggle. The day of suspicion and antagonism was about to be succeeded by one of confidence and good will. Now it is proposed to set aflame, in this country, the suspicion that in conquering a great European militaristic power, bent on continental control and ultimately world conquest, we have set up another in Asia, and as the first whetting of the appetite of the new Moloch, we have fed to it a great Chinese province, with forty million people thus transferred to an alien sovereignty, and have opened the door to Japanese dominance of an area equal in size, resources and potential wealth to the United States, with a population four times our own, thus putting within the grasp of one power as big a possibility of world conquest as that which lured Germany to her doom.

For her single-hearted, one-minded devotion to Japanese interests at the peace table, Japan is not to be condemned. There are many Americans who regret that this almost fanatical national devotion is met only by a willingness to sacrifice American interests, traditions and ideals on our own part. Before Japan, now almost within her grasp, lies the prize of dominance over China which has possessed her statesmanship for years. It is a tremendous temptation; a temptation which will not be lessened by the cession of the province of Shantung unreservedly to her. The statement that the province will be turned back to China is doubtless made in good faith. It was made in good faith at the time of the capture of Kiaochow four years ago. The Chinese delegates to the peace conference do not expect it will be easier to fix a date for the surrender, which is entirely left to the option of Japan, ten years from now than it is now. The principle involved is to be settled now. It is proposed that the province be turned over to Japan at this time, and that the title be confirmed and recorded by the league of nations, so that if China wishes to defend her sovereignty we may be bound to send troops to suppress her aspirations to free nationality. It is no defense of the act of selling a child into slavery to say, in reply to critics, that the purchaser agrees to emancipate the slave in due time. It is only an aggravation of the offense.

We may not be able to save China from partition, despite our success up to this time in doing so against the intrigue of most of the other powers of the world. Secret treaties incident to the war, and possibly necessary to its successful prosecution, seemingly stand in the way. But what we can do, as a nation, is to avoid becoming parties to the thing. We can avoid joining in the transaction, and from guaranteeing, through Article X of the proposed league of nations covenant, title to the spoil thus taken from a republic created in emulation of the American example, which had its inspiration in admiration of the traditional policy of unselfish friendship for all nations and championship of the rights of weak and helpless peoples as exemplified in our conduct in the Orient in earlier days. But we may even save China from Japan, and Japan from herself, by organized, public protest.

Write your senators your views on this matter, and on Article X of the constitution of the league of nations by which it is proposed to bind the bargain. Powerful, organized influences are urging those desiring the adoption of what is brought over from Paris, without amendment in behalf of the United States, to flood the capitol with letters and telegrams. Get YOUR views before your representatives charged with joint responsibility in this momentous matter; it is your only opportunity to be heard. This is the

most important crisis in national history since 1861. Do YOUR duty,—a duty vastly easier of performance than that which has fallen to the millions who have offered their all on the altar of patriotism that this republic might live for the fulfillment of its high mission among men.
—May 10, 1919.

Is it any wonder that the old soldier loves the flag under whose folds he fought and for which his comrades shed so much blood? He loves it for what it is and for what it represents. It embodies the purposes and history of the government itself. It records the achievements of its defenders upon land and sea. It heralds the heroism and sacrifices of our Revolutionary fathers who planted free government on this continent and dedicated it to liberty forever. It attests the struggles of our army and the valor of our citizens in all the wars of the republic. It has been sacrificed by the blood of our best and our bravest. It records the achievements of Washington and the martyrdom of Lincoln. It has been bathed in the tears of a sorrowing people. It has been glorified in the hearts of a freedom-loving people, not only at home but in every part of the world. Our flag expresses more than any other flag; it means more than any other national emblem. It expresses the will of a free people, and proclaims that they are supreme and that they acknowledge no earthly sovereign but themselves. It never was assaulted that thousands did not rise up to smite the assailant. Glorious old banner!—William McKinley.

Every time we do honor to the soldiers of the republic, we reaffirm our devotion to the country, to the glorious flag, to the immortal principles of liberty, equality and justice, which have made the United States unrivaled among the nations of the world. The union of these states must be perpetual. That is what our brave boys died for.

The unity of the republic is secure so long as we continue to honor the memory of the men who died by the tens of thousands to preserve it. The dissolution of the union is impossible so long as we continue to inculcate lessons of fraternity, unity and patriotism.

But we must not forget, my fellow-countrymen, that the union which these brave men preserved, and the liberties which they secured, places upon us, the living, the gravest responsibility. We are the freest government on the face of the earth. Our strength rests in our patriotism. Anarchy flees before patriotism. Peace and order and security and liberty are safe so long as love of country burns in the hearts of the people.

It should not be forgotten, however, that liberty does not mean lawlessness. Liberty to make our own laws does not give us license to break them. Liberty to make our own laws commands a duty to observe them ourselves and enforce obedience among all others within their jurisdiction. Liberty, my fellow-citizens, is responsibility, and responsibility is duty, and that duty is to preserve the exceptional liberty we enjoy within the law and for the law and by the law.—William McKinley.

On primal rocks she wrote her name,
    Her towers were reared on holy graves;
The golden seed that bore her came
    Swift-winged with prayer o'er ocean waves.

The Forest bowed his solemn crest,
    And open flung his sylvan doors;
Meek Rivers led the appointed Guest
    To clasp the wide-embracing shores;

Till, fold by fold, the broidered Land
    To swell her virgin vestments grew,
While sages, strong in heart and hand,
    Her virtue's fiery girdle drew.

O Exile of the wrath of Kings!
    O Pilgrim Ark of Liberty!
The refuge of divinest things,
    Their record must abide in thee.

First in the glories of thy front
    Let the crown jewel, Truth, be found;
Thy right hand fling, with generous wont,
    Love's happy chain to furthest bound.

Let Justice, with the faultless scales,
    Hold fast the worship of thy sons;
Thy Commerce spread her shining sails
    Where no dark tide of rapine runs.

So link thy ways to those of God,
    So follow firm the heavenly laws,
That stars may greet thee, warrior browed,
    And storm-sped angels hail thy cause.

O Land, the measure of our prayers,
    Hope of the world, in grief and wrong!
Be thine the blessing of the years,
    The gift of faith, the crown of song!
                —Julia Ward Howe.

THE TREATY'S BETRAYAL OF A
SISTER REPUBLIC

The camouflage with which the true significance of the Shantung decision is being concealed from the American people is only another proof that you can put almost anything over in world politics if your press agents are equal to the emergency. That decision, amounting to the surrender of the territory and sovereignty, the sacrifice of the independence of the world's most populous republic,—a republic associated with the United States in the war,—to the imperial ambitions of the greatest military and commercial power of the Orient,—is a travesty upon the high pretensions of the American delegation at the peace conference to an idealism at war with all the ancient standards of diplomacy.

The partition of Poland by the enemies of that nation was an act of humanity as compared with the partition of helpless China by her "friends" at Paris. The effort to soften the ugly outlines of this procedure cannot hide the fact that in consenting to this arrangement America will betray a nation which, with pathetic confidence in American idealism and unselfishness based upon our traditional policies, has looked to the great republic whose institutions the Chinese people have sought to emulate, but looked in vain. And why? Because our representatives at Paris, without a mandate for their action from the American people, have chosen to involve this country in the entanglements of European politics.

Doubtless the decision against China was assented to by the American delegation reluctantly. But we have cast in our lot with other powers; we have surrendered our right to independent action; the surrender of China to Japan is the result of sundry bargainings to which we have been made party. It foreshadows what we may expect as the result of yielding up our traditional policy of independent action in the world's affairs, by being "yoked with unbelievers" in a partnership for world domination. We are told, for instance, that Japan looks to the proposed league of nations by a subsequent decision, to open our doors to unrestricted Japanese immigration.

At the end of the peace conference, as the first important decision of the proposed league of nations, China is delivered bound hand and foot into the suzerainty of Japan against the wishes and over the protest of the Chinese people. In effect we have confirmed, in addition, the secret treaties and arrangements whereby

Japan, during the war, took a blanket mortgage on the natural resources and trade opportunities of China in exchange for some seventy million dollars in loans. This is the natural consequence of the Lansing-Ishii secret agreement, whereby the United States, without the knowledge or consent of the American people, gave sanction to the doctrine of "special interests" of Japan in China. That agreement closed the "open door" of Hay and Knox and recognized, in principle, the right of Japan to control the destinies of China.

We have no right to complain of the ambition of Japan to dominate China. It is a natural ambition; as natural as that of the central powers to dominate Europe; if it can be peacefully achieved through American consent or connivance, it represents a triumph of Japanese diplomacy almost without parallel in history. Japan is a nation of limited area and pressing population; a nation of hiving tendencies and ambition for expansion; autocratic and militaristic. The Japanese combination of industry, thrift, ingenuity and low living standards for wage earners, makes Japan a formidable contestant for world trade supremacy. Backed by the teeming population and vast untouched natural resources of China, Japan can dominate any market through low production costs. With control of China, Japan may easily become the richest and most powerful nation in the world.

Thus ends pathetically the struggle of the Chinese republic for independent existence, as the first decision of the proposed league of nations. It will be of interest to recount the story.

The Boxer rebellion, believed to have been fostered by the Dowager Empress, resulted in the slaughter of many Europeans and Americans. We had at the time many veteran soldiers in the Philippines. A considerable detachment was sent to China to join the allied expedition for the relief of the foreigners penned up in the legations at Pekin. The American forces had read to them by the commanding general before beginning the march to Pekin, the American code of warfare, prepared more than a half century ago by Francis Lieber, prohibiting injury or robbery of non-combatants. The American forces did not indulge in the looting which characterized the marches and occupations of the forces of some of the associated powers.

When Pekin had fallen, indemnities were imposed upon China to reimburse the various nationals for life and property destroyed. Alone among all the powers, the United States, after paying all claims, returned the unexpended balance to China. In recognition of this act China created from this repayment, a fund for the education of Chinese students in American colleges and universities. Germany compelled the Chinese to erect a statue to the murdered imperial minister at the spot in Pekin where he fell, and required the cession of an entire province to Germany. It is the title thus obtained that the preliminary league of nations has just confirmed in Japan.

When Japan took Shantung from the Germans early in the war, it was with the public declaration, especially addressed to the United States, that it was for the purpose of returning the province to China. The province has now been turned over to Japan without reservation as to its future disposition, and the public is fed the statement that Japan intends ultimately to return the territory to China. Of course, if there were such an intention, no reason exists for not carrying it out at once, and no date being given for the return, it is not surprising that the Chinese delegates to the peace conference regard the announcement of such an intention as mere camouflage. Possession is nine points of the law, and assuming that the present purpose is to return the territory some time, it is not binding upon future Japanese governments, and the covenant of the league of nations confirms the right of Japan to hold the territory forever.

In this connection it is worthy of note that when President Yuan Shi Kai attempted to make himself emperor of China, he had the assistance of an opinion rendered by Professor Goodknow, of Johns Hopkins University, an American adviser who presumably was at the court of Pekin with the consent of the American government, that a monarchy was a form of government better suited to the Chinese than a republic. The people of China confuted this professorial sophistry by driving the would-be emperor from power. This was the first public proof given to the world of the foothold which European conceptions of government have gained in America, especially in American universities in recent years. The loans recently accepted by the present Chinese government in exchange for exclusive concessions amounting to a mortgage on China, had been made over the protest of the republican elements in China, temporarily out of power through the exercise of military force at Pekin.

There is nothing to be gained, and much to be lost by stirring up ill will between Japan and the United States. With such good grace as we can, we may as well face the facts, which are that Japanese diplomacy has outplayed us at the peace table, gaining for Japan the obliteration of the Hay policy and making China a Japanese dependency. At the same time the administration, through President Wilson and Secretary Baker, is urging that we abandon the Philippines and with them all responsibility in the Orient. Surely republican China is disillusioned. But republican China should understand that the cause of republicanism and of Chinese political independence and territorial integrity would not have been abandoned by the party of McKinley and Hay. It is to be hoped that the advocates of the league of nations are satisfied with this first sample of its operations in behalf of international justice and in the abandonment of American traditions.

AMERICANISM

But will the United States Senate care to accept joint responsibility for such a betrayal? Perhaps we cannot help this betrayal, but we can at least refuse to accept joint responsibility for it.
—May 10, 1919.

It appears to me probable that Monroe had but little conception of the lasting effect which his words would produce. He spoke what he believed and what he knew that others believed; he spoke under provocation, and aware that his views might be controverted; he spoke with authority after consultation with his cabinet, and his words were timely; but I do not suppose that he regarded this announcement as his own. Indeed, if it had been his own decree or ukase it would have been resented at home quite as vigorously as it would have been opposed abroad. It was because he pronounced not only the opinion then prevalent, but a tradition of other days which had been gradually expanded, and to which the country was wonted, that his words carried with them the sanction of public law. A careful examination of the writings of the earlier statesmen of the republic will illustrate the growth of the Monroe Doctrine as an idea dimly entertained at first, but steadily developed by the course of public events and the reflection of those in public life. I have not made a thorough search, but some indications of the mode in which the doctrine was evolved have come under my eye which may hereafter be added to by a more persistent investigator.

The idea of independence from foreign sovereignty was at the beginning of our national life. The term "continental," applied to the army, the Congress, the currency, had made familiar the nation of continental independence. This kept in mind the nation of a continental domain. Moreover, in the writings, both public and private, of the fathers of the republic, we see how clearly they recognize the value of separation from European politics, and of repelling, as far as possible, European interference with American interests.—Daniel C. Gilman, 1883.

From all the combinations of European politics relative to the distribution of power or the administration of government the United States have studiously kept themselves aloof. They have not sought, by the propagation of their principles, to disturb the peace, or to intermeddle with the policy of any part of Europe. In the Independence of Nations, they have respected the organization of their governments, however different from their own, and they have thought it no sacrifice of their principles to cultivate with sincerity and assiduity peace and friendship even with the most absolute monarchies and their sovereigns.—John Quincy Adams, 1823.

A LEAGUE TO PERPETUATE INTERNATIONAL INJUSTICE?

A more appropriate name for the proposed league of nations, in the light of the Shantung decision, would be a League of Force for the Perpetration and Perpetuation of International Injustice. The name given to the proposed organization by the Chinese themselves, viz., "The League of Thieves," is perhaps a bit too drastic. It is certain that the American people never gave their consent to the organization of such a league as that. It is certain that the American people do not approve the proposed abandonment of the American policy of fair play for China in order to enter into a partnership for putting the world's most populous republic in a strait-jacket and forming a league to guarantee that the bonds shall not slip.

It is scarcely necessary to point out the gross injustice of delivering to Japan, on the basis of a "title" transferred from Germany, and obtained by Germany in the same way that she got title to Belgium, the province of Shantung, comprising 10,000 square miles of territory and more people than inhabit all that part of the United States lying west of the Great Lakes; all Chinese, and yet placed beneath the sovereignty and subjected to the exploitation of a power that has similarly absorbed Korea and has a definite, determined policy of territorial absorption.

The injustice to China did not stop there. Germany is not the only European country that has by force taken from China pieces of her territory on one pretext and another. These land-grabs of the European powers are called "concessions." They are the same kind of concession that an unarmed pedestrian hands over to a footpad at the point of a gun. If there were any sincerity whatever in the pretense of the preamble of the proposed league of nations about a mutual determination of the powers to usher in a reign of international justice, this "swag" would have been handed back. What greater moral right has Great Britain to Hong Kong than China to Liverpool? What higher ethics is involved in the "internationalization" of Shanghai, or the exercise of sovereignty over Pekin soil by the several European powers than in the German claim to Brussels? Will anyone believe that Europe has turned over a new leaf while it holds to these concessions, desired and held only for the purpose of pressing commercial advantage, and with no purpose whatever to serve or assist the Chinese people?

AMERICANISM

But not only are these concessions of China's late European associates in the war not turned back to the owner, but the "concessions" grabbed by Germany, instead of being handed back to China, are by treaty "internationalized," in other words taken over by the nations benevolently associated to prevent future war and injustice throughout the world!

It is not fair to the Paris conferees, of whom President Wilson is, by his press agents, pronounced the master spirit, to say that they did nothing for China. One clause in the peace treaty requires that Germany shall return to China the astronomical instruments taken to Berlin during the Boxer uprising. These instruments were presented to China by Louis XVI. Their return to Pekin as the sole measure of fair play to China is appropriate, for the diplomacy exemplified in the Shantung decision seems to be of the Louis XVI period.
—May 17, 1919.

We think that nothing is powerful enough to stand before autocratic, monarchical or despotic power. There is something strong enough, quite strong enough,—and, if properly exerted, will prove itself so,—and that is the power of intelligent public opinion in all the nations of the earth. There is not a monarch on earth whose throne is not liable to be shaken by the progress of opinion, and the sentiment of the just and intelligent part of the people. It becomes us, in the station which we hold, to let that public opinion, so far as we form it, have a free course. Let it go out; let it be pronounced in thunder tones; let it open the ears of the deaf; let it open the eyes of the blind; and let it everywhere be proclaimed what we of this great republic think of the general principles of human liberty.—Daniel Webster.

Individuals may wear for a time the glory of our institutions, but they carry it not to the grave with them. Like rain-drops from Heaven, they may pass through the circle of the shining bow and add to its luster, but when they have sunk to the earth again the proud arch still spans the sky and shines gloriously on.
—James A. Garfield.

Peace, liberty and personal security are blessings as common and universal as sunshine and showers and fruitful seasons; and all sprang from a single source—the principle declared in the Pilgrim covenant of 1620—that all owed due submission and obedience to the lawfully expressed will of the majority. This is not one of the doctrines of our political system, it is the system itself. It is in our political firmament, in which all other truths are set, as stars in heaven. It is the encasing air, the breath of the nation's life.—James A. Garfield.

"PARTISANSHIP" AND THE
LEAGUE OF NATIONS

The Omaha World-Herald, a Democratic party paper published by Senator Hitchcock, of Nebraska,—from which one may draw conclusions as to the sincerity of the declaration at the head of the editorial column that it is "an independent newspaper,"—says there is no difference between the rank and file of both parties in their desire to have enduring peace, and to have in the world a "sacred document" for the prevention of wars.

There is no difference between the rank and file of both parties in their desire to have enduring peace,—that is true. If there ever was in this country a man who wanted war, the experiences of the past two years would have cured him. Not only have we experienced the horrors of the battlefield as portrayed by the World-Herald in the campaign of 1916, with the assurance that the election of Wilson meant that we would not be called upon the undergo them,—but we have passed through an era of extravagance, waste, mismanagement, control of public opinion by propaganda and coercion, in itself sufficient to prove that when Sherman said war was hell, he didn't fully rise to the occasion.

There is a very serious difference of opinion about the "sanctity" of the covenant cooked up by Mr. Wilson and the European diplomats, however, even when it is presented with the Pecksniffian pretense that it is going to keep us out of war by the same politicians and editors who handed us the same bunk in 1916, with an aftermath it is unnecessary to recall. The dishonesty of many of the advocates of this covenant is demonstrated by their crooked claim that opposition to it is based upon a desire that this country shall become involved in war, and by the assertion that the foes of the scheme are inspired by "partisan" motives, when everybody understands that such organs as the World-Herald and such politicians as Senator Hitchcock would be howling their heads off against the whole arrangement if it had been proposed by the McKinley or Roosevelt administrations.

The British-Wilson covenant is opposed by the sturdy Americanism of this country because it not only sacrifices the sovereignty and independence and prosperity of the American people, but because it makes every war of the future an American war, and binds us to send our sons to fight it. Instead of partisanship being responsible for the opposition to it, the scheme as proposed would not have formidable support except for partisanship, coupled with the wholesale prostitution of the publicity agencies of the country to propaganda for this alien scheme of internationalization. It is a well known fact that privately more than half of the Democratic members of the Senate are in their hearts against the scheme and it is only the lash of party discipline which prevents revolt against it. It is worthy of note that as soon as Senator James Hamilton Lewis got out of the Senate and from under the official lash, he experienced as sudden a change of heart as came to Saul of Tarsus. Among Republicans most of the disposition not to war upon it results from that meanest kind of partisanship which fears the immediate effect upon the party or personal fortunes of taking a bold and unequivocal stand for the right, even in a matter involving the very fate of the republic.

The World-Herald says that The National Republican is distorting the "ideals" for which America, alias Mr. Wilson, is "striving at the peace table." These "ideals" have emerged from the realm of rhetoric to that of practical application. In compliance with secret treaties the province of Shantung, with 10,000 square miles of territory and a population of 40,000,000,—the sacred province of China inhabited only by Chinese,—is torn from the heart of the world's most populous republic and handed over to Japan, the great military autocracy of the Orient, whose emperor's person is "sacred," just like the "covenant" under which we guarantee the territorial integrity of every kingdom, empire and principality on earth. You can't "distort" such "ideals" as that. Just as well talk about blackening a coal mine or darkening a railway tunnel. Such transactions as this represent reaction to feudalism, not progress toward that glad day when there shall be peace on earth, good will to men, when cannons shall become plow-shares and swords pruning hooks and Colonel Bryan's army of farmers in Fords, armed with corn knives, shall be sufficient to keep safe the shores of the republic.
—May 24, 1919.

There is not an idea or sentiment in Washington's Farewell Address which may not be found, more or less extended, in different parts of Washington's writings; nor, after such a perusal, can any one doubt his ability to compose such a paper. It derives its value, and is destined to immortality, and chiefly from the circumstances of its containing wise, pure and noble sentiments, sanctioned by the name of Washington at the moment when he was retiring from a long public career, in which he had been devoted to the service of his country with a disinterestedness, self-sacrifice, perseverance and success, commanding the admiration and applause of mankind.—Jared Sparks, 1837.

SHALL WE NOW BE GUIDED MORE BY OUR HOPES THAN BY OUR FEARS?

The Saturday Evening Post, one of the active propagandists of the national administration and particularly of the administration plan for a world constitution, says that the objections urged to the "covenant" are mere "senatorial bogies." Others may discover some uncertainty in the provisions of the document, but the Saturday Evening Post finds it all as clear as the noonday sun. It required nearly a century of debate and judicial interpretation, legislative contention and finally civil war, to decide the meaning of the American Constitution, but concerning the provisions of the divinely inspired Versailles constitution, which has been written and re-written, patched and half-soled a number of times, it is unnecessary to go beyond the sanctum of the Saturday Evening Post to discover that they mean nothing the unfriendly interpreters fear they do and everything the partisans of the scheme say they mean. The Post continues:

"Any possible federation of nations must be essentially like a partnership among individuals. If each prospective partner is going to assume, to begin with, that the other prospective partners are seeking a partnership in order to take every possible advantage of him and injure him at every opportunity the partnership will never be formed, for legal ingenuity cannot frame a compact under which a set of rogues, working together, will not find a chance to gouge each other. But if each prospective partner takes the common-sense view that, as the partnership is for the mutual benefit of all concerned, every partner will wish to keep on good terms with the other partners and will act toward them with a reasonable degree of honesty and good faith, then a legal document, satisfactory to all of them, can be drawn."

The Saturday Evening Post would not advise any one of its readers, presumably, to sign any legal contract, affecting his rights or interests, without making the closest possible investigation of not only the surface meaning, but the implications, of every clause in the contract. The company which published the Post would not enter into any legal contract without submitting it to the scrutiny of a high-priced lawyer, whose business it would be to seek out the possibilities of danger involved in every phrase. This would be true, particularly, if the contract had been prepared not by his client, but by the parties of the other part, possibly by their lawyers. It is admitted that the constitution for a league of nations prepared by the American delegation was rejected, and the pending covenant, written by Lord Cecil on the basis of General Smuts' outline, substituted. What the American proposal was we have never been permitted to know in this day of open covenants openly arrived at, so there is no way of telling how far the British plan varies from the American scheme. But the Post advises its readers to get a copy of the league of nations covenant, read it, and then reach their own conclusions as to its meaning; the Post, thoughtfully, however, instructs them what to think.

* * * * *

We repeat that the sensible man who plans to abandon a prosperous independent business and merge it into a partnership would consider it not only his right, but his duty, to give even greater weight to the possible disadvantages than to the possible benefits of the arrangement. Of the state of his own business and the sincerity of his own intentions he could be certain. The man who, in considering the merging of his own business with another business, consults his hopes and his imagination more than his fears and suspicions will have luck to thank if he does not find himself worsted in the bargain. It is all very well for special pleaders for the covenant like the Post to say that in going into a "partnership" we do not surrender our own right to independent action; but any man of common sense knows that the thought of partnership is inconsistent with that of independence. Those who paint in bright colors the alleged advantages, or the alleged service to humanity in general, of the proposed covenant, bear the same relationship to the American people that the promoter of an oil, mining or land development does to the prospect who is asked to buy stock. It is the business of the promoter to leap over all the possible limitations of the property and hold before his possible customer the big profits that are in sight. And if the prospect were to propose to submit the prospectus to an attorney or an expert, doubtless the promoter would advise him as the Post does, just to look at the pretty pictures on the stock certificate and use his own horse sense without listening to the "bogies" raised by flaw picking lawyers. The Post says, and the argument is quite commonly used by partisans of the covenant as proposed: "Picking flaws, and magnifying them, is to be expected. * * * Keep the official texts and read them over for yourself, with plain horse sense, not of course forgetting that the sincerity of the signatory powers is the essence of the contract."

The competent lawyer advising a client who is proposing to enter a partnership will tell him that if the essence of a contract is dependent upon the sincerity of the parties signing it, then no written contract would be necessary. The very existence of a written instrument demonstrates that sensible men prefer to have mutual obligations clearly defined, to leave nothing to chance and to depend upon no verbal representations outside the text of the agreement. The man who, in making a contract with you, objects to having a complete meeting of minds in the construction of an agreement, for instance, when you mean Monroe Doctrine, saying "Monroe Doctrine" instead of "such regional understandings as the Monroe Doctrine in the interests of peace," will bear watching. There is a reservation of some sort in his mind which prompts him to beat around the bush. The history of European diplomacy proves the existence of a disposition in some quarters to consider language a means of concealing thought. Double meaning is more perilous in a contract than in an ordinary joke.

What of the meeting of minds between America and the other signatory powers which after all is the essence of the contract? Do we have, as a matter of fact, the same ideals, purposes and interests which make a partnership agreement an assurance of amicable relations? What light is thrown upon this by the proceedings of the peace conference? We have asked nothing there; we ask no recompense for the billions of dollars expended, the seventy-five thousand priceless lives lost, the hundreds of thousands of minor casualties, the heavy burden of debt we have shouldered, the sacrifices, material and moral, the people of this country have made during the war. What about our prospective partners? What about Great Britain? Have her representatives revealed at the peace table the same self-sacrificing altruism? Have the national interests of that great world empire been in any wise surrendered for the sake of the rest of the world? What about France? Has France been in the peace conference to give or to take? What about Italy? Fiume. The downfall of the Orlando ministry because it went too far in compromising with the one demand made by President Wilson for surrender of the spoils of war by any other nation. What about Japan? Shantung is the answer. What about even the new governments which have sprung up as the result of a war partly waged for their liberation? Have they been in Paris seeking an opportunity for sacrifice, or a chance for national advantage? All this is not said by way of censure of these nations. It is evident, from the universality of their spirit, that there is something quite human about it. It is not for us to condemn, but it is certainly for us to recognize, this stubborn clinging to the ancient rivalries, jealousies and clashing ambitions of European and Asiatic nations. It is with these we are asked to go into partnership. It requires the optimism of a Mulberry Sellers to find the prospect of peace for America in the process of involving ourselves in a covenant the essence of which is the sincerity of these nations in desiring to sacrifice national advantage upon the altar of international good will!

Taking it for granted, however, that our proposed partners are as sincere as the Saturday Evening Post thinks they are in their desire to end the system of which they have for centuries been a part, and of which we have never been a part; that the hearts of these nations are for the moment filled with the passion for world service, free from the taint of national selfishness, the desire for territorial aggression, naval supremacy or trade advantage, what about these partners tomorrow or day after tomorrow? Governments come, and governments go; especially in Europe in these days, they go. The Russia of yesterday and the Russia of today may not be wider apart than the England or France of today and the England or France of tomorrow. When the average man takes a partner he would like to know what he is going to look and act like a year hence. A few days ago we were dealing with one Italy, now, before the peace conference is over, by political revolution there is another and different Italy. By an act of the Italian parliament the official status of Premier Orlando is extinguished. No obligation of the Russia of the Czar or even of Kerensky is recognized by the Russia of Trotzky and Lenine. This is an extreme example, but it illustrates the fact that no government of today can in matters of vital national concern and particularly in matters of idealism, bind the government of a few years hence. This matter is worthy of consideration in arriving at the weight that is to be attached to the "sincerity" of the contracting parties as the "essence" of a contract of permanent partnership.

* * * * *

That, by the partnership proposed, these European and Asiatic powers might profit, is a fair argument. That we might be able to act as a peace-maker to some extent as member of such a combination, is true. But in entering a partnership, or rather a corporation in which we are a minority stockholder, it would probably be well, instead of depending entirely on our own hopefulness, our own child-like faith in the good intentions of others, to listen as carefully to the pickers of flaws as the painters of rainbows; to listen to the voice of experience as well as to voices in the air. Perhaps some significance should be attached to the fact that the chief proponent of the present plan for keeping us out of war were the more or less inspired leaders who rhetorically reduced the high cost of living and introduced the simplicity and economy befitting a democratic government in 1912 and kept us out of war in 1916. Even stock in a solvent corporation is not helped through being offered by agents who in the past have achieved a reputation for floating fake securities. We are now confronted with an alluring prospectus which invites us to become minority stock holders in a world corporation in which we furnish the assets and the other partners the experience; and by these very political Micawbers and Wallingfords!

Let it be admitted that the Republicans in the Senate are acting in the capacity of attorneys for only one of the parties to the proposed covenant. As such, it is their business to be partisans for the party of the first part. It is their business to "pick flaws" and to create "bogies," if you will. Once adopted, the covenant will be subject to the interpretation of those whose interests are adverse to ours, as well as of those who have our national interests at heart. The theory that we can get out of the league if we do not find it to our liking seems fair enough; but it is always easier to get into a partnership than to get honorable and profitable release from a partnership that turns out to be disadvantageous. The theory that we can amend the covenant to our advantage hereafter carries with it the implication that in a combination in which we can be out-voted it may be amended to our disadvantage.

* * * * *

Let the people deal with this proposed covenant just as they would with any contract of partnership or corporate association they are invited to sign. Let them not fail to give as careful scrutiny and as interested consideration to the perils and penalties as to the suppositious advantages of the arrangement. Let them see to it that any contract executed says what its proponents say it means, leaving nothing to guess-work. No sensible man would fail to follow such a course in his own private business. Why would he not act with as much caution in a matter affecting the destiny of the nation, the welfare of himself, his children and his children's children? Would any man competent to protect his own rights and interests in private life, yield to the demand to "sign here" made in behalf of a contract of wide terms and implications, and to the plea that any effort on his part to change these terms and implications for his own protection would be interpreted as "delaying the game" and as a dishonorable repudiation of the acts of a self-constituted agent never authorized by him to enter into any such agreement? And whatever contract we sign, let us expect to execute to the letter, however seriously it may affect our national rights and interests. The time to protect these rights and interests is now, before the contract is made. —June 28, 1919.

Washington reminds us of the quality of great citizenship. His career is at once an inspiration and rebuke. Whatever is lofty, fair and patriotic in public conduct instinctively we call by his name; whatever is base, selfish and unworthy is shamed by the lustre of his life. Like the flaming sword turning every way that guarded the gate of Paradise, Washington's example is the beacon shining at the opening of our annals and lighting the path of our national life. Washington's conduct of the war was not more valuable to the country than his organization of the government, and it was not his special talent but his character that made both of those services possible. In public affairs the glamor of arms is always dazzling. But while military glory stirs the popular heart it is the traditions of national grandeur, the force of noble character which nourish the sentiment that makes men patriots and heroes. It is not only Washington the soldier and the statesman, but Washington the citizen, whom we chiefly remember. Americans are accused of making an excellent and patriotic Virginia gentleman a mythological hero and demigod. But what mythological hero or demigod is a figure so fair? We say nothing of him today that was not said by those who saw and knew him, and in phrases more glowing than ours, and the concentrated light of a hundred years discloses nothing to mar the nobility of the incomparable man.—George William Curtis.

We ought not to undertake the task of policing Europe, Asia and northern Africa; neither ought we to permit any interference with the Monroe Doctrine or any attempt by Europe or Asia to police America. Mexico is our Balkan peninsula. Some day we will have to deal with it. All the coasts and islands which in any way approach the Panama Canal must be dealt with by this nation in accordance with the Monroe Doctrine. * * * Let each nation reserve to itself and for its own decision, and let it clearly set forth, questions which are nonjusticable. Finally, make it perfectly clear that we do not intend to take a position of an international "Meddlesome Mattie." The American people do not wish to undertake the responsibility of sending our gallant young men to die in obscure fights in the Balkans or in central Europe or in a war we do not approve of; moreover, the American people do not intend to give up the Monroe Doctrine.—Theodore Roosevelt.

It is the long-settled conviction of this government that any extension to our shores of the political system by which the great powers have controlled and determined events in Europe would be attended with danger to the peace and welfare of this nation. * * * It is nothing more than the pronounced adherence of the United States to principles long since enunciated by the highest authority of the government, and now, in the judgment of the President, firmly inwoven as an integral and important part of our national policy.—James G. Blaine.

Having lavished all her honors, his (Washington's) country had nothing more to bestow upon him except her blessing. But he had more to bestow upon his country. His views and his advice, the condensed wisdom of all his reflection, observation and experience, he delivers to his compatriots in a manual worthy of them to study, and of him to compose.—John M. Mason, 1800.

Throughout the whole web of national existence we trace the golden thread of human progress toward a higher and better estate.—James A. Garfield.

SHALL WE BE JOINED IN THE SHAME
OF SHANTUNG?

The plea is made that Japan has shed her blood in war for the conquest of the province of Shantung, and should not be denied the fruits of victory. Is the United States Senate not acting the part of a big bully in refusing to help turn over to Japan the Chinese soil taken from Germany, we are seriously asked?

Is Japanese blood more precious than American blood? Have Americans, too, not shed blood and spent treasure in this war, far beyond anything yielded up by Japan? Did we, too, not take territory from Germany? Are we demanding that this territory be given to us? Or, to draw a parallel, are we asking that a slice of Belgian soil be given to the United States on the ground that our men and money helped expel the late claimant to Belgium?

And if we did not shed that blood and spend that treasure to despoil an enemy, or rob a friend of territory, is there any injustice in declining to join in a compact whereby one ally shall rob another of her fairest province? Is there cause of offense in declining to fix for Japan a lower standard of international morality than we are willing to accept for ourselves?

What did Japan do in comparison with what we did to win the struggle against the central empires? And since we armed four million men for the war, sent half of them across the Atlantic to grapple with the enemy, laid down sixty thousand precious lives on the battlefields of France, and gave three hundred thousand additional names to the casualty lists; since we saddled ourselves with a debt of thirty billions, and made all the sacrifices necessary for the achievement of victory and peace, shall it be said that, asking nothing by way of indemnity or territory from the vanquished foe we may not at least have the feeble satisfaction of refusing to help an autocratic and militaristic nation that has done vastly less, to satisfy her imperialistic ambitions at the expense of an ally we induced to go into the war with the assurance that it would be to her advantage?

We went into the war with clean hands and a clear conscience. Let us come out of it without the loss of either. We did no secret bargaining behind closed doors; no deception of our allies was committed by the United States government; we demanded no price for our service to the common cause. We have proclaimed to the world that our purpose was to bring mankind the justice of a new and better order of world affairs. We have borne our part in the fight. What crime have we committed, that in violation of our high professions, in repudiation of our long record as the champion of the open door in the Orient and justice for China, we should be compelled to become parties to a compact whereby the great republic of the Orient formed in emulation of our own, is delivered to the domination of a power whose claim is based upon the fact that she is armed to the teeth and able to take territory by violence from her weaker neighbor?

If we are to be parties to international thievery, shall we have none of the loot? If we are to be assistant burglars, do we get none of the spoil? If we insist on sharing the dishonor of the crime of violence against China, shall we not be paid off for our participation? Otherwise why should we accept partnership in such a violation of international justice and good faith for no reason whatever except that we have gone to war and come out victorious?

We are told that if we refuse to give our approval, as a nation, to the seizure of Shantung by Japan, it will throw us into the shadow of war and we are asked if we are willing to send our sons to fight for the freedom of China. Is it a cause of war that we, asking nothing for ourselves in return for our vast sacrifice in blood and treasure, will not help another nation despoil her neighbors? We are not proposing to force Japan out of Shantung. We are merely declaring, by our action, that we are unwilling to approve and underwrite the transaction whereby China parts with her property and her self respect and her sovereignty at the command of allies who proclaim to the world that they went to war to end the very practices they thus commit. By refusing to assent to this arrangement, we are adopting the only means we have of protest; any other protest would be like that of the man who helps commit a crime and then cards the newspapers with a sig expression of disapproval of the deed he has joined in doingd

If we are to get nothing out of the war, let us at least not accept disgrace from it by reason of giving our assent to an arrangement whereby the unhappy nation we induced to enter this struggle, is despoiled of many thousand square miles of territory and thirty-eight millions of people. If we did not, after all, go to war in the cause of freedom, let us not make it of record that we went to war in behalf of enslavement. If it be said that we must accept the promise of Japan to negotiate with China for the restoration of her province, let it be answered that if this were the intention, no excuse whatever could be offered for not making the restoration at once or fixing a date when it will be done. A note without a due date is of no value. An agreement to return territory without fixing a time for the return is worthless, because it promises nothing whatever. To all this talk the word "Korea," the steady record of Japanese aggression in China, is sufficient answer.

When the advocates of the league of nations defend this Shantung transaction the people of this country get an insight into the sincerity of their professions of purpose to introduce into the world, through this covenant, a new order of world affairs. Search the history of the United States from the beginning and you will find no instance in which we have ever indulged in such an act of injustice and betrayal toward a friendly nation as we are asked to commit in the approval of this Shantung transaction. If this be the new pathway along which we are to be led, well may we hesitate to take a step further. If this be the sort of "new order" the league of nations is to introduce, let us cling to the old.
—September 6, 1919.

It is only when our rights are invaded, or seriously menaced, that we resent injuries, or make preparations for our defense. With the movements in this hemisphere we are, of necessity, more immediately connected, and by causes which must be obvious to all enlightened and impartial observers. The political system of the allied powers is essentially different in this respect from that of America. This difference proceeds from that which exists in their respective governments; and to the defense of our own, which has been achieved by the loss of so much blood and treasure, and matured by the wisdom of their most enlightened citizens, and under which we have enjoyed unexampled felicity, this whole nation is devoted.

We owe it, therefore, to candor, and to the amicable relations existing between the United States and those European powers, to declare that we should consider any attempt on their part to extend their system to any portion of this hemisphere as dangerous to our peace and safety.

With the existing colonies and dependencies of any European power, we have not interfered, and shall not interfere. But with the governments who have declared their independence and maintained it, and whose independence we have, on great consideration and on just principles, acknowledged, we could not view any interposition for the purpose of oppressing them, or controlling in any other manner their destiny by any European power, in any other light than as the manifestation of an unfriendly disposition toward the United States.—From the message of President Monroe, December, 1823.

We ought always to act fairly and generously to other nations. In international matters I hold that we should have the same standard of morality that we have in private matters. But we must remember that our first duty is always to be loyal and patriotic citizens of our own nation, defenders of her rights, maintaining her noblest traditions. These two facts should always be uppermost in our mind when we take up any proposal for a league of nations. We can then be loyal to great ideals as well as true to ourselves.—Theodore Roosevelt.

Oh, say, can you see by the dawn's early light
What so proudly we hail'd at the twilight's last gleaming—
Whose broad stripes and bright stars through the perilous fight,
O'er the ramparts we watch'd, were so gallantly streaming?
And the rocket's red glare, the bombs bursting in air,
Gave proof through the night that our flag was still there;
Oh, say, does that star-spangled banner yet wave
O'er the land of the free, and the home of the brave?

On that shore, dimly seen through the mists of the deep,
Where the foe's haughty host in dread silence reposes,
What is that which the breeze, o'er towering steep,
As it fitfully blows, now conceals, now discloses?
Now it catches the gleam of the morning's first beam,
In full glory reflected, now shines in the stream;
'Tis the star-spangled banner; oh, long may it wave
O'er the land of the free, and the home of the brave!

And where are the foes who so vauntingly swore
That the havoc of war and the battle's confusion
A home and a country should leave us no more?
Their blood has wash'd out their foul footsteps' pollution.
No refuge could save the hireling and slave
From the terror of flight, or the gloom of the grave;
And the star-spangled banner in triumph doth wave
O'er the land of the free and the home of the brave.

Oh, thus be it ever, when freemen shall stand
Between their loved homes and the war's desolation!
Blest with victory and peace, may the heaven-rescued land
Praise the Power that hath made and preserved us a nation.
Then conquer we must, when our cause it is just;
And this be our motto: "In God is our trust;"
And the star-spangled banner in triumph shall wave
O'er the land of the free, and the home of the brave.
　　　　　　　　　　　　　　　　　　—Francis Scott Key.

We should do nothing inconsistent with the spirit and genius of our institutions. We should do nothing for revenge, but everything for security; nothing for the past, everything for the present and the future.—James A. Garfield.

PEOPLE DEMAND REAL, NOT NOMINAL
TREATY CHANGES

Reservations or amendments in the covenant of the league of nations should be written by those who have shown themselves alive to the perils of the proposed world constitution, not by those who have shown themselves willing to sacrifice American rights, interests and ideals by the swallowing whole of the plan as brought home from Europe, and who are willing to have protective changes made only as a necessary concession to public sentiment.

The feeling of the American people against any alien entanglement effected at the sacrifice of American nationalism, American independence or American welfare, is not only great, but it is growing. That sentiment demands not the mere camouflaging of the defects of the covenant, but actual changes which will prevent the proposed sacrifice of all that Americans have striven for and fought for throughout nearly a century and a half of national existence.

Unless the treaty is so changed that it ceases to become an instrument to be used for the subordination and ultimately the destruction of a free and independent United States of America, then it should be rejected by those in the Senate whose hearts are still beating in sympathy with traditional Americanism.
—September 13, 1919.

Under the influence of rapidly increasing knowledge, the people have begun, in all forms of government, to think, and to reason, on affairs of state. Regarding government as an institution for the public good, they demand a knowledge of its operations, and a participation in its exercise. * * * When Louis XVI said, "I am the state," he expressed the essence of the doctrine of unlimited power. By the rules of that system, the people are disconnected from the state; they are its subjects, it is their lord. These ideas, founded in the love of power, and long supported by the excess and the abuse of it, are yielding, in our age, to other opinions; and the civilized world seems at last to be proceeding to the conviction of that fundamental and manifest truth, that the powers of government are but a trust, and that they can not be lawfully exercised but for the good of the community. * * * Let our object be, our country, our whole country, and nothing but our country. And,

AMERICANISM

by the blessing of God, may that country itself become a vast and splendid monument, not of oppression and terror, but of wisdom, of peace and of liberty, upon which the world may gaze with admiration forever!—Daniel Webster.

We sit here in the Promised Land
That flows with Freedom's honey and milk;
But 'twas they won it, sword in hand,
Making the nettle danger soft for us as silk.
We welcome back our bravest and our best;—
Ah me! not all! some come not with the rest,
Who went forth brave and bright as any here!
I strive to mix some gladness with my strain,
But the sad strings complain,
And will not please the ear:
I sweep them for a paean, but they wane
Again and yet again
Into a dirge, and die away, in pain.
In these brave ranks I only see the gaps,
Thinking of the dear ones whom the dumb turf wraps,
Dark to the triumph which they died to gain:
Fitlier may others greet the living,
For me the past is unforgiving;
I with uncovered head
Salute the sacred dead,
Who went, and who return not.—Say not so!
'Tis not the grapes of Canaan that repay,
But the high faith that failed not by the way;
Virtue treads paths that end not in the grave;
No bar of endless night exiles the brave;
And to the saner mind
We rather seem the dead that stayed behind.
Blow, trumpets, all your exultations blow!
For never shall their aureoled presence lack:
I see them muster in a gleaming row,
With ever-youthful brows that nobler show;
We find in our dull road their shining track;
In every nobler mood
We feel the orient of their spirit glow,
Part of our life's unalterable good,
Of all our saintlier aspiration;
They come transfigured back,
Secure from change in their high-hearted ways,
Beautiful evermore, and with the rays
Of morn on their white Shields of Expectation!
                              —James Russell Lowell.

WHAT IS THE ALTERNATIVE TO THE PENDING COVENANT?

One of the stock arguments of the proponents of the unamended league of nations covenant is that the opposition has no alternative, constructive program.

It is the chief offense of the makers of this covenant that in un-American, unconstitutional fashion, they have excluded from any constructive part in the formulation of the scheme any and all persons not willing to accept their opinions, hand-me-down style, from the one official and political leader who is alleged to possess the exclusive prerogative of representing the people of America in this matter. Clearly enough he, alone, does not represent the people of America, because on the basis of a direct appeal that he be given a rubber stamp Senate committed to this very doctrine, a majority of more than a million votes was rolled up against him at the ballot boxes last November. The Constitution of the United States, moreover, defines clearly a division of this responsibility between the President and the Senate. Yet, throughout, in the appointment of his commission, in the formulation of the treaty and covenant, in the effort to put the thing over without yielding to the Senate the slightest voice in the matter, President Wilson has deliberately and stubbornly sought to ignore and even to defy this coordinate treaty making branch of government. What opportunity has there been for constructive action in this matter by anyone but President Wilson himself? Who, then, is responsible for this condition of affairs?

If, through the refusal of the administration senators to give consideration to the views of those who believe that the rights, interests and ideals of America are sacrificed in this treaty and covenant as it stands, and through their bourbon opposition to any modification or amendment or reservation in the treaty, members of the Senate more interested in the preservation of America than in the vindication of the administration are forced to vote against ratification of the treaty and covenant, and it thereby is defeated, who must accept the responsibility in the eyes of all fair-minded men? Those, surely, who take the position that the treaty and covenant must be accepted, defects, dangers and all, or rejected in toto.

If modification of the treaty and covenant so as to protect American sovereignty, American rights, American ideals and just American interests is refused by the agents of the administration in the Senate, then the duty of the Senate is clear—to reject.

Then will come the opportunity for constructive suggestion. So far as the treaty is concerned, whether or not we are parties to it does not much matter. The treaty deals with the imposition of penalties and the distribution of spoils in territory and money, and the police and military duty incident to guaranteeing that the allied powers shall "get theirs." As we get nothing, we will lose nothing but trouble if we are not in on this particular job.

The world's longing for some plan whereby the peace of the world may be preserved, so far as this is humanly possible, remains. Without the realization of this longing the war must be set down as a gigantic failure, out of which can come no compensation adequate to the sacrifices entailed. That longing finds no response in the peace treaty and covenant except in the resounding rhetoric of those who defend it before the world. There can be no guaranteed peace unless the world, at least gradually, lays down its arms. Despite all the claims to the contrary, there is absolutely no provision for disarmament, or any provision whereby it is at all likely that any step will be taken in that direction, in either the treaty or covenant. The big military and naval programs proposed by the men who made this treaty, both in Europe and in the United States, prove that they themselves have no faith in their own professions in this respect.

There is no provision in this treaty for the settlement of international disputes on the basis of international law and equity rather than of force. For the covenant sets up, not a world court, but a world legislature; not a tribunal which is to decide international questions by judicial interpretation, but a legislative body, with powers of coercion, which is to decide such matters on the basis of interest.

What the world needs is a complete body of international law, dealing with all matters capable of becoming subjects of dispute between nations,—a body of international law formulated by a world conference, composed of representatives not merely of kings, emperors and presidents, but of the people acting through their legislative representatives, chosen just as our representatives in the Congress which formulated our Constitution were selected; representing in each case not merely one party, or faction, or person but the people as a whole, thus commanding the support and confidence of all elements. Then, for the interpretation of this law, dealing entirely with international as differentiated from domestic questions, the world needs, as Colonel Roosevelt put it, "an amplified Hague court, acting in a judicial and not a representative capacity;" a court, which, like our own Supreme Court, because of its separation from every interest in conflict, will command for its decisions the world's confidence and acquiescence.

Then if there be good faith in the declared desire of the powers with which we are associated for world peace, there will be an agreement for disarmament to that point below which the nations could not go with due regard for their domestic safety. The absence of such an agreement from the Paris treaty and covenant demonstrates that those who wrote it had, as a matter of. fact, no intention whatever of substituting the rule of justice for the rule of might among nations. The continuance of the spirit of imperialism, as exemplified in the desire for world trade and territorial domination, backed up either by military or naval supremacy, is utterly inconsistent with the true spirit of a league of nations for the establishment and maintenance of peace in the world,—a fact which millions of people who at one time accepted the alluring prospectuses of the league of nations covenant as a substitute for any guarantee of the results desired in its actual contents, are beginning to realize.

If, through the stubborn, autocratic, un-American refusal of the proponents of the pending treaty and league of nations to accept reasonable modifications, the defeat of the treaty is assured, the way will have been opened for entering upon an honest effort to secure a real arrangement for world cooperation for the maintenance of peace, security and liberty throughout the world. Because of that hope there are millions of liberal-minded men in America and throughout the world who hope that the defenders of the covenant will persist in their present destructive course. It is impossible for any unprejudiced student of this treaty and covenant to believe that it represents a forward step in the deliverance of humanity from the curse of war, the sway of tyranny or the clash of contending territorial, trade and dynastic ambitions whetted by fresh acquisitions as the spoils of war. The program prepared at Paris has the voice of progress, but the hand of reaction.

Let us have, through the deliberate and free action of all the nations of the world, assembled upon our government's initiative in conference at Washington, the capital of the one nation which went into this war for the high purposes it is sought to fulfill in the new world order, a world congress, not to legislate in restriction of the rights or interests of any nation, but to lay down broad legal principles of international cooperation, fundamental principles rather than a specific program, and then to erect a great world court to whose decisions these powers agree to bow as willingly as the American people bow to the decisions of their Supreme Court. Then, as a guarantee of good faith, let the nations of the earth agree to cease the maintenance of vast armies and navies, abolish conscription for military or naval service, tear

down and keep down to the limitations of domestic necessity, establishments for the manufacture of the enginery of warfare, and thus make it impossible for any nation to war upon its neighbors without, by definite preparations, serving long notice of a declaration of war not only against the specific enemy, but against the world's desire for freedom from the sacrifices of that organized butchery we call war.
—September 13, 1919.

The great rule of conduct for us in regard to foreign nations is, in extending our commercial relations, to have with them as little political connection as possible. So far as we have already formed engagements, let them be fulfilled with perfect good faith. Here let us stop.

Europe has a set of primary interests which to us have none or a very remote relation. Hence she must be engaged in frequent controversies, the causes of which are essentially foreign to our concerns. Hence, therefore, it must be unwise in us to implicate ourselves by artificial ties in the ordinary vicissitudes of her politics or the ordinary combinations and collisions of her friendships or enmities.

Our detached and distant situation invites and enables us to pursue a different course.

Why forego the advantages of so peculiar a situation? Why quit our own to stand upon foreign ground? Why, by interweaving our destiny with that of any part of Europe, entangle our peace and prosperity in the toils of European ambition, rivalship, interest or caprice?

It is our true policy to steer clear of permanent alliances with any portion of the foreign world, so far, I mean, as we are now at liberty to do it; for let me not be understood as capable of patronizing infidelity to existing engagements. I hold the maxim no less applicable to public than to private affairs, that honesty is always the best policy. I repeat it, therefore, let those engagements be observed in their genuine sense. But in my opinion it is unnecessary and would be unwise to extend them.

Taking care to keep ourselves by suitable establishments on a respectably defensive posture, we may safely trust to temporary alliances for extraordinary emergencies.—George Washington.

I do not believe that the United States should enter into a worldwide career of disinterested violence for the right; because where both the lands and the issues involved are remote from us our people wouldn't know with certainty where the right lay and wouldn't feel that we ought to go into the quarrel. We have enough to do that is our business.—Theodore Roosevelt.

THE PEOPLE GROW WEARY OF GOVERNMENT BY FEAR

The people have grown weary of government by fear. They accepted many repressive measures during the war, in the necessity of some of which they did not believe. When American soldiers are fighting at the front, it is the duty of every citizen to stand by what his government says is essential to standing by the flag. At that time, "Their's not to answer why."

But the war is over; the enemy is defeated and disarmed. The people grow weary of having their disposition to do whatever is bidden or suggested by executive authority taken for granted. They want a return to that government of public opinion for which American institutions fundamentally stand. They are tired of being called "pro-Germans" and "disloyalists" if they fail to accept without shadow of question whatever is handed down from high places as the law and the gospel.

The people are tired of being bullied and threatened into doing things their judgment does not approve. They are weary of such treatment at the hands of their representatives in authority; they are doubly tired of it as it emanates from private groups and classes and elements engaged in swishing clubs around the ears of the people and telling them to stand and deliver on penalty of the terrible things that are going to be done to them by individual or mass movement.

It is a poor student of popular psychology who does not recognize and reckon with this state of the public mind. Bullyism in politics, in industrial relations and in public affairs not only will not win hereafter, but it will bring reaction seriously harmful to those who keep on keeping on in this practice.

One cause of the tremendous popular uprising against the un-amended, made-in-Paris covenant is that an organized effort has been made to put it over simply by ordering the people to accept it by authority. In this attempt the fact has been overlooked that in this country the authority to make contracts for the whole American people is not centered in one man's hands, but is divided under the Constitution between the legislative and executive branches of government.

Depending upon the impetus of the disposition of the people during the war to look to the White House for orders, the attempt has been made to put this thing over on the people by the pretense that any disagreement with President Wilson is treason. This in the face of the fact that President Wilson has not recognized his mutual obligation to the American people. He has treated the negotiation of the treaty and covenant as a matter of personal prerogative. He did not ask the people to authorize him to represent this country in writing a world constitution; he did not even ask them if they wanted a world constitution. He did not appoint a representative peace delegation, and when it proved to be stronger than he supposed it was, he ignored the advice of its members whenever it failed to coincide with his preconceived notions. He did not proceed with the "advice and consent" of the Senate. On the contrary he has ignored and defied the Senate and is today traveling over the country in a special train at public expense endeavoring to arouse the people against their representatives in the legislative body which legally has as much to do with making a treaty as he has, and is guilty only of the crime of doing its sworn duty under the Constitution by considering this vital national matter upon its merits.

And what are the arguments whereby President Wilson attempts to coerce Congress to do his bidding? They represent clearly a phase of government by fear. He resorts naturally to the weapon of the autocrat. He appeals to the fears of the senators and to the fears of the people. He declares that the senators who fail to agree with him are going to be "gibbeted." He calls them names: "Contemptible quitters," "intellectual pigmies," "reactionaries," "men without vision," "cowards" and the like. He tells the people that if they do not swallow this treaty and covenant without the crossing of a "t" or the dotting of an "i" terrible things are going to happen to them. They will have strikes, war, bolshevism, high cost of living and a whole brood of troubles now perilously present after Mr. Wilson has been for six and a half years in the White House under pledge to eliminate them.

At the same time private organizations, representing the special interests of groups and elements closely associated politically with President Wilson, have moved upon Congress threatening the representatives of the people with paralysis of industry unless they adopt certain governmental policies which would mark the beginning of complete state socialism. Heretofore we have determined political questions in the court of public opinion. Now we are told they are going to be settled with a club brandished under the noses of the people of this country.

We repeat, the people of the United States are getting weary of threats and orders, of bulldozing and scares. The backs of the great masses of the people of this country,—the overwhelming majority of the people of this country,—of the workers of this country,—are to the wall. They have been the "goats" of the situation up to the present time. They have been soaked and bilked, exploited and run over. They are getting ready to tell the demagogues and the doctrinaires of all breeds and varieties where to head in. This great popular majority includes most of the men who were called to the colors to serve their country during the past two years at great personal loss, discomfort and sacrifice, while many of the most loud-mouthed of those who are now telling the people what they have got to do, or get a rough-house, were having the time of their lives at the expense of the general public.

There is going to be an election in this country little more than a year hence. The people of this country are getting ready to make a house cleaning at that time. They are going to clean up on the politicians who have wasted the people's substance in riotous living, and sacrificed their rights and interests for personal and political ends. The voters of this country are going to strike a blow at the polls in November, 1920, for government of the people, for the people, by the people, as contrasted with government of the people for the benefit of groups, classes, partisans and crowds, having in mind in their exploitation of the public only their own selfish interests, until the whole country, even the members of these very groups, have found themselves far worse off than they ever were before, while profiteering, speculation and thimblerigging of the public has become the regular order of the day. Production has been curtailed, efficiency has been impaired, prices have been enthroned, laziness and inefficiency have been rewarded, honest business has been penalized and oppressed, speculative adventurers have been given free reign, honest competition has been destroyed, monopolistic exploitation has gone unpunished; all this to the tune of high-flown phrases about the people's rights and interests thus so ruthlessly sacrificed.

And as the fitting climax of all this carnival of demagogy, waste, incompetency, discrimination, carried on at the very time the fighting men of the republic have been writing in their own red blood a new and glorious chapter in the annals of Americanism, we have the proposition to sacrifice the rights, interests and ideals of America in a covenant covertly connived at by the very influences and elements which have put all this over on the American people here at home. And, again,—government by fear,—we are threatened that if we do not do this thing, after all we have done to bring peace to the world through the sacrifice of our blood and treasure, we will become pariahs in the community of nations, and that the rest of the world will run amuck, commit suicide and take us along with them, unless we take on the job of policing and providing for the rest of the world for all time to come.

The people of this country are not cowards. Their traditions are not those of timidity. They are not a people to be scared or threatened or bullied into doing things. They never have been and they never will be. Government by fear does not go here.

AMERICANISM

The people of America still have in their hearts the spirit of the Declaration of Independence. No combination of classes or elements, no propagandists of any mere caste or dynasty or alien interest, can permanently put anything over on them. Never was that clearer than it is today. In the splendid rise of American public opinion to meet the fateful emergency of this hour has come anew the triumphant vindication of real democracy; free, independent, deliberative American democracy which bows its neck to no master, foreign or domestic, but carries its sovereignty beneath its own hat.

The people of this country, themselves not cowards, nor the sons of cowards, want brave, true, modest, devoted men in public place; men who can think of public questions in terms other than those of their own interests and advantage; who at the command of their own judgment and conscience are willing on occasion to take a chance by telling elements which seek to govern by fear that they will get nothing from government that is not for the general good. The people are tired of truckling, fawning opportunists in public place who think of no public problem except in terms of votes; not the votes of the majority, but the votes which stand ready to be delivered in blocks in exchange for special advantage surrendered at the sacrifice of the general welfare. This lesson should not be lost upon the leadership of either great party. For in this hour of turmoil and anxiety and uncertainty and unrest, the cry of the American people is, echoing the words of J. G. Holland:

"God give us men! A time like this demands
Strong minds, great hearts, true faith and willing hands:
   Men whom the lust of office does not kill;
Men whom the spoils of office can not buy;
Men who have honor; men who will not lie;
   Men who can stand before a demagogue
And damn his treacherous flatteries without winking,
   Tall men, sun crowned, who live above the fog
In public duty and in private thinking."
—September 20, 1919.

We are bound to maintain public liberty, and, by the example of our own systems, to convince the world that order and law, religion and morality, the rights of conscience, the rights of persons and the rights of property, may all be preserved and secured in the most perfect manner, by a government entirely and purely elective. If we fail in this, our disaster will be signal, and will furnish an argument stronger than has yet been found, in support of those opinions which maintain that government can rest safely on nothing but power and coercion.—Daniel Webster.

SOME FLIMSY SOPHISTRY ON THE SHAME
OF SHANTUNG

President Wilson said at San Francisco: "Which of these gentlemen who are now objecting to the cession of the German rights in Shantung to Japan were prominent in protesting against the original cession? It makes my heart burn when some men are so late in doing justice."

According to President Wilson's present claims as to why we went to war with Germany, his own heart, then, ought to burn brightly over his own deliberate processes of espousing the cause of justice.

But this talk about our failure to protest over the German seizure of Shantung being a bar to protest now is sophistry of the flimsiest sort. We were not parties to that transaction any more than we were parties to the hundred other cases of similar injustice in China and elsewhere throughout the world.

But we are parties to this treaty President Wilson has brought home from Paris. We are asked to sign the contract under which the territory of one ally is taken and handed over to another ally. We are requested by President Wilson to join in committing this injustice. Then we are asked, under Article X of the league, to guarantee the permanency of the seizure.

Is President Wilson unable to differentiate between our failure to protest against the dismemberment of Poland and the right or wrong of our joining in a treaty to steal territory from one country and hand it to another in fulfillment of secret treaties to which we were not parties? Is he unable to tell the difference between one's failure to pursue every thief who comes into the neighborhood, and acting as a thief's accomplice?

"It is the first time in the history of the world anything has ever been done for China," declared President Wilson. It is not the first time, but only the last time, that anything has been done to China. But China is not so completely lacking, as President Wilson professes himself to be in knowledge and appreciation of what has been done for China by this nation in the past. China knows that while the other powers with whom President Wilson would permanently ally us, and in whose last foray upon China he would have us join, have been robbing China, this country has been helping her. China knows that this country prevented the execution of a general policy of partition in China by the European powers following the Boxer uprising. China knows that alone among the powers the United States returned the unexpended portion of the indemnity exacted from China after the capture of Pekin by the allied forces to pay for personal injuries done foreigners. Of this episode President Wilson professes himself ignorant. He knows nothing of the "open door" policy of Hay and McKinley. He says, "for the first time in the history of the world" something has been done for China.

Well, if this service done China is the realization of all the beautiful purposes and lofty ideals professed in behalf of the league of nations covenant, if this be the new order they are talking about, then God help the weak nations of the earth. For if robbery can be camouflaged under the rhetoric of pseudo-idealism to look like philanthropy, we must be well on the way toward the establishment of what the Chinese themselves, unconscious of the philanthropic objects of the new world government, have already dubbed: "The league of thieves."
—September 27, 1919.

Thou, too, sail on, O Ship of State!
Sail on, O Union, strong and great!
Humanity with all its fears,
With all the hopes of future years,
Is hanging breathless on thy fate!
We know what Master laid thy keel,
What Workmen wrought thy ribs of steel,
Who made each mast, and sail, and rope,
What anvils rang, what hammers beat,
In what a forge and what a heat
Were shaped the anchors of thy hope!

Fear not each sudden sound and shock,
'Tis of the wave and not the rock;
'Tis but the flapping of the sail,
And not a rent made by the gale!
In spite of rock and tempest's roar,
In spite of false lights on the shore,
Sail on, nor fear to breast the sea!
Our hearts, our hopes, are all with thee,
Our hearts, our hopes, our prayers, our tears,
Our faith triumphant o'er our fears,
Are all with thee—are all with thee!
                                —Henry W. Longfellow.

Let us have faith that right makes might; and, in that faith, let us, to the end, dare to do our duty as we understand it.— Abraham Lincoln.

SOME QUESTIONS

Special appeal has been made by propagandists of the unamended covenant of the league of nations to business men, ministers of the gospel and wage earners. For these three influential groups of American citizens we have a few questions.

TO THE BUSINESS MAN: Would you sign a contract, affecting your private interests, concerning the meaning of which there is serious disagreement among friends equally intelligent, some of them believing it means your ruin, without clearing up all doubts by inserting in the contract your interpretation of it in terms nobody could misunderstand? If those of your friends who say this contract means nothing to your detriment, insist that if you make sure of that by saying so in the contract the other parties to the agreement will refuse to sign it, have you not room to doubt their good faith or the good faith of the other parties in interest? Suppose it should be suggested to you to sign the contract and ask the other parties to change it afterward; what would you think of the intelligence of such advice? Now if you would not sign an uncertain contract affecting your private property or personal rights without meeting in it every objection your lawyer could offer, would you show less concern for the rights and interests of your country by committing yourself unreservedly to an argeement, as presented, in the original making of which you had no part, knowing that this agreement would affect vitally the future of your country?

TO THE MINISTER OF THE GOSPEL: Would you consent to the formation of a league of religions, including Mohammedanism, Christianity, Buddhism. Confucianism, Shintoism and all other forms of religion, which would have the power over the churches of the world that the league of nations is to be given over the governments of the world? Would you agree to divide up the people of the world among the existing religious faiths on the basis of the status quo, and to defend the integrity of these other religious bodies upon call? Would you agree to such a form of government even for Catholics and Protestants in the United States? Would you agree to it if your own particular religious body were to be in a minority in the world church government, and some other body of similar size were to be given six votes in one of the two branches of the world religious parliament to your one? If you wouldn't make this sacrifice of your church, why would you make it of your country? Are the political ideals of America and Japan more

115

remote than the ideals of Christianity and Shintoism? How may political and religious ideals best be established in the world, by force or by example?

TO THE WAGE EARNER: Are you ready to sacrifice the American standard of wages and living, with all that it implies of comfort and pleasure and opportunity, in the vain hope that the leveling down of our standard will lift that of the hundreds of millions of peasant, coolies and peons in the rest of the world? Does the common standard of life proposed in the league of nations covenant and its world government of labor appeal to you as meaning anything to wage earners in the land of labor's best estate and highest opportunity? Are you seeking the "removal of economic barriers and quality of trade opportunity" which means that labor's rewards and opportunities are to be standardized throughout the world? Do you believe there is really any good reason why Americans should divide up with the rest of the world the rich heritage which has come down to them by the favor of God, the sacrifices of our fathers and the beneficent influence of institutions which have given us a nation without caste or class? Shall we level ourselves down to the rest of the world, or shall we invite the rest of the world to lift itself to our standards? Are you willing to be bound to fight for the defense of your country, and for the defense of the rest of the world as well, only in order that American markets may be thrown open, under the Third of the Fourteen points and the sway of the league of nations, to the exploitation of alien producers who have had nothing to do with upbuilding your country and will have nothing to do with maintaining it? Do you believe it is up to us to become "the servants of mankind," rather than the masters of our own destiny and the world's great working model of progress and prosperity under genuine representative republican democracy: do you prefer pretended democracy under imperial institutions?
—September 27, 1919.

I trust I understand and truly estimate the right of self-government. My faith in the proposition that each man should do precisely as he pleases with all which is exclusively his own, lies at the foundation of the sense of justice there is in me. I extend the principle to communities of men as well as individuals.

I so extend it because it is politically wise in saving us from broils about matters which do not concern us. Here, or at Washington, I would not trouble myself with the oyster laws of Virginia, or the cranberry laws of Indiana. The doctrine of self-government is right—absolutely and eternally right.—Abraham Lincoln, in debate with Douglas, 1854.

PATRIOTS MUST MEET THE CHALLENGE
OF LAWLESSNESS

Whence comes the spirit of lawlessness prevalent in the country to an extent hitherto unknown, and which in recent months has found increasing expression in violence of utterance and action without parallel in previous American history?

Partly, of course, it is the aftermath of the war, which has disturbed conditions, let loose passions, stirred desires and spread unrest throughout the world, to such an extent that civilization itself demands the active effort for its preservation of every man who has anything at stake in the salvation of the world from chaos. In the present unsettled condition of affairs the agitator who plays upon human discontent for the fulfillment of sinister ends, finds fruitful opportunity. The strain of the situation has told upon the impractical idealists who are the natural, though involuntary, partners of the designing demagogue in the creation of human hells paved with good intentions. The result is a situation perilous in the extreme to humanity. Only the courage and persistence of devoted, thoughtful, sane, unselfish men stands between society and the chaos produced by the demagogues and the doctrinaires in Russia, where in the name of human welfare humanity has been crucified en masse.

To what extent is lawlesness on the pavement due to exhibitions in high places of the spirit of lawlessness, of rebellion against the restraints of orderly governmental procedure under the Constitution of this republic, or arbitrary exercise of power and of attacks upon the supreme legislative power of the land, not for its opinions and convictions alone, but for the very act of exercising legal, constitutional functions in the discharge of sworn duty?

To what extent is the disposition to overthrow law and order and government by fear and force due to attacks upon the fundamentals of American government by officials sworn to their protection and the applause and emulation of that example by partisans of such procedure? To what extent is all this due not only to preachments in the past that this is a government of, by and for the special interests, and that the time is at hand for the ushering in of the new freedom from the checks and balances of representative republicanism, of deliberative democracy, but to representations now that a Senate of the United States, jointly charged under the Constitution with the responsibility of perfecting international engagements of the United States, is guilty of usurpation in the mere act of deliberation upon a pact which involves for all time the very destiny of the United States?

With one branch of the treaty making power assaulting another for the mere exercise of its constitutional functions, and demanding for itself the sole and exclusive right of doing a thing the Constitution clearly charges both branches of government with performing, and accompanying these attacks with threats of political punishment; with such words being used in the belittling of that coordinate branch of government as "intellectual pygmies," "cowardly quitters," men without vision or altruism or any motives but the meanest for that attitude upon the most important public question that has arisen since the sixties; with all this going on, and with partisans of the administration echoing this lawless talk, what wonder that words are converted into deeds in Oklahoma, and a senator of the United States is mobbed by partisans of the administration?

There has not been in the whole history of the United States so violent and unreasonable a campaign of misrepresentation as that which has persistently been carried on for weeks by partisans of the administration against the majority membership of the Senate of the United States. And, strangely enough, this violent, objurgatory, proscriptive, intolerant assault upon men guilty of the mere crime of doing their sworn duty, has not been confined to leaders or followers of the political party in power. It has been taken up by many men professing political independence, and lack of partisan bias, but who have given to the country the most astounding exhibition of partisan bias, using that phrase in the narrowest sense, this country has ever seen. This hateful mob spirit, so destructive of all that deliberative democracy stands for, has been reflected in magazines professing freedom from personal or partisan partiality, but which in some instances are controlled by influences far more sinister than political party affiliation. It has reflected itself even in the columns of the religious press and pulpit, in the school room, and in other agencies which, for their own good and the country's good, should have been kept free from this lawless factionalism that has sought to break down the barriers imposed by the Constitution between any one man or set of men and this country's dearly bought rights, interests and ideals.

To what extent is the decay of patriotism due to the preaching of internationalism; the socialistic internationalism of the anti-patriot and the idealistic internationalism of the well meaning but misguided altruists who have been misled by dreams of an earthly millennium to be produced by man-made rearrangements of political forms? Whatever the motive of the internationalist, whether it be hatred of this country or a sickly sentimentalism which in saving the world would lose the world's best hope of freedom and of progress,—the free and independent republic of the United

118

States; whatever the motive, the effect of it all is the same; the breaking down of the devotion of the people of this country to their own nation and their own flag.

The level-headed, soundly patriotic, undeluded people of the United States of America, men who in attaining world "vision" have not lost their national eyesight, must rally to the defense of their institutions, of their country and its laws. They must preach persistently and fearlessly the doctrine of obedience to law and regard for the checks and balances of free government which alone stand between the individual and tyranny,—the tyranny of the autocrat or the tyranny of the mob; the one as dangerous as the other. Wherever the laws or institutions of this country are assailed, whether by the mob in the streets, whose weapons are the bludgeon, the rope and the torch, or the orator on the soap box or the pulpit or the platform or the stump, whose weapons are words which seek to sway the crowd to break down the authority of the representatives of the people in the discharge of their sworn, sacred duty to the people; there those must rally to the defense of their country who believe with Lincoln that they who war upon the Constitution or the laws trample into the dirt the memory of our forefathers whose blood and treasure were poured out that we might enjoy the priceless heritage of liberty guaranteed and protected by law.

Let us have an end of the doctrine that there is anything in this world of human devising that is "bigger" or dearer to the American people than the American government. The brain of the idealist may weave a fabric of gossamer that shines in the sunlight for a day, but the government of the republic of the United States is something more than a cob-web spun in the imagination of dreamers. Into the fabric of that government have been woven the labors and the prayers, the dreams and the tears, the blood and the treasure, of five generations of strivers after the light of freedom and order who lived and labored in liberty's behalf before America was born.

The drums of '76, of '12, of '61, of '98, of '17 are beating once again. They call to the colors of peaceful but militant endeavor every citizen of America worthy of the name. It is their duty and opportunity to preserve against external and internal aggression all that Washington fought for and Lincoln died for; this government of laws rather than of men; this republic of institutional liberty; this nation where every citizen is a sovereign but none can be a tyrant; this land where public opinion, deliberately formed and freely and constitutionally expressed is the only power to which free men yield allegiance; a government which can never be made the personal property of any leader, or element, or faction, or party, but belongs to all the people and to every branch of their government, exercising its powers in the calm light of reason and justice, without usurpation or intimidation.

AMERICANISM

In every community in this country let the forces of law and order under the free institutions of the republic of the United States, dedicate themselves to the national service not only of obedience to law on their own part, but of requiring, and compelling, if necessary, the observance of national, state and local law and respect for American institutions, in letter and in spirit, by all others, regardless of station, that
"Government of the people, by the people, for the people
"Shall not perish from the earth."
—October 11, 1919.

Monticello, October 24, 1823.
To the President (James Monroe):
Dear Sir,—The question presented by the letters you have sent me, is the most momentous which has ever been offered to my contemplation since that of Independence. That made us a nation, this sets our compass and points the course which we are to steer through the ocean of time opening on us. And never could we embark on it under circumstances more auspicious. Our first and fundamental maxim should be, never to entangle ourselves in the broils of Europe. Our second, never to suffer Europe to intermeddle with cis-Atlantic affairs. America, north and south, has a set of interests distinct from those of Europe, and peculiarly her own. She should therefore have a system of her own, separate and apart from that of Europe. While the last is laboring to become the domiclie of despotism, our endeavor should surely be, to make our hemisphere that of freedom.

* * *

Its object is to introduce and establish the American system, of keeping out of our land all foreign powers, of never permitting those of Europe to intermeddle with the affairs of our nations. It is to maintain our own principle, not to depart from it. * * *
I have been so long weaned from political subjects, and have so long ceased to take any interest in them, that I am sensible I am not qualified to offer opinions on them worthy of any attention. But the question now proposed involves consequences so lasting, and effects so decisive of our future destinies, as to rekindle all the interest I have heretofore felt on such occasions, and to induce me to the hazard of opinions, which will prove only my wish to contribute still my mite towards anything which may be useful to our country. And praying you to accept it at only what it is worth, I add the assurance of my constant and affectionate friendship and respect.

THOMAS JEFFERSON.

WITH MALICE TOWARD NONE AND CHARITY FOR ALL

It has been necessary in the discussion of the dangers of the league of nations covenant as brought home from Europe to call attention to the dangers of American entanglement in European affairs; to cite the enormous territorial acquisitions of other great powers as the result of the treaty of peace; to refer to the tendency of these nations to keep their own interests first in mind, and to warn the American people that the history and traditions of these European and Asiatic powers does not justify the belief that they are ready to participate in a new world order from which extreme nationalism is, according to the writers of the prospectuses, to be excluded.

This does not express hostility to these alien powers on the part of the special champions of American interests. It merely means that the America-first elements in this country do not propose to delude themselves or their countrymen as to the real purposes of these foreign powers. We have no right in this country to criticize the disposition of Great Britain, France, Japan and Italy to add to their own wealth, power and economic opportunity. In fact there are many people in this country who only wish that our representatives at Paris had shown the same loyalty to and interest in their own land as the representatives of European and Asiatic powers did in the welfare of the peoples for whom they spoke at the peace conference.

The true American nationalist, anxious above all else for the welfare of his country and his countrymen, desires the closest and most friendly relations with foreign nations through which the peace and prosperity of his own country may be ensured. No true American can but feel the highest admiration and the most lively good will toward nations, such as France, Great Britain and Italy, with whom we have recently been fighting shoulder to shoulder for the safety of civilization. Bad feeling or war between this country and these nations is unthinkable. But this does not prevent the level-headed American from recognizing the fact that the tendencies and traditions and impulses and prejudices and rivalries of these countries, rooted in centuries of experience, must be taken into account in any common sense adjustment of the world's affairs. Shutting one's eyes to the conditions which have kept Europe almost constantly at war for the last century and a third

121

while this nation has been nearly all the time free from war and the menace of war, does not change these conditions. Big talk, musical rhetoric, imaginative oratory, will not of themselves create a new heaven and a new earth, despite the superstitious faith some people have in their ability to make the world over by the free use of the contents of the dictionary.

The policy of the America first people of the United States is the policy of the founders of this republic, as expressed in the words of Washington,—good will toward all nations, entangling alliances with none. This is not an expression of hostility, but of the most intelligent friendship toward the rest of the world. Nothing breeds misunderstanding and war like international relationships based upon imperfect understanding. The Senate of the United States, in making clear the meaning of this country in entering a league of nations, is clearing away multiplied causes of war, and is thus performing the best possible service to this republic and to civilization, despite the stupid, unpatriotic outcry against the course of this coordinate treaty making branch of our government.
—October 11, 1919.

Without attempting extended argument in reply to these positions it may not be amiss to suggest that the doctrine upon which we stand is strong and sound because its enforcement is important to our peace and safety as a nation and is essential to the integrity of our free institutions and the tranquil maintenance of our distinctive form of government. It was intended to apply to every stage of our national life, and cannot become obsolete while our republic endures. If the balance of power is justly a cause for jealous anxiety among the governments of the Old World, and a subject for our absolute non-interference, none the less is an observance of the Monroe Doctrine of vital concern to our people and their government. * * * The Monroe Doctrine finds its recognition in those principles of international law which are based upon the theory that every nation shall have its rights protected and its just claims enforced.—Grover Cleveland, 1895.

This is a republic, and neither Mammon nor Anarchy shall be king. The American asks only for a fair field and an equal chance. He believes that every man is entitled for himself and his children to the full enjoyment of all he honestly earns. But he will seek and find the means for eradicating conditions which hopelessly handicap him from the start. In this contest he does not want the assistance of the red flag, and he regards with equal hostility those who march under that banner and those who furnish argument and excuse for its existence.—Chauncey M. Depew.

WHAT REALLY HAPPENED AT THE PARIS
PEACE CONFERENCE

Gradually the whole truth about what happened to us at Paris is coming out. We are beginning to understand why, when Lloyd George mentioned the league of nations in parliament, he was compelled to "beg" the lords, gentlemen and commoners there assembled "not to laugh."

On November 11th a thirty days armistice was signed, ending the World war. This armistice imposed conditions on the enemy which well began the work of rendering him impotent from a military and naval standpoint. Because there had been an abortive effort to secure a negotiated peace a few weeks before, causing general protest in the United States where the proposition was seriously entertained by the government, and because Germany announced that she was entering into an armistice with the expectation of a peace based on Mr. Wilson's Fourteen points, the allies believed it was necessary to make it impossible for President Wilson to be the determinative factor in the peace conference. In this they succeeded.

Measures to this end were proposed by Clemenceau and accepted by Lloyd George. Though Germany on November 12th asked President Wilson to begin arrangements for a peace parley, and on November 18th President Wilson announced he would attend the conference, the opening of the peace conference was set on December 5th, one day after President Wilson sailed for France, not immediately, as might have been expected in the ordinary method of procedure and in courtesy to President Wilson, but for the first week in January, a full month later. As President Wilson arrived in Paris, the first thirty-day armistice expired, and the opportunity came for the prolonging of the armistice, but with additional conditions rendering Germany still more impotent. The peace conference was not called the first week in January or until after another period of renewal of the terms of the armistice on January 13th. These new armistice terms, drawn by the supreme war council, laid Germany flat on her back. The German army was now being rapidly demobilized. The American army was on the way home. The British army was being withdrawn. The French army was held intact. It was now master of the situation. It could march to Berlin at any moment without serious opposition. The terms of armistice were such that a peace treaty was necessary only to write the will of Clemenceau into it. President Wilson began to play the game with every high card in the hands of his friendly antagonists.

But Clemenceau found Mr. Wilson willing to still further postpone the consideration of a peace treaty until a league of nations covenant was prepared. Clemenceau and Lloyd George found Mr. Wilson willing to surrender most of his Fourteen points not only as respected the treaty but in the formulation of a scheme of world government, from which Europe would reap the advantages and to which America would make the sacrifices. The so-called peace conference was kept busy until February 15th considering the details of the league of nations covenant; then President Wilson left for a visit to the United States.

Meanwhile terms of peace with Germany were being made by the allies through the armistice method. On March 7th a parley for the renewal of the armistice was broken off when Germany refused to give up ships demanded. Next day Germany decided to give up the ships on the promise of food.

So the parley continued. The terms of peace were left entirely to the allies. President Wilson was interested only in the league of nations covenant. France and Great Britain were far more anxious than President Wilson could be for the adoption of a league of nations which would be a means of maintaining the status quo in the world after the vanquished had been stripped of her territorial possessions and these had been added to the far-flung empire of England and France.

This is what happened at Paris. If President Wilson went to Europe with the idea of dominating the situation he must have come away with the knowledge that he had been outwitted at every point, and that his league of nations covenant was as far from being a realization of the altruistic world order outlined in his Fourteen points as old-fashioned European diplomacy, in compiete command of the situation, could make it.

If President Wilson, realizing the situation, had risen from the council table when the secret treaties were brought forth, and the knowledge came that the peace was one in which our allies were to secure all the material advantages and we were to be compelled to surrender the ideals we had so widely advertised as the cause of our entry into the war through the speeches and writings of President Wilson, and had sailed back to the United States with his report of a futile effort made in behalf of humanity and peace and a new world order, he would have loomed large in history an'd in American esteem. But President Wilson came home defeated, tricked, outwitted, with the claim of complete victory rather than the confession of defeat. Upon these claims the facts as they are understood by all who know the inner workings of the peace conference constitute an illuminating commentary.

—October 11, 1919.

HOW THE LEAGUE OF NATIONS COVENANT
WAS ADOPTED

The proceedings at Paris were covered by a horde of hand-picked newspaper correspondents. And the proceedings were successfully covered—up. If the world had been told the real story of the manipulation and intrigue which led up to the decisions at Paris, universal would have been the wonder and regret that President Wilson did not rise from the council table and come home until such time as Europe was ready for a permanent peace of justice rather than a patched up truce founded on the flimsy basis of the satisfaction of the sordid, selfish greed for domination of certain powers that were talking one way and acting another. It was once said that in diplomacy language is a means of concealing thought. With Creel at one end of the cables and Burleson at the other, journalism during the peace conference was merely a means of concealing or camouflaging the facts.

A participant in the plenary session of the peace conference at which the league of nations covenant was adopted has given to The National Republican a verbal account of the proceedings in connection with the "adoption" of this world constitution. For weeks three men had been working on the league of nations covenant. Clemenceau, Lloyd George and Wilson sat behind closed doors in exemplification of that soulful phrase: "Open covenants openly arrived at." Inquiries as to what was going on in the sanctum sanctorum were met by the whispered shibboleth: "League of Nations."

At last the doors were thrown open and a plenary session was announced. The representatives of the allied and associated powers assembled. The hall was more than half full of the members of the delegations from the Big Five powers, with their numerous secretaries and attaches. The delegations of the other many but minor powers gathered around the edges. The announcement was made by Clemenceau that a plan for a league of nations had been evolved. President Wilson spoke eloquently on the covenant, reading extracts from it, and printed copies were distributed among the delegations present, of course no time being given for reading of the document thus for the first time brought to the light, much less deliberation or discussion upon it. Lloyd George added a few words in support of the covenant. The announcement was made that inquiries would be permitted. When they were called for hands went up all over the house. The desire for more light was apparently pretty general. President Wilson then made a second speech. He declared that two courses were open: One the immediate adoption of the covenant, or extended debate which might indefinitely prolong the proceedings, which by word and manner he deprecated. Clemenceau then took the situation in hand. He called for a vote. Some hands went up, the whole miscellaneous audience, secretaries, attaches, experts and all, amid the great confusion prevailing in the hall, participating.

"C'est decidee," (It is decided), declared Clemenceau, and the subject was changed. Soon the assemblage was dissolved. The whole transaction occupied only a short time.

Here was a covenant involving the fate of the world, affecting the destiny of every nation, large or small, there represented. Yet the whole thing was jammed through without the slightest semblance of that deliberation and debate which in this country we have learned, in the school of republican institutions, to understand as an essential preliminary to public decisions. It was put over with as little regard for the real opinion of the world, even as represented in that body, as a delegate slate in a Tammany caucus in the darkest days of strong arm methods in municipal politics.

What wonder that President Wilson has chafed because of the disposition of a legislative body in the United States to actually debate this matter! Why should there be surprise that so many of President Wilson's followers have been indignant because there has been free discussion of this fundamental matter in the forum of the Senate and in the larger forum of public opinion?

Thank God there is one country in the world where the people do discuss and have some hand in deciding questions affecting the national destiny!

Judged by our experience in connection with the adoption of the league of nations covenant there is not another country in the world where the great body of the people have taken the slightest interest in the moral or economic or political issues involved in the most important proposal affecting the world's future that has ever been presented.

In Europe the masses of the people have been content to accept what was handed down to them by authority from on high.

But here, public decisions are handed, not down from thrones and palaces, but up from the hearts and minds of the millions.

This is genuine democracy. No nation in which there has not been general debate upon this matter among the people is a democracy, because it is lacking in the very fundamentals of real popular government.

The most encouraging sign of the times, the surest guarantee of the beneficence and the permanency of American institutions, is that this great question, over the protest of those who are possessed by European conceptions of government, has been discussed thoroughly and intelligently and courageously in the Senate of the United States and by the great body of the people; that in the streets and the stores, in the trains and in the offices, in the shops and the mills, on the farms and in the pulpits and the school houses, this great issue has been debated. The tide of public opinion, as this great debate has proceeded, has risen higher and higher against the sacrifice of American ideals and interests involved in the acceptance of the covenant without reservations and amendments.

The deliberative democracy of America still lives and rules. And it is the world's one hope of a better political and economic and social order, because this is the one government, as demonstrated by the great test just given, where there actually is

"Government of the people, by the people, for the people."
—October 18, 1919.

I shall stand by the Union, and by all who stand by it. I shall do justice to the whole country, according to the best of my ability, in all I say, and act for the good of the whole country in all I do. I mean to stand upon the Constitution. I need no other platform. I shall know but one country. The ends I aim at shall be my country's, my God's and truth's. I was born an American; I live an American; I shall die an American; and I intend to perform the duties incumbent upon me in that character to the end of my career. I mean to do this, with absolute disregard of personal consequences. What are personal consequences? What is the individual man, with all the good or evil that may betide him, in comparison with the good or evil which may befall a great country in a crisis like this, and in the midst of great transactions which concern that country's fate? Let the consequences be what they will, I am careless. No man can suffer too much, and no man can fall too soon, if he suffer, or if he fall, in defense of the liberties and Constitution of his country.—Daniel Webster.

On this auspicious occasion we may well renew the pledge of our devotion to the Constitution, which, launched by the founders of the republic and consecrated by their prayers and patriotic devotion, has for almost a century borne the hopes and the aspirations of a great people through prosperity and peace and through the shock of foreign conflicts and the perils of domestic strife and vicissitudes.—Grover Cleveland.

We want a man who standing on a mountain height sees all the achievement of our past history and carries in his heart the memory of all its glorious deeds and who looking forward prepares to meet the labor and dangers to come.—James A. Garfield.

AMERICANISM

Hail, Columbia! happy land!
Hail, ye heroes! heaven-born band!
    Who fought and bled in Freedom's cause,
    Who fought and bled in Freedom's cause,
And when the storm of war was gone,
Enjoyed the peace your valor won.
    Let independence be our boast,
    Ever mindful what it cost;
    Ever grateful for the prize,
    Let its altar reach the skies.

        Firm, united, let us be,
        Rallying round our liberty;
        As a band of brothers joined,
        Peace and safety we shall find.

Immortal patriots! rise once more:
Defend your rights, defend your shore:
    Let no rude foe, with impious hand,
    Let no rude foe, with impious hand,
Invade the shrine where sacred lies
Of toil and blood the well-earned prize.
    While offering peace sincere and just,
    In Heaven we place a manly trust
    That truth and justice will prevail,
    And every scheme of bondage fail.

Sound, sound, the trump of Fame!
Let Washington's great name
    Ring through the world with loud applause,
    Ring through the world with loud applause;
Let every clime to Freedom dear,
Listen with a joyful ear.
    With equal skill, and godlike power,
    He governed in the fearful hour
    Of horrid war; or guides, with ease,
    The happier times of honest peace.

        Firm, united, let us be,
        Rallying round our liberty;
        As a band of brothers joined,
        Peace and safety we shall find.
                —Joseph Hopkinson.

    The Constitution is a sacred instrument; and a sacred trust is given to us to see to it that its preservation in all its virtue and its vigor is passed on to the generations yet to come.—William McKinley.

SHALL WE BE A PATCH IN EUROPE'S CRAZY QUILT?

It is stated that in one New England town the result of an election held last week was determined by the vote of Italians who were dissatisfied with the decision of the peace conference on the Fiume question, and who took this opportunity to express their resentment by voting against the Democratic candidates.

This is only faintly suggestive of the results sure to follow, in domestic politics, our entanglement in the affairs of Europe. Every nation in Europe is represented in our population. Europe is a crazy quilt of national and racial antagonisms and rivalries from the effects of which we here in this country have hitherto been free. It is a remarkable fact that in this country we have taken all the warring elements of Europe and fused them into a fairly homogeneous whole; a more homogeneous whole than is to be found in any one European country, for the theory of separatism is there so strongly intrenched that there are dialects even for mere neighborhoods in many of these nations.

The relations of nations and the domestic politics of these European countries are based upon the racial, religious and economic group antagonisms we in this country have managed to eliminate as controlling phases of political action. Our great political parties in this country have united men of many faiths, occupations and racial origins. In the European nations these groups are arrayed in political organizations, against one another. It is a sort of tong or feud system, from which we in this country had been emancipated. The big movement to Europeanize the United States has brought with it the attempt to base our politics upon the group system; to divide it into a number of voting bodies, each representing a special interest and considering itself at war with all other elements. It is this Europeanization of our politics and industry, with the introduction of the caste and class spirit on the European model, and the passionate antagonisms which accompany their conflicts, that has most of all seemed to be leading us away from the old America we had learned to love as something different than the world had ever before experienced, a realization of the true spirit of democracy in which men connect themselves with party organizations or other political movements solely on the basis of the general good.

Europeanism is fundamentally race, class, group, caste con-

129

sciousness rising above national or people-consciousness. Americanism is fundamentally national or people-consciousness rising above race, class, group, caste loyalty. At one end of Europeanism is the autocracy of the aristocracy. At the other is the autocracy of the proletariat. From one of these extremes Europe is rushing to the other, and threatening to engulf the world in the attendant disaster. Americanism is at war with both these fundamental manifestations of Europeanism. That is to say, it always has been, but today America is menaced by the movement, strongly championed, to substitute the European for the American system.

What should have been attempted at the peace conference was the Americanization of Europe, rather than the Europeanization of America. For America has taught Europe that the caste and class and group interest system are inconsistent with true democracy and are "rotten survivals of by-gone circumstances." America has also taught Europe that it is unnecessary to have a nation for every racial group; that these groups can be fused, and will fuse if they are permitted to do so. But Europe has been Balkanized at the peace conference, not Americanized. It has been further divided, not federated. Any intelligent program for world peace, lifted above the level of sordid self-interest on the part of the European nations, or futile idealism on the part of our spokesman, would have resulted in the federation of European peoples, rather than the creation of a dozen new states similar to the little Balkan powers, each with the seed of war in it because of its economic and territorial insufficiency, and the bitterness of the racial, religious and dynastic hatred the creation of these new governments intensifies. The creation of a United States of Europe, with each of the twenty or thirty little states made independent by the treaty as one commonwealth in a great federated republic, would have done far more to preserve the peace of the world than any league of nations, based upon the perpetuation of the old order.

But the basing of politics upon the demands of racial, religious and class groups is an evil certain to bring to America new perplexities, embarrassments and dangers. Entangled in the affairs of Europe, we encourage every European power, with interests at stake in the new world government, to cultivate, primarily through its own nationals in the United States, influence in American politics. With the United States concerned in every decision affecting these age-old hatreds, jealousies, rivalries and ambitions of Europe, we will have as many groups contending for dominance in our national affairs as we have nationalities represented in the United States. The new hyphenism will be vastly more perilous than any we have hitherto known. This election result in New England is a suggestion of what will happen. The Irish question, the Fiume question, and a hundred other international questions arising under the operations of the new world government, will divide our people in campaign periods to the exclusion of domestic matters which so much need the attention of the people, entirely free from influences arising out of the European mess the millions who have come here from the Old World thought they had turned their backs on forever.

How unfortunate that after more than a century of successful experience as an independent nation, with a wide ocean rolling between each of our coasts and the older worlds with all their heritage of hatred and bloodshed, poverty and oppression, we have developed in this country so powerful a faction that would Europeanize the United States, and turn back the prow of the Mayflower and of all the pilgrim ships that have succeeded it, to the conditions many generations of emigrants left the older lands to escape.

How much to be deplored it is that Old World books and Old World associations and Old World propaganda have blinded the eyes of so many Americans to the very meaning of America.

Here we have fused all the Old World elements into a united people, at peace with themselves and with the world until we were drawn into the vortex of a war growing out of the European system into which we are now asked to permanently involve our country.

God knows we have problems enough of our own, many of which are unsolved, and that there never was a time in our history when it was so important that we Americans should devote ourselves whole-heartedly and single-mindedly to the working out of the destiny to which America was dedicated by the fathers.

The task of pacifying Europe is absolutely hopeless so long as Europe clings to the system of separateness and aloofness instead of turning to the solution of federated republicanism, presented by this nation as a guide to the goal of peace and unity among peoples. And the problem of keeping the peace within our own country is going to be a serious, and maybe an impossible one, if we continue to Europeanize our politics under the leadership of men who seem blind to what this republic was founded for and what it stands for; if we divide, in this country, as they have in Europe, along racial, religious, class and caste lines, and make of our politics only a sort of civil war with elements and combinations of elements, warring on one another as, under the influence of the new order, they are now beginning to do.

The Republican party should make the fight for single track, single allegiance, single thought, single heart Americanism.

We are being led down the pathway of internationalism to the bottomless pits of European conflict, intrigue and travail.

It is for the Republican party, which was born to save the nation, and which brought it to the highest pinnacle of prosperity and power and true democracy ever attained by a people in all the history of mankind, to rescue this republic from the danger to

which it is now exposed by those whose alien sympathies and ideals would make of this country only one more patch in the political and social crazy quilt of Europe.
—October 25, 1919.

When Freedom from her mountain'height,
Unfurled her standard to the air,
She tore the azure robe of night,
And set the stars of glory there.
She mingled with its gorgeous dyes
The milky baldric of the skies,
And striped its pure, celestial·white,
With streakings of the morning light;
Then from his mansion in the sun
She called her eagle-bearer down,
And gave into his mighty hand
The symbol of her chosen land.

Majestic monarch of the cloud,
Who rear'st aloft thy regal form,
To hear the tempest-trumpings loud,
And see the lightning lances driven,
When strive the warriors of the storm,
And rolls.the thunder drum of heaven,
Child of the sun! to thee 'tis given
To guard the banner of the free,
To hover in the sulphur smoke,
To ward away the battle stroke,
And bid its blendings shine afar,
Like rainbows on the cloud of war,
The harbingers of victory!

Flag of the free heart's hope and home!
    By angel hands to valor given;
Thy stars have lit the welkin dome,
    And all thy hues were born in heaven.
And fixed as yonder orb divine,
    That saw thy bannered blaze unfurled,
Shall thy proud stars resplendent shine,
    The guard and glory of the world.
Forever float that standard sheet!
    Where breathes the foe but falls before us,
With Freedom's soil beneath our feet,
    And Freedom's banner streaming o'er us?
                              —Joseph Rodman Drake.

AN AMERICANIZED COVENANT

The Senate of the United States will perform its full duty in the matter of Americanizing the league of nations covenant. In the face of malicious misrepresentation and violent assault the Senate majority has proceeded calmly with a great debate on the treaty, which is now followed by votes on effective reservations ensuring to the American people full protection of the rights, interests and ideals of their republic.

The battle for the Americanization of the league of nations compact has been fought with great courage and ability, against all the pressure it has been possible for the national administration to bring to bear through its agents in the Senate, its party organization throughout the country and all the vast agencies for the control of public opinion at its command.

The National Republican began the battle for the Americanization of the covenant as soon as the provisions of the compact were made known. There was a time when there was some justification for the belief that this struggle was against the preponderance of public opinion. But this paper has an abiding faith in the ultimate judgment of the American people, and has never for a moment lost faith that the ultimate demand of public sentiment would be for drastic changes in the treaty.

The debate in the Senate has been one of the greatest, if not the greatest, in the entire history of Congress. This discussion, followed throughout the country by press and public, has served to bring public sentiment to the support of those who have from the beginning demanded that the Senate of the United States should perform its constitutional duty by so revising the league of nations covenant as to make it compatible with American traditions and American institutions.

The attempt of President Wilson to ignore and even defy the Senate in the exercise of its lawful prerogatives, has miserably failed. The attempt to force the covenant through the Senate as a rider to the peace treaty on the theory that the coordinate treaty making branch of government must either accept or reject the covenant in toto has broken down. The Senate has not been bluffed or bullied. It has done far more than merely to make changes in the treaty essential to the protection of American rights, interests and ideals. It has asserted anew the independence and self respect and lawful authority of the legislative representatives of the people of the United States, which rubber-stamp

representatives and weak-kneed adversaries of the administration were ready to sacrifice. It is not probable that any other President, in the light of this precedent, will proceed upon the theory that the whole treaty making power of the American government is vested in the one individual who for the time being happens to occupy the presidency, or that it will be possible for any executive to bargain away his country's welfare without being called to account by the people of the United States and their representatives in the legislative branch of government.
—November 15, 1919.

No other people have a government more worthy of their respect and love, or a land so magnificent in extent, so pleasant to look upon, and so full of generous suggestion to enterprise and labor. God has placed upon our head a diadem, and has laid at our feet power and wealth beyond definition or calculation. But we must not forget that we take these gifts upon the condition that justice and mercy shall hold the reins of power, and that the upward avenues of hope shall be free for all the people.

I do not mistrust the future. Dangers have been in frequent ambush along our path, but we have uncovered and vanquished them all. Passion has swept some of our communities, but only to give us a new demonstration that the great body of our people are stable, patriotic and law-abiding. No political party can long pursue advantage at the expense of public honor, or by rude and indecent methods, without protest and fatal disaffection in its own body. The peaceful agencies of commerce are more fully revealing the necessary unity of all our communities, and the increasing intercourse of our people is promoting mutual respect. We shall find unalloyed pleasure in the revelation which our census will make of the swift development of the great contributions of the states. Each state will bring its generous contributions to the great aggregate of the nation's increase. And when the harvests from the fields, the cattle from the hills and the ores from the earth, shall have been weighed, counted and valued, we will turn from all to crown with the highest honor the state that has most promoted education, virtue, justice and patriotism among its people.—Benjamin Harrison.

To all our means of culture is added that powerful incentive to personal ambition which springs from the genius of our government. The pathway to honorable distinction lies open to all. No post of honor so high but the poorest boy may hope to reach it. It is the pride of every American, that many cherished names, at whose mention our hearts beat with a quicker bound, were worn by the sons of poverty, who conquered obscurity and became fixed stars in our firmament.—James A. Garfield.

PRESIDENT WILSON TAKES FULL RESPONSIBILITY

The responsibility for the defeat of the peace treaty, as for the many months of delay in securing action upon it, rests squarely upon President Wilson.

The President's letter to Senator Hitchcock, ordering the administration senators to vote against the treaty with the Lodge reservations effecting its Americanization, was the death warrant of the document. It served notice on the Senate, the country and the world, that President Wilson did not propose to accept any treaty or covenant in the formulation of which the Senate had played its constitutional part, or in which reservations had been inserted protective of American rights, interests and ideals.

From the beginning President Wilson has displayed this irreconcilable and intolerant attitude. He boasted that he would not permit the Senate to pass upon a treaty of peace without at the same time either accepting or rejecting in toto the plan for a world constitution perfected at Paris. He ordered the administration senators to resist all amendments or reservations. He refused to permit any program of compromise or conciliation. He would have the treaty and covenant without the dotting of an "i" or the crossing of a "t" or he would not have it at all.

The criticism of the covenant was that it sacrificed American rights and interests and involved this country in responsibilities and dangers out of proportion to the promised benefits. The answer to this criticism was that the dangers alleged to lurk in the covenant were imaginary. The reservations proposed by Senator Lodge and his associates gave to the treaty in letter the interpretation its proponents claimed was the real meaning of the document. And when these reservations had been included the document was no longer acceptable to President Wilson..

In view of the fact that President Wilson and his senators will not accept an Americanized covenant, the people of this country will be glad, as an alternative, to accept no entanglement with Europe at all. Congress should pass a resolution declaring the war at an end, and make an end of the business. The purpose of President Wilson has been to make of the matter a personal and political issue contributory to the fortunes of himself and his party organization. He has evidently decided to accept the responsibility of killing the treaty and covenant in order that a cam-

paign issue may be made of this international problem. That being his choice the Republican party stands ready to meet him upon the issue of America First.
-—November 22, 1919.

If anything be found in the national Constitution, either by original provision or subsequent interpretation, which ought not to be in it, the people know how to get rid of it. If any construction unacceptable to them be established, so as to become practically a part of the Constitution, they will amend it at their own sovereign pleasure. Gentlemen do not seem to recollect that the people have any power to do anything for themselves. The people have not trusted their safety in regard to the general Constitution to other hands. They have required other security, and taken other bonds. They have chosen to trust themselves, first, to the plain words of the instrument, and to such construction as the government themselves, in doubtful cases, should put on their own powers, under their oaths of office, and subject to their responsibility to them; just as the people of a state trust their own state governments with a similar power. Secondly, they have reposed their trust in the efficacy of frequent elections, and in their own power to remove their own servants and agents whenever they see cause. Thirdly, they have reposed trust in the judicial power, which, in order that it might be trustworthy, they have made as respectable, as disinterested and as independent as was practicable. Fourthly, they have seen fit to rely, in case of necessity or high expediency, on their known and admitted power to alter or amend the Constitution, peaceably and quietly, whenever experience shall point out defects or imperfections. * * *

If the people in these respects had done otherwise than they have done, their Constitution could neither have been preserved, nor would it have been worth preserving. And if its plain provisions shall now be disregarded, and these new doctrines interpolated in it, it will become as feeble and helpless a being as its enemies, whether early or more recent, could possibly desire.

But although there are fears, there are hopes also. The people have preserved this, their own chosen Constitution, for forty years, and have seen their happiness, prosperity and renown grow with its growth, and strengthen with its strength. They are now, generally, strongly attached to it. Overthrown by direct assault it cannot be; evaded, undermined, nullified, it will not be, if we and those who shall succeed us here as agents and representatives of the people shall conscientiously and vigilantly discharge the two great branches of our public trust, faithful to preserve and wisely to administer it.—Daniel Webster.

THE PEOPLE'S THANKS ARE DUE THE
AMERICAN SENATE

The expedition with which the Senate, debate concluded, passed the Lodge reservations Americanizing the covenant of the league of nations, seems to have stunned those who have been, up to this time, deceived by the campaign of misrepresentation carried on in behalf of the administration. The people of this country, and the world in general, have been assured that opposition to the President's program in the Senate was merely a game of party politics; that in the end, after much loud talk, the Senate would swallow the covenant whole, just as it was brought home from Paris. There has, of course, never been any justification for such statements. This paper has been able to inform its readers for many weeks that just what has happened in the Senate would happen; that the Senate would either Americanize the treaty, or reject it.

Now those who have been accusing the Senate of a mere desire to "play politics" with the situation, and after "grand-standing" for a season give in to the administration, are loudly crying that the Senate has "cut the heart from the covenant." It has been claimed by the senators opposing the adoption of the covenant without change that it contained certain provisions and implications which menaced American rights, interests and ideals. The President and his friends have replied that these dangers did not lurk in the treaty, but that they had been read into it by the President's critics. But now the Senate has proceeded to incorporate into the treaty reservations making impossible such an interpretation of the treaty as its friends say would be unjustified, the administration's press agents insist that the covenant has been ruined, and that it would be rejected by the other signatory powers. Thus they confess publicly that they have been trying to deceive the American people as to the true inwardness of the treaty.

Imperialist newspapers in Paris and London still cling to the stupid theory that opposition to President Wilson's program as it was brought home from Paris is based merely upon partisan and personal prejudice. The trouble with these publications is that they have been content to feed themselves on administration propaganda without letting any real knowledge of the situation interfere with their preconceived notions. The truth is that this

137

is the only country in the world in which the covenant of the league of nations as concocted at Paris, has been considered, debated and passed on upon its merits. In France, England and other European countries, it has simply been accepted on authority.

It was reasonable to assume that the statesmen of Europe knew something of the Constitution of the United States when they proceeded upon the theory that Mr. Wilson had the right to constitute himself the sole and final arbiter of American purposes in the peace conference at Paris. If these statesmen knew that the Senate of the United States had anything to do with the making of international contracts, they chose to ignore the provisions of the American Constitution, even after more than one-third of the members of the Senate, a sufficient number to defeat any treaty, had served written notice on them that the constitution of the league of nations in "its present form" should not be accepted by the United States and urging that a peace treaty with Germany be at once concluded and the subject of a league of nations be left for more deliberate determination. In this course the representatives of European government gave deliberate affront to a majority of the members of a coordinate treaty making branch of the United States government, and also to the majority sentiment of the American people.

The American people and the American government have not broken faith with Europe. They never gave President Wilson carte blanche to commit them to any proposition his personal judgment might favor in the matter of a world constitution. It has not been the practice in the United States to permit constitutions to be framed by the mere ukase of an executive. A matter of this kind may be settled in Japan by a decree of the Mikado, but there are a few other preliminaries in the United States of America, despite the activities of our home-grown monarchists against the traditions and institutions and laws of this republic.

The Senate of the United States has performed a service of immeasurable value to the people of the United States in its courageous and effective fight in behalf of its own constitutional prerogatives, and in behalf of the rights, interests and ideals of the American people. It may reasonably be assumed that never again in the history of the republic will a chief executive attempt to establish the novel and unconstitutional doctrine that it is within the power of the one man who at the time being happens to be the chief executive of the nation, to sign, seal and deliver a contract involving the sovereignty and the independence, the rights and the interests of the whole American people. Such an effort must hereafter, as it has on this occasion, result in the defeat and humiliation of the President who would so far forget his limitations as to undertake this autocratic abuse of power.

The Senate has Americanized the covenant of the league of nations. It may be within the power of the President to stand in the way of the signing of a treaty of peace on the ground that he will join in no treaty in the formulation of which the Senate of the United States has participated. He cannot, however, prevent the declaration of a state of peace by the Congress of the United States. Peace would have come to the world early in the present year if it had not been for the stubborn insistence of President Wilson upon the incorporation in the peace treaty of the covenant of the league of nations in order that the Senate might be coerced into its acceptance. The administration responsible for so much delay in the conclusion of the war cannot well afford to assume still further responsibility by further delaying the ratification of the treaty.

—November 22, 1919.

The one effective move for obtaining peace is by an agreement among the great powers, in which each should pledge itself not only to abide by the decisions of a common tribunal, but to back its decisions with force. The great civilized nations should combine by solemn agreement in a great world league for the peace of righteousness. A court should be created—a changed and amplified Hague court would meet the requirements—composed of representatives from each nation, these representatives being sworn to act as judges in each case, and not in a representative capacity. * * * The nations should agree on certain rights that should not be questioned, such as territorial integrity, their right to deal with their own domestic affairs and with such matters as whom or whom not they should admit to citizenship. All should guarantee each of their number in possession of these rights. All should agree that other matters at issue between any of them, or between any of them and any one of a number of specified outside civilized nations, should be submitted to the court as above constituted. * * * Each nation should absolutely reserve to itself its right to establish its own tariff and general economic policy, and to control such vital questions as immigration and citizenship. * * * Let us explicitly reserve certain rights—to our territorial possessions, to our control of immigration and citizenship, to our fiscal policy and to our handling of our domestic problems generally—as not to be questioned and not to be brought before any international tribunal.

As regards impotent or disorderly nations or peoples outside the league, let us be very cautious about guaranteeing to interfere with or on behalf of them, where they lie wholly outside our sphere of interest; and let us announce that our own sphere of special concern in America (perhaps limited north or somewhere near the equator) is not to be infringed on by European or Asiatic powers.

Moreover, let us absolutely decline any disarmament proposition that would leave us helpless to defend ourselves. Let us absolutely refuse to abolish nationalism; on the contrary, let us base a wise and practical internationalism on a sound and intense nationalism. * * * When all this has been done, let us with deep seriousness ponder every promise we make, so as to be sure that our people will fulfill it. * * * Let us go into such a league. But let us weigh well what we promise, and then train ourselves in body and soul to keep our promises. Let us treat the formation of the league as an addition to but in no sense as a substitute for preparing our own strength for our own defense. And let us build a genuine internationalism—that is, a genuine and generous regard for the rights of others—on the only healthy basis—a sound and intense development of the broadest spirit of American nationalism.—Theodore Roosevelt.

"O Beautiful, my country!"
　　Be thine a nobler care,
Than all thy wealth of commerce,
　　Thy harvest waving fair;
Be it thy pride to lift up
　　The manhood of the poor;
Be thou to the oppressed '
　　Fair freedom's open door.

For thee our fathers suffered,
　　For thee they toiled and prayed;
Upon thy holy altar
　　Their willing lives they laid.
Thou hast no common birthright;
　　Grand memories on thee shine,
The blood of pilgrim nations,
　　Commingled, flows in thine.

O beautiful, our country!
　　Round thee in love we draw;
Thine is the grace of freedom,
　　The majesty of law.
Be righteousness thy scepter,
　　Justice thy diadem;
And on thy shining forehead
　　Be peace the crowning gem.
　　　　　　　　　　—Frederick L. Hosmer.

All free governments, whatever their name, are in reality governments by public opinion; and it is on the quality of this opinion that their prosperity depends.—James Russell Lowell.

AMERICA FIRST! NOW AND FOREVER!

Frequently we hear talk of what "we" the American people, owe this, that or the other country, and the world in general.

The American people are not the debtors of the world or of any nation in it; the world owes us.

The world owes America because this country for a century and a third has given to the world a working model of popular government, which, if it had been adopted by other nations, would have spared them the necessity of fighting the great war we have just concluded, and many another war beside.

The world owes America because we have welcomed to this country millions of the poverty stricken people of other lands, and given them here a home and country they could call their own; and America has divided, with generous hand, its wealth with their poverty; it has fused all these alien, discordant elements into a homogeneous whole, furnishing to Europe evidence that the racial and national differences which have kept that continent at war or preparing for war for a century, can be composed and peace be brought to the world, through the mere emulation of our national example.

The world owes America because this is the one powerful nation in the world that has not used its strength to rob or oppress its neighbors or distant peoples, and that has not been looking with jealous and designing eyes upon the property and territory of other nations.

The world owes America because it went into the great World war at a time when the strength of this country was necessary to prevent a great combination of military powers from setting up a world empire on the ruins of other nations, and because America poured out her blood and treasure without limit until the tide of conquest had been stopped and turned back.

The world owes America because for all this, at a time when other nations were dividing up the rich spoils of victory, this country asked nothing, in territory or indemnity; asked nothing but a peace of justice and of right.

Isn't it about time to cease talking about what America owes the rest of the world and begin to think a little bit about what America owes herself?

We think so. We think that is the thought of most of the American people. We believe they believe that the problems which confront us are big enough to tax our strength in their solu-

tion. We think they think that it is time to quit chasing trans-
oceanic rainbows and begin to pay close attention to the chores
that need to be done right here on the old place.

Lloyd George has not been afraid to say recently that England's
first thought now must be of England, whose very self preservation is at stake in these anxious days. Clemenceau does not hesitate to say his first thought is of France. We know what is first
in the thought of Italy and Japan. We, too, must think of our
own country first; not in the sense of antagonism to other countries,—with friendship for all,—but with first interest in our own.

While the thought of some of our leaders has been centered on
European affairs and world destiny, things here in our own land
have been drifting,—and drifting toward what? Not an hour
should be lost in fixing the thought of our nation and our government exclusively upon the immediate needs of America. We are
solicitous for the welfare of the world; yes. But what shall it
profit us if we try to help the whole world and lose our own national
existence through failure to meet and solve the great special problems which involve the very existence of our civilization?

The debt Americans owe the rest of the world is an imaginary
debt. If we owed such a debt we would gain the curses and not
the blessings of the world by thrusting ourselves into the political
control of their affairs, and involving them in the ordering of our
national business.

The debt Americans owe America is a real obligation. The discharge of that debt to the great republic, born of the dreams and
maintained by the sacrifices of our fathers, is the first duty of
Americans.

America First. America Always First. America not above, but
before, all. Now and Forevermore. Amen.
—November 29, 1919.

Venerable Men! you have come down to us from a former generation. Heaven has bounteously lengthened out your lives, that
you might behold this joyous day. You are now where you stood
fifty years ago, this very hour, with your brothers and your neighbors, shoulder to shoulder, in the strife for your country. Behold,
how altered! The same heavens are indeed over your heads; the
same ocean rolls at your feet; but all else, how changed! You
hear now no roar of hostile cannon, you see no mixed volumes of
smoke and flame rising from burning Charlestown. The ground
strewed with the dead and dying; the impetuous charge; the
steady and successful repulse; the loud call to repeated assault;
the summoning of all that is manly to repeated resistance; a thousand bosoms freely and fearlessly bared in an instant to whatever
of terror there may be in war and death,—all these you have witnessed, but you witness them no more. All is peace; and God has

granted you the sight of your country's happiness, ere you slumber in the grave. He has allowed you to behold and to partake the reward of your patriotic toils; and he has allowed us, your sons and countrymen, to meet you here, and in the name of the present generation, in the name of your country, in the name of liberty, to thank you!

But alas! you are not all here! Time and the sword have thinned your ranks. Prescott, Putnam, Stark, Brooks, Read, Pomeroy, Bridge! our eyes seek for you in vain amid this broken band. You are gathered to your fathers, and live only to your country in her grateful remembrance and your own bright example.

But the scene amidst which we stand does not permit us to confine our thoughts or our sympathies to those fearless spirits who hazarded or lost their lives on this consecrated spot. We have the happiness to rejoice here in the presence of a most worthy representation of the survivors of the whole Revolutionary army.

Veterans! you are the remnant of many a well-fought field. You bring with you marks of honor from Trenton and Monmouth; from Yorktown, Camden, Bennington and Saratoga. Veterans of half a century! when in your youthful days you put everything at hazard in your country's cause, good as that cause was, and sanguine as youth is, still your fondest hopes did not stretch onward to an hour like this! At a period to which you could not reasonably have expected to arrive, at a moment of national prosperity such as you could never have foreseen, you are now met here to enjoy the fellowship of old soldiers, and to receive the overflowings of a universal gratitude.

May the Father of all mercies smile upon your declining years, and bless them! And when you shall here have exchanged your embraces, when you shall once more have pressed the hands which have been so often extended to give succour in adversity, or grasped in the exultation of victory, then look abroad upon this lovely land which your young valor defended, and mark the happiness with which it is filled; yea, look abroad upon the whole earth, and see what a name you have contributed to give to your country, and what a praise you have added to freedom, and then rejoice in the sympathy and gratitude which beam upon your last days from the improved condition of mankind!—Daniel Webster to the veterans of the Revolution on the 50th anniversary of the Battle of Bunker Hill.

Let us then, with courage and confidence pursue our own federal and republican principles, our attachment to union and representative government. Kindly separated by nature and a wide ocean from the exterminating havoc of one-quarter of the globe; too high-minded to endure the degradations of the others; possessing a chosen country, with room enough for our descendants to the hundredth and thousandth generation; entertaining a due sense of our equal right to the use of our own faculties, to the acquisitions of our own industry, to honor and confidence from our fellow citizens, resulting not from birth, but from our actions and their sense of them; enlightened by a benign religion, professed, indeed, and practiced in various forms, yet all of them inculcating honesty, truth, temperance, gratitude, and the love of man; acknowledging and adoring an overruling Providence, which by all its dispensations proves that it delights in the happiness of man here and his greater happiness hereafter—with all these blessings, what more is necessary to make us a happy and a prosperous people?—Thomas Jefferson.

Though many and bright are the stars that appear
   In that flag, by our country unfurled—
And the stripes that are swelling in majesty there
   Like a rainbow adorning the world—
Their light is unsullied as those in the sky,
   By a deed that our fathers have done;
And they're leagued in as true and as holy a tie
   In their motto of "Many in One."

From the hour when those patriots fearlessly flung
   That banner of star-light abroad,
Ever true to themselves to that banner they clung,
   As they clung to the promise of God;
By the bayonet traced at the midnight of war,
   On the fields where our glory was won—
Oh! perish the heart or the hand that would mar
   Our motto of "Many in One."

We are many in one while there glitters a star
   In the blue of the heavens above;
And tyrants shall quail, 'mid their dungeons afar,
   When they gaze on that motto of love.
It shall gleam o'er the sea 'mid the bolts of the storm—
   Over tempest, and battle, and wreck;
And flame where our guns with their thunder grow warm,
   'Neath the blood on the slippery deck.

Then up with the flag! Let it stream in the air
   Though our fathers are cold in their graves;
They had hands that could strike, they had souls that could dare,
   To do and to die. Where it waves,
The emblem of justice and freedom for all,
   Our millions shall rally around;
And a nation of freemen that moment shall fall
   When its stars shall be trailed on the ground.
               —George Washington Cutter.

KEYNOTE OF CAMPAIGN WILL BE "AMERICANISM"

The keynote of the next Republican national platform will be found in the one word "Americanism."

"Americanism" in the true sense means, to Americans, America always first; America, not above all, but before all, in the minds and hearts of those who profess allegiance to America.

"Americanism" means first thought of the rights, interests and ideals of America. It does not mean enmity to other nations. It means recognition of the indisputable truth that as other nations and peoples look first after their own, so the American people should think first of the preservation of the heritage that has come down to them through the labors and sacrifices of the founders of this republic and the generations that have toiled and sacrificed that this nation might be the strongest and happiest of earth.

"Americanism" means that America shall not, without some better reason for doing than has yet been advanced, bankrupt herself in order that some insolvent nation may be saved from financial disaster. "Americanism" means that the assets of this country shall not be traded for the liabilities of other countries to such an extent that America shall be dragged down to that level of life for the ordinary man which has for centuries prevailed in other lands.

It is not necessary that America be wrecked to save other nations from economic disaster in order that the generosity of this nation shall be demonstrated. We have just emerged from a war in which the American people poured out their money by the billions and their soldiers by the millions to save civilization from disaster. The theory that such sacrifice only involves this nation in the obligation to take on the debt and disaster of all the rest of the world seems to be entertained only by a few theorists and doctrinaires, ambitious for world fame, with their deluded dupes, and with interests not so well stocked with ideals, but heavily loaded with foreign securities and the ambition to take on more to their own profit, even if all this be done by the sacrifice of the rights and interests of their own country and countrymen.

"Americanism" means, in short, a return to the well settled Clay so well called the "American system" of protection to American manufactures, American agriculture and American labor. It means first change in the American market for producers who live here, pay taxes here, build up this country through labor and investment, and upon whom rests the obligation to protect this country in time of war as well as support it in time of peace. It means the abandonment of a fiscal policy which robs the American treasury and throws heavier burdens on the American taxpayer in order that alien rather than domestic industrial interests may be fostered.

"Americanism" means the protection of the lives and the property of American citizens abroad as well as at home. It means that to be an American citizen will again be as much of a protection to those who yield allegiance to the American government, as it is to be a citizen of Great Britain or of any other great, self-respecting power. It will mean an end of the policy of treating American citizens, American rights and American interests with open contempt in any country on this or the other hemisphere.

"Americanism" means the turning of the thought of American statesmanship to the problems that affect the homes of the American people. It may not mean so much high-sounding talk about tranquilizing the world, but it will mean practical measures taken toward the restoration of domestic peace and order. We talk of settling the world's problems by subordinating the United States in a world parliament, when we seem to be unable to prevent the settlement of domestic industrial disputes by any method but that of civil war.

"Americanism" means the preservation of an obedience to the American Constitution and form of government. It means an end of usurpation of all functions of government by any one of the three coordinate branches of government. It means government by public opinion, and by the common counsel of the people's leadership. It means an end of opinionated autocracy. It means an end of thinking of public problems only in terms of votes. It means government of, by and for the people rather than by whatever interests may be able to bring upon the government, for the time being, the heaviest political pressure or brandish under the noses of the people the biggest club and assail their ears with the most menacing threats.

"Americanism" means, in short, a return to the well settled precedents and policies which made this nation the richest and the greatest and the happiest on earth long before the "new freedom" was thought of. It means turning our backs upon European imperialism and European socialism. It means the re-establishment of the right of the American people to conduct their national affairs in their own way, with malice toward none and with friendship for all the governments of earth.

Here at home it means resistance to the movement to transfer from Europe to America the idea of class division, class consciousness, class government and class war, or to introduce here as a factor in our politics the complex racial and national hatreds and rivalries of Europe. It means the perpetuation of the republic under which the government is the creature of the people, as opposed to the effort to establish in its stead the socialist state under which the people are to be dependents and creatures of the government.

. "Americanism" means the return to the more economical and common sense methods of conducting the national government. It means an end of the system, introduced by the present national administration, whereby there are coming to be more office holders supported by the people, than private citizens to support the job holders.

"Americanism" means the establishment of those policies under which honest private enterprise is encouraged, rather than struck down; by which industry and ability, usefully employed, are regarded, rather than penalized; whereby initiative and invention and exploration which add to the general wealth are honored rather than attacked. It means, too, that the government shall halt enterprise at the border line of selfish exploitation, and shall treat as criminal all conspiracies directed toward the oppression of the general public, by whomsoever hatched.

"Americanism" means an end of government by fear, of the misuse of government for the control of public opinion either by threat or persuasion. It means that coercion of government or of the general public by the threat of any individual or combination of individuals to do the public injury shall cease.

Involved in the next campaign will be the fundamental matter of the very character of our government and the attitude of national administration toward it. The very atmosphere of Washington needs to be changed. The windows of public place must be thrown open and the fresh air of the old Americanism let in. To bring this about is the mission of national Republicanism in the next campaign. The people eagerly await the opportunity to put the seal of their approval upon this enterprise.
—December 20, 1919.

Friends, our task as Americans is to strive for social and industrial justice, achieved through the genuine rule of the people. This is our end, our purpose. The methods for achieving the end are merely expedients, to be finally accepted or rejected according as actual experience shows that they work well or ill. But in our hearts we must have this lofty purpose, and we must strive for it in all earnestness and sincerity, or our work will come to nothing. * * *

The leader for the time being, whoever he may be, is but an instrument, to be used until broken and then to be cast aside; and if he is worth his salt, he will care no more when he is broken than a soldier cares when he is sent where his life is forfeit in order that the victory may be won. In the long fight for righteousness the watchword for all of us is, "Spend and be spent." It is of little matter whether any one man fails or succeeds; but the cause shall not fail, for it is the cause of mankind.

We, here in America, hold in our hands the hope of the world, the fate of the coming years, and shame and disgrace will be ours if in our eyes the light of high resolve is dimmed, if we trail in the dust the golden hopes of men. If on this new continent we merely build another country of great but unjustly divided material prosperity, we shall have done nothing; and we shall do little if we merely set the greed of envy against the greed of arrogance, and thereby destroy the material well-being of all of us. To turn this government either into a government by a plutocracy or government by a mob, would be to repeat on a larger scale the lamentable failures of the world that is dead.

We stand against all tyranny, by the few or by the many. We stand for the rule of the many in the interest of all of us, for the rule of the many in a spirit of courage, of common sense, of high purpose; above all, in a spirit of kindly justice toward every man and every woman. We not merely admit, but insist, that there must be self-control on the part of the people, that they must keenly perceive their own duties as well as the rights of others; but we also insist that the people can do nothing unless they not merely have, but exercise to the full, their own rights.

The worth of our great experiment depends upon its being in good faith an experiment—the first that has ever been tried—a true democracy on the scale of a continent; on a scale as vast as that of the mightiest empires of the Old World. Surely this is a noble ideal, an ideal for which it is worth while to strive, an ideal for which at need it is worth while to sacrifice much; for our ideal is the rule of all the people in a spirit of friendliest brotherhood toward each and every one of the people.—Theodore Roosevelt.

There is no point in which an American, long absent from his country, wanders so widely from its sentiments as on the subject of its foreign affairs. We have a perfect horror at everything like connecting ourselves with the politics of Europe. It would indeed be advantageous to us to have neutral rights established on a broad ground; but no dependence can be placed in any European coalition for that.—Thomas Jefferson.

Freedom of the press; freedom of person under the protection of the habeas corpus; and trial by juries impartially selected—these principles form the bright constellation which has gone before us, and guided our steps through an age of revolution and reformation.—From the first inaugural address of Thomas Jefferson, March 4, 1801.

"AMERICANISM" IS THE REPUBLICAN KEYNOTE

The keynote of the Republican national campaign of 1920 is the single word "Americanism."

Americanism means, not a race, nor a language, nor a mere area on the map, but a working program of government which has withstood the test of a century's practical experience, and has more to the welfare of mankind than any other plan for the regulation of human relations the world has yet devised.

Americanism means the maintenance and further development of representative republican government as conceived by the founders of this nation and embodied in a written constitution, the most beneficent charter of ordered liberty ever evolevd by the hand and brain of man.

The basic principle of that constitution is that governments exist for the service of men, not men for service of governments. The motto of the nation that constitution established and which it has safeguarded since 1787 is "E Pluribus Unum,"—out of many one,—out of many states, one nation, out of many races and tongues and religions, one people, out of all classes and conditions of men, one body politic, existing for the service of all and the oppression of none.

Europeanism means separatism. It means a continent divided into a half hundred jealous, hostile, contending nationalities. Americanism means the union, not the division, of peoples. Americanism means the unity of all the heterogeneous elements of Europe into the homogeneity of a single national allegiance.

* * * * *

The Republican party, under Lincoln, saved the Union. In so doing it saved this continent from Europeanization. . Had secession triumphed, what is now the United States of America, the most powerful nation of earth, would have been two, three, five or more petty nations, glaring at one another across armed border lines, arrayed against one another by European intrigue,. involved in European entanglements through the necessity of foreign alliances to maintain national integrity.

Because each of the sectional nations thus created would have lacked economic independence, there would have been continual conflict among these new-world powers, or an armed neutrality such as Europe preserved before the World war. Only because the calamity of disunion was averted by the Republican party in the years of its youth, we have preserved a united and peaceful

AMERICANISM

America while Europe, during all the years since Lincoln's day, has been constantly either in conflict or within the shadow of war.

The European war began, naturally, in the Balkans, where the doctrine of "self determination of peoples" has flowered in a half dozen little nationalities which became pawns in the great game the principal powers of Europe were playing. The two Balkan wars were curtain raisers for the big fight. They were prophetic to thoughtful men of what was to come. The World war has closed with the creation of a dozen more new small nations on the Balkan model,—a dozen more causes of war. Instead of giving to Europe ˙ that one hope of peace that would have come with larger federation, we have de-federalized Europe. Under the leadership of men who are European in their conceptions of politics, the effort has been made, not to Americanize Europe, but to Europeanize America. Yet Americanism has meant unity and peace; Europeanism has meant division and war, and will continue to mean disunion and war. The very statesmen who have talked of world-wide peace as the harvest of the World war, have sown the seed of future wars thick in the soil of Europe and of Asia.

* * * * *

Americanism means a classless, casteless republic. It stands opposed to the idea of border lines of hostility between people and people, class and class. Americanism stands for the self-determination of the individual, but for the unity of all the variant strains of European race and tongue in loyalty to one nation and one flag.

This ideal no true, comprehending American would risk by involving the destiny of his republic with that of nations whose very being is imbedded in a conception of nationality our very nationality forswears. This conception of the scope and purpose of government the true, understanding American would not yield up for American inclusion in a world government dominated by nations fully resolved to maintain the European system of nationality.

Americanism means the maintenance of the American Constitution against the foes from within who would destroy it either in mass or piecemeal, or the enemies from without who would carry it down in the world chaos to which Europe's system of warring nationalities, of contending caste and class, has led Europe and will lead us if we unreservedly cast in our lot with the proposed world government in which we are to play a subordinated part.

* * * * *

Americanism means the preservation of the American standard of life for the masses of the people through the maintenance of American industry and agriculture on the basis of superiority to the standards of other lands. That program has made this republic the Mecca of the European millions seeking a land of richer reward and broader opportunity for the toilers who are the social and economic mud-sills of older lands, and of lands to the south of the United States in this hemisphere, which have been fashioned after the European model.

Americanism means that those who must be depended upon in time of war to protect and in time of peace to support this government, are entitled to the protection and support of the government, as compared with the peoples of other lands. Americanism means that the resources, the markets, the industrial opportunities of the United States are first of all the possessions of the people of the United States, and that the welfare of the American employer and the American wage worker, who must pay the taxes and carry the rifles for America's support and protection should be the first, not the second or the last, thought of the makers and administrators of American l   s.

* *aw* * *

Americanism means, as Lincoln declared in his first political announcement, the protection and development of American industries and American resources.

It means the development of an American merchant marine, not as a government charity, but as a business enterprise carried on by American initiative and enterprise.

It means the holding of all the territory now beneath the American flag not merely because of what that may mean to this nation commercially and from a naval and military standpoint, but because of the blessings that flow from American government to all the peoples who yield allegiance to the American flag.

It means the establishment of the authority of the national government in industrial relations rather than the dictatorship, real or attempted, of any one class or element in industry. It means turning the thought and effort of the American people away from European problems of which they know little, to the solution of home problems which heretofore they have so successfully solved that this republic, through the mere power of successful example, has been the most powerful influence in world politics.

Americanism means the restoration in practice as well as theory, of the three independent and coordinate branches of government established in the American Constitution. It means an end of executive dictatorship, real or attempted, and the resumption of orderly, constitutional government through the Congress and the executive, with their powers limited by the Constitution under its interpretation by the Supreme Court.

It means a real return to "that simplicity and economy befitting a democratic government," as mentioned in the Democratic platform of 1912 and never thought of by Democratic leadership since.

Americanism means the abandonment of all the schemes of politicalized industry, of state socialism, of either the Prussianized or Russianized scheme of the exaggerated state, under which citizenship is only a form of slavery to government.

AMERICANISM

Americanism means a restoration, in public affairs, of the doctrines and ideals of Washington, Lincoln, McKinley and Roosevelt.

* * * * *

Upon this simple platform of Americanism the Republican party can confidently stand in the campaign near at hand. The issue involved is far more important than any mere detail of political or economic policy.

Great national campaigns deal with fundamentals, and no question more fundamental in our national life has been raised since 1860 than this question of whether America is to become a mere European annex, a patch in Europe's crazy quilt.

In his determination to make the un-Americanized covenant a campaign issue President Wilson has thrown down the gage of battle, and it again becomes the duty and the privilege of the Republican party to make the fight for American ideals of nationality.

As the minute men at Lexington said: "The fight may as well start here."

—March 6, 1920.

The revolutions of time furnish no previous example of a nation shooting up to maturity and expanding into greatness, with the rapidity which has characterized the growth of the American people. It is pleasing and instructive to look backwards upon the days of our youth; but in the continual and essential changes of a growing subject, the transactions of that early period would be soon obliterated from the memory, but for some periodical call of attention to aid the silent records of the historian. Such celebrations arouse and gratify the kindliest emotions of the bosom. They are faithful pledges of the respect we bear to the memory of our ancestors, and of the tenderness with which we cherish the rising generation. They introduce the sages and heroes of ages past to the notice and emulation of succeeding times; they are at once testimonials of our gratitude, and schools of virtue to our children. These sentiments are wise; they are honorable; they are virtuous; their cultivation is not merely innocent pleasure, it is incumbent duty.—John Quincy Adams.

We shall feel more than ever the want of an efficient general government to * * * connect the political views and interests of the several states under one head in such a manner as will effectually prevent them from forming separate, improper or indeed any connection with the European powers which can involve them in their political disputes. For our situation is such as makes it not only unnecessary, but extremely imprudent, for us to take a part in their quarrels.—Washington to Jefferson, 1788.

SILENCE, NOT DEBATE, HAS BEEN DISGRACEFUL

Colonel William J. Bryan, speaking in New York on the evening of the day the treaty of Paris failed of ratification, said:

"The debate on the treaty has been a disgrace."

He added that the rules of the Senate should be changed to permit the ratification of a treaty by majority vote, and to shut off debate.

Whether or not the debate on the treaty and league of nations covenant has been a "disgrace," and whether debate upon such questions should in future be prevented and ratification of treaties by a bare majority be provided for, depends upon the point of view.

Naturally those who wanted the treaty and covenant swallowed just as it was brought home from Europe, with its sacrifice of American sovereignty, ideals, interests and independence, regret the debate and regret the inability of the administration senators, with a few additional votes, to put the unchanged compact over.

To those who would thus have sacrificed American interests and ideals the debate in the Senate and throughout the country has been regrettable, because it has opened the eyes of the people to the perils of some of the provisions of the treaty, such as the Shantung clause approving the theft of a Chinese province by the Japanese empire, and Article X, of the league of nations covenant, providing that American blood and treasure should be pledged to the preservation of the national boundaries established in the Paris treaty.

The position of Mr. Bryan in this matter has been especially discreditable. He gave approval to the imperialistic treaty and the un-Americanized covenant, by silence, until the Senate debate to which he objects had aroused public sentiment to the menace of American ideals, interests and independence involved in certain provisions of the treaty. Finally, at a Democratic party banquet, Colonel Bryan, on purely partisan grounds, urged Democrats to join in accepting provisions of the treaty which he admitted were objectionable from an American standpoint.

Think of a politician too solicitous for the welfare of his party to protest against treaty provisions which he now admits were objectionable, to say a word while the debate on these matters was proceeding, but who now, while admitting that the protective reservations proposed were proper, denounces the Senate for having put up a fight against the attempted sacrifice of the highest and best interests of the American people!

AMERICANISM

No, the Senate debate has not been disgraceful. It constitutes one of the most inspiring chapters in American legislative history. Colonel Bryan's silence at such a time WAS disgraceful to him.

The failure of this scheme to subordinate the United States to the sovereignty of a super-state, controlled by European and Asiatic powers, does not demonstrate any weakness in the constitutional provision for a two-thirds vote in the Senate as an essential of treaty ratification. On the contrary it proves anew the wisdom of the founders of our nation in declining to make it possible for any one official and his partisan following to surrender the rights, interests and even the independence of the United States of America through a compact with other nations.

Colonel Bryan has apparently never thought of the treaty and league of nations covenant except in connection with its influence upon the election day outlook for the Democratic party. It is fortunate indeed that there were enough senators on Capitol Hill, of both political parties, who placed the national safety above mere partisan strategy. Through their courageous fight for fundamental Americanism, this nation has been saved for the fulfillment of its destiny as a great free nation, the world's exemplar of ordered liberty under a constitution establishing a representative republic which Colonel Bryan has for years been trying to destroy in favor of a constitution establishing a "pure" democracy, —another name for pure demagogy
—March 27, 1920.

Soldier and statesman, rarest unison;
High-poised example of great duties done
Simply as breathing, a world's honors worn
As Life's indifferent gifts to all men born;
Dumb form himself, unless it were to God,
But for his barefoot soldiers eloquent,
Tramping the snow to coral where they trod,
Held by his awe in hollow-eyed content;
Modest, yet firm as Nature's self; unblamed
Save by the men his nobler temper shamed;
Never seduced through show of present good
By other than unsetting lights to steer
New-trimmed in Heaven, nor than his steadfast mood
More steadfast, far from rashness as from fear;
Rigid, but with himself first, grasping still
In swerveless poise the wave-beat helm of will;
Not honored then or now because he wooed
The popular voice, but that he still withstood;
Broad-minded, higher-souled, there is but one
Who was all this and ours, and all men's—Washington.
                              —James Russell Lowell.

TRUE DEMOCRACY AND TRUE INTERNATIONALISM

This paper has frequently called attention to the fact that in all the talk of "saving the world for democracy" that has been proceeding from high places, the determination has persisted to use the word "democracy" in its European, rather than in its true and American sense. True democracy finds its expression in the republic; in representative government. That democracy safe for the world, providing both liberty and security, is the republicanism of the American Constitution. And the true internationalism, as this paper has often pointed out, is found in the peaceful residence under the American flag, of all the varied elements of European race and nationality; in not merely their residence here, but their absorption of a common spirit of nationality based upon common conceptions of government, rather than upon age-old predilections and prejudices.

The ideals of this true democracy, this true internationalism, were lost sight of even by those who were supposed to represent America at the peace conference. No attempt was made to carry the ideals of this country to Europe, but an effort was made to transfer the ideals of Europe to America. Neither true democracy nor world peace are consistent with the European system of caste and class, of racial and dynastic jealousies and hatreds, of multiplication of nationalities, which lie at the bottom of European civilization, caused the world war, and remain as causes for wars yet to come.

Curiously enough this truth which some Americans, steeped in European conceptions, are unable to understand, some European students of government clearly comprehend. Lady Frances Evelyn Warwick, Countess of Warwick, seems to have a better comprehension of fundamental Americanism than some of those who stand in the forefront of American public life. In a speech recently delivered she revealed an understanding of the fact that the existence of hereditary titles and caste based upon birth is not the mere unimportant survival of tradition some of our Europeanized Americans would have us believe, but that it is a symbol of a system entirely out of harmony with the underlying principles of Americanism,—that it is something, we may add for ourselves, with which we should not readily enter into partnership in any league of kingdoms and empires in which our national sovereignty is in any degree yielded. Let Europe give evidence of real conversion to the doctrines of true democracy,—which are something more than patronizing the poor or rule by class conscious "proletarians," —before we surrender our own real democracy and genuine internationalism for the spurious and pretended sort.

These words by a titled Englishwoman should be read by every American who wishes to have a truer understanding of what his own republic stands for in the eyes of a comprehending foreign student of our institutions:

"I deplore kingship—it is the eternal foe of peace. I see no security for Europe until democracy has grown up, learning to act as well as talk, until the prostitution of titles, honors, decorations and the rest, has been carried so far that even the most ignorant can see them for what they have become, until the anr̄-rower patriotism has seen light of the international.

"The face of Europe is seamed and riddled with kingship and hereditary right. France alone, that nation of genius, has thrown it off. But when I look across the Atlantic it is to millions of miles that have never felt the footprint of a monarch.

"Freedom, so long a fact with us here in England, a fact subject to a score of modifications, and yet a fact for all that, is now merely a name and threatens to become a memory. In the United States, in spite of unfavorable labor conditions in certain industrial centers, freedom is a fact, and there is universal recognition of the worth of man. What wonder if those of us here who feel as I do turn to the greatest republic of the world that day by day is carrying out the supreme experiment of amalgamation, proving that there are no races under the sun that given ample scope and equal liberty cannot dwell side by side in peace."

Believing that, despite the acute problems of reconstruction, British women are still chiefly concerned with the recurrence of a war that has taken millions of their sons, Lady Warwick said:

"The internationalist contends that the people who understand one another properly will not mass themselves into vast companies for mutual destruction.

"They say there is nothing in race to justify antagonism, that the Englishman, Frenchman, German and Jew can live side by side in amity under proper conditions of life. The United States, where men of all countries live in peace, has demonstrated the truth of this theory—it is the greatest supporter of internationalism on the planet.

"Our European system of rule and manners makes flunkies of honest men. America makes men out of slaves who have fled from European misrule. I have long been thinking that I will end my days in America."
—April 3, 1920.

PROVINCIALISM: WHAT IS IT IN THE UNITED STATES?

The National Republican recently received a letter in which the statement was made that opponents of the un-Americanized covenant of the league of nations are guilty of "provincialism."

The very use of that term demonstrates that those who employ it think they are living in a European colony rather than in a free and independent nation. The provincial is the inhabitant of a province who exalts local above national interests. What inhabitants of the United States who imitate President Wilson in talking about American "provincialism" need to learn is that this is not a province or colony, but a nation.

The real provincials in the United States are those who possess the provincial spirit; who cannot comprehend the separateness and the greatness of their own country; who suppose it still to be a sort of European back yard, like Africa or the East Indies. These real provincials are so obsessed with European ideas and ideals that the thing we call Americanism has never soaked through.

American nationalism is not provincialism, because the United States is something more than a European appendage; remarkable as this may seem to our home-grown aliens, America has an identity, a history, traditions and a destiny that are of importance independent of their relationship to any nation or set of nations in Europe. Our American provincials need to be awakened to the fact that they live in a nation, not a colony. And while they are acquiring a comprehension of this situation it would be well for them to drop this accusation of "provincialism" as applied to people who understand that the United States would be of some consequence in world history even if Europe were to sink tomorrow beneath the waves and become as much a forgotten continent as Atlantis.

—April 24, 1920.

The dangers of the commonwealth subsided at the close of his second administration, he (Washington) felt himself justified, after dedicating forty-five years of his valuable life to her service, in withdrawing to receive with resignation the great change of nature, which his age and his toils demonstrated to be near. When he declined your future suffrages, he left you a legacy. What! like Caesar's to the Romans, money for your sports? Like Attalus', a kingdom for your tyranny? No; he left you not such baubles, nor for such purposes. He left you the records of wisdom for your government; a mirror for the faithful representation to your own view, of yourselves, your weaknesses, your advantages, your dangers; a magnet which points to the secret mines and windings of party spirit, faction, foreign influence; a pillar to the unity of your republic; a band to inclose, conciliate and strengthen the whole of your wonderful and almost boundless communities. Read, preserve the sacred deposit; and lest posterity should forget the truth of its maxims, engrave them on his tomb, that they may read them when they weep before it.—George R. Minot, 1800.

Mine eyes have seen the glory of the coming of the Lord:
He is trampling out the vintage where the grapes of wrath are
    stored;
He hath loosed the fateful lightning of his terrible swift sword;
    His truth is marching on.

I have seen Him in the watch-fires of a hundred circling camps;
They have builded Him an altar in the evening dews and damps;
I can read His righteous sentence by the dim and flaring lamps,
    His day is marching on.

I have read a fiery gospel, writ in burnished rows of steel:
"As ye deal with my contemners, so with you my grace shall deal;
Let the Hero, born of woman, crush the serpent with his heel,
    Since God is marching on."

He has sounded forth the trumpet that shall never call retreat;
He is sifting out the hearts of men before His judgment-seat:
Oh! be swift, my soul, to answer Him! be jubilant, my feet!
    Our God is marching on.

In the beauty of the lilies Christ was born across the sea,
With a glory in his bosom that transfigures you and me:
As He died to make men holy, let us die to make men free,
    While God is marching on!
            —Julia Ward Howe.

The great doctrines of the Declaration germinated in the hearts of our fathers, and were developed under the new influences of this wilderness world; by the same subtle mystery which brings forth the rose from the germ of the rose-tree. Unconsciously to themselves the great truths were growing under the new conditions, until, like the century-plant, they blossomed into the matchless beauty of the Declaration of Independence, whose fruitage, increased and increasing, we enjoy today.—James A. Garfield.

MR. WILSON PERSISTS IN A PECULIAR OBSESSION

In a letter to former Representative Jouett Shouse, of Kansas, read at the Kansas Democratic state convention, President Wilson said:

"The issue which it is our duty to raise with the voters of the country involves nothing less than the honor of the United States and the redemption of its most solemn obligations, its obligations to its associates in the great war and to mankind, to whom it gave the most explicit pledge when it went to war, not merely to win a victory in arms, but also to follow up that victory with the establishment of such a concert of nations as would guarantee the permanence of a peace based on justice."

President Wilson is still indulging the modest theory that he is the United States. The Congress of the United States, which acts on behalf of the American people in declaring war, said nothing in the declaration about promising the world that it would not only win the war but establish a concert of nations that would guarantee eternal peace on earth. That would have been a fool promise to make, because no man or body of men with any regard for its word would promise something it would manifestly be impossible to certainly fulfill. Whether or not eternal world peace is possible is still a moot question, and whether or not the contraption rigged up at Paris would accomplish that end is, to say the least, a debatable proposition.

The only declarations of purpose on the part of this country in entering the war other than that given in President Wilson's message to Congress calling for a declaration of war against Germany and in the declaration of war itself,—the defense of the rights and interests of the American people,—were made by President Wilson himself. These were not" promises" to our associates in the war and to mankind; we didn't have to promise anything in order to get into a fight from which we expected nothing and where the effect manifestly was to save from defeat the allies to whom President Wilson now declares we made "solemn promises." As for the rest of mankind, it can scarcely be claimed that we had to make promises to Germany, Austria, Turkey and company in order to get the privilege of entering the war; they would not have given their consent if we had.

President Wilson used the war as a frame upon which to spread a great many declarations that had nothing to do with the war or our part or purpose in it. Just as the greedy contractor used the war as an excuse for putting things over on the public, so President Wilson employed it as a background for an attempt to make the world over on the pattern of the new freedom. In so doing he did not ask the consent of anybody, and he had no mandate from the people for the formulation of the Fourteen points which were so completely abandoned by him and repudiated by his associates in the preparation of the treaty of Paris. The well remembered fact is that President Wilson put up to the people of the country in October, 1918, the issue of whether or not he was their fully authorized representative in all that had to do with settling the issues of the World war, and the verdict at the polls was such that any chief executive with less of an obsession as to his own omniscience and omnipotence would have taken the hint and called in a few other people to cooperate in defining the policies of the country.

The statement that all these personal declarations of President Wilson, made not only without authority but even in the face of direct repudiation of the people, are binding upon the United States as "solemn obligations" which this country must fulfill "as a matter of honor" is mere rhetorical flapdoodle. Some of the diplomats who skinned Mr. Wilson out of his marbles at Paris might be excused for an ignorance of the division of powers under the American Constitution which make such declarations preposterous, but President Wilson has posed as a student and writer on the American Constitution, and undoubtedly knows better.

It isn't at all necessary in this country to wage a campaign to induce the American people to preserve the honor of this nation in its relations with the rest of the world. The great American republic has always kept its "solemn obligations," and it always will. If an instrumentality to hold the United States to the keeping of its pledges were necessary, the job would hardly be turned over to the party and the leadership which declared for a single presidential term, for economy in public expenditures, reduction of the high cost of living, destruction of the monopolist and the profiteer, free Panama Canal tolls for American coastwise shipping and a few little things like that, beside promising somewhat "solemnly" to "keep us out of war."
—May 1, 1920.

As the United States is the freest of all nations, so, too, its people sympathize with all people struggling for liberty and self-government, but while so sympathizing it is due to our honor that we should abstain from enforcing our views upon unwilling nations and from taking an interested part, without invitation, in the quarrels between different nations or between governments and their subjects.—U. S. Grant.

THE AMERICAN CHURCHES AND THE LEAGUE
OF NATIONS

At the national convention of the Southern Baptists, just closed at Washington, a distinguished preacher of the denomination spoke to a large audience assembled at the east front of the capitol for a Sunday evening service. He declared in the course of his address that he "dared to say" within the shadow of the American Senate chamber that the American people were for some form of world organization that would guarantee the world's peace, and that the dream of Tennyson of a "parliament of man" would yet be realized in fulfillment of the hope of the "stricken man in the White House."

No one need fear to say in the shadow of the Senate chamber that he favors a form of world organization that would ensure world peace. There is not a man in the United States Senate, of any party, who would not favor such an organization. The little matter which propagandists of the Wilson brand of internationalism overlook is that there is a very radical difference of opinion as to the service which the league of nations, as proposed by President Wilson, would render to world peace. There are millions of people in this country, just as much devoted to peace as this speaker could be, who cannot understand how a scheme which would bind this country to participation in every war that might spring out of the age-old rivalries, hatreds and ambitions of the continent of Europe, can be accepted by reasonable people as a contribution to the peace of this continent and especially of the American people.

The United States has not been a warlike nation. This government has never fought a war which did not have behind it a high and holy purpose, if we except the Mexican war, beneficent in its results to the people of the territory thus acquired by the United States, even if not immediately justifiable. This nation does not need a world government dominated by the chancellories of warring Europe, to keep it from engaging in unjustifiable war, and the assumption that the peace of our nation will be safeguarded by the treaty and league covenant concocted at Paris is entirely without warrant in common sense.

It is as true today as it was in Washington's time that the soil of Europe is strewn thick with the seed of war. The settlement of the great struggle just ended has added to rather than subtracted from these causes of war. In this republic we have welded a hundred and ten millions of people into a homogeneous nation. In Europe are multiplied lines of division, based upon commercial rivalries, territorial ambitions, dynastic hatreds, differences in language, ideals, religious faith and national aspirations. We have established in Europe a dozen new nations, no one of which is in position to achieve its economic independence, and every one of which, therefore, is looking enviously at the territory or trade of its neighbors for the means of expansion deemed necessary to national life. Already several wars have been waged on the basis of these differences; some are in progress now.

Now it is claimed by the Wilsonian internationalists that in some way, as the result of our unselfish participation in the World war, and presumably because we came out of it asking and getting nothing by way of territorial acquisitions, we are bound to link our destiny with that of Europe and assume the ungrateful task of keeping the peace of Europe and of the world. If we as a people were looking for a means of making ourselves the most hated nation in the world this would give us the opportunity desired. We have already made considerable progress toward the attainment of that unenviable distinction by our course at the Paris peace conference.

Those who talk glibly of the beauties of peace, and then assume that this sort of oratory justifies the provisions of the Paris peace treaty and league of nations covenant, either are exceedingly ignorant of the provisions and implications of the treaty and covenant, or are willing to help the national administration put it over on the people of this country. The truth is that the Wilsonian covenant makes every boy in the United States a possible soldier in every war of the world. It takes from this country the defense of our peculiarly fortunate situation, and requires Uncle Sam to take pot luck with Europe. Talk of "idealism" and superior "morality" and larger devotion to world welfare in connection with this undertaking is a mere continuance of the habit of mindless thinking and senseless speaking which became all too common under the sway of war psychology.

It occurs to a layman to suggest that some of the clerical leaders who, in violation of the sentiments of the vast majority of the plain Americans who sit in the pews of the churches, are endeavoring to commit religious bodies to the sacrifice of American ideals, rights and interests through the subordination of this republic to the authority of a super-state, might with considerable propriety begin a little nearer home in their labors for world unity. So long as single denominations of a single branch of a single religion in the United States are unable because of mere sectional differences, to accept a common government there ought to be a little more modesty about asking Americans to merge their nation into a world corporation in which the United States will held only about two per cent of the stock. Until those of our religious leaders who are using their posts of authority to promote the Wilson covenant, are ready to accept not only a common government for all branches of single denominations, but even a common government for Protestantism and Catholicism, and then a world government of Mohammedanism, Judaism, Buddhism, Confucianism, Shintoism, Zoroastrianism and Christianity in which Christianity shall play a minority role, then they ought to go a little slow in proposing that Americans merge their ideals and sovereignty with the world's empires, kingdoms and quasi republics. The misuse of church organizations and publications in behalf of the un-Americanized covenant is exceedingly distasteful to the vast majority of the men and women who go to make up the churches of this country. Far more harm has been done to the churches than good to the administration by the vast effort which has been made to commit the churches of the United States to support of the super-government devised by the diplomats at Paris. For the people understand that the effect if not the purpose of this scheme of world government as Mr. Wilson brought it home was to guarantee the spoils of victory to certain great European and Asiatic powers, flatten out weaker nations like China, and link the destiny of this republic with that of many nations which are as far from acceptance of this nation's ideals as they were when Washington warned Americans against entanglement with the primary concerns of Europe.

—May 22, 1920.

How many, like the great Emmet, have died and left only a name to attract our admiration for their virtues, and our regret for their untimely fall, to excite to deeds which they would but could not effect? But what has Washington left behind, save the glory of a name? The independent mind, the conscious pride, the ennobling principle of the soul,—a nation of freemen. What did he leave? He left us to ourselves. This is the sum of our liberties, the first principle of government, the power of public opinion, the only permanent power on earth. When did a people flourish like Americans? Yet where, in a time of peace, has more use been made of the pen, or less with the sword of power? When did a religion flourish like the Christian, since they have done away with intolerance? Since, men have come to believe that physical force cannot effect the immortal part, and that religion is between the conscience and the Creator only. He of 622, who with the sword propagated his doctrines through Arabia, and the greater part of the barbarian world, against the power of whose tenets the physical force of all Christendom was opposed in vain, under the effective operations of freedom of opinion, is fast passing the way of all error. Napoleon, the contemporary of our Washington, is fast dying away from the lips of men. He who shook the whole civilized earth; who, in an age of knowledge and concert among nations, held the world at bay;—at whose exploits the imagination becomes bewildered,—who, in the eve of his glory, was honored with the pathetic appellation of "the last lone captive of millions in war,"—even he is now known only in history. The vast empire was fast tumbling to ruins while he yet held the sword. He passed away, and left no successor there! The unhallowed light which obscured is gone; but brightly beams yet the name of Washington!

This freedom of opinion, which has done so much for the political and religious liberty of America, has not been confined to this continent. People of other countries begin to inquire, to examine, to reason for themselves. Error has fled before it, and the most inveterate prejudices are dissolved and gone. Such an unlimited remedy has in some cases, indeed. apparently proved injurious, but the evil is to be attributed to the peculiarity of the attendant circumstances, or the ill-timed application. Let us not force our tenets upon foreigners. For, if we subject opinion to coercion, who shall be our inquisitors? No; let us do as we have done, as we are now doing, and then call upon the nations to examine, to scrutinize, and to condemn! No! They cannot look upon America, today, and pity; for the gladdened heart disclaims all woe. They cannot look upon her and deride; for genius and literature and science are soaring above the high places of birth and pageantry. They cannot look upon us, and defy; for the hearts of thirteen millions are warm in virtuous emulation—their arms steeled in the cause of their country. Her productions are wafted to every shore; her flag is seen waving in every sea. She has wrested the glorious motto from the once queen of the sea, and high on our banner, by the stars and stripes, is seen:

"Columbia needs no bulwark,
  No towers along the steep,
Her march is o'er the mountain wave,
  Her home is on the deep."
—Cassius Marcellus Clay.

There is a rising tide of socialism which threatens the foundations of representative democracy the world over. There are well-meaning men in their ranks. They believe that the millennium is coming, that the government can exercise the functions of all private enterprise and that all fields of human endeavor can be equalized. It is an old, old dream, which the world has discarded again and again since the dawn of civilization. The best guarantees to the people of this country for the security of our institutions are those principles embodied in the Bill of Rights, which have been tried by the experience of ages and are firmly fixed in the Constitution of this land.—Senator Frank B. Kellogg, of Minnesota.

"WHY QUIT OUR OWN TO STAND UPON
FOREIGN GROUND?"

The acceptance of a "mandate," another name for protectorate, over Armenia, as now formally proposed by President Wilson, would definitely involve the American people in the complications of Old World international politics.

Our associates in the World war have divided up, through annexations and mandatories, all the spoils of war which represent assets rather than liabilities. We are asked to take over and administer the affairs of an area which has for centuries been the scene of the most intense racial and religious conflict. The powers have taken from the area originally belonging to Armenia all those portions which possess wealth or commercial possibilities, and are asking the United States government to take under its care the pitiable remainder and maintain it on an eleemosynary basis.

The risk of the undertaking would not arise primarily from the mere fact of our control of the affairs of the republic of Armenia, but from the establishment of an American outpost in the Near East which would physically involve us in all the mutations of European politics in this battle ground of Old World intrigue. It would mean keeping an armed force in the Near East for many years to come, and it would mean that this country would not be free to either enter or refuse to enter the future wars that may, and probably will, result from the failure of the peace conference to settle the problems arising out of the war.

Curiously enough this demand that we involve ourselves in European and Asiatic politics through the acceptance of such responsibility in Armenia, comes from the very politicians who have always denounced the United States for the work it has done in the Philippine Islands. In the Philippine archipelago, having full authority as well as responsibility, this country has done a great work for the ten million people who as the result of the war with Spain came beneath American sovereignty. Mr. Wilson and his party denounced the extension of American authority to the Philippines, and they have all along been demanding that we abandon these islands to their fate. They will doubtless declare at San Francisco that it is the duty of the United States to abandon the Philippine Islands to Mexicanization or Japanization.

This project of an American outpost in the Near East comes, moreover, from the same politicians who have for the past seven years successfully resisted the demand that we do something to compose conditions menacing us as a people immediately next door in the republic of Mexico. Conditions in Mexico are not much better, for the masses of the people, than they are in Armenia. Yet we are told by Mr. Wilson and his party that it would be an act of criminal aggression for us to use the great power of this republic to bring tranquility and prosperity and safety of life and property even to the Mexican people in Mexico, much less to defend our own people, rights and interests there. In this our Democratic friends are much like the man who preaches loudly the benefits of certain social and political nostrums to cure all the ailments of the human race, but who neglects and abuses his own family in his own home.

The appeal in behalf of an American mandate in Armenia is made in the name of suffering humanity. We are told of the terrible conditions prevailing in that hapless country, and of our duty to alleviate the suffering of the people there. There is much more human suffering in the world than it will ever be possible for the generosity of America to alleviate. It is to be feared, moreover, that some of the people who are asking the American people to fare abroad as crusaders, overlook the gravity of home problems, which, if not solved within the next few years, may send this republic on the rocks. Have the American people met all the claims upon their aid and cooperation which may fairly be made within the borders of this republic and upon this continent?

The American people do not want to shirk any responsibility that has or may properly come to them as the result of the World war. Many of us cannot comprehend, however, the talk of those who seem to think that we have earned by the great sacrifices of blood and treasure made in the great conflict, sacrifices which saved Europe from the domination of an autocratic military power, only the duty of making further sacrifices while our associates in the war are busily engaged in annexing territory and indemnities. There is a mawkish sentimentality to which some people are given that may lead an individual, as well as a nation, far astray. We have had a great deal of this over-wrought sentimentality on tap during the whole war period. It is high time for the re-enthronement, in our national thinking, of old-fashioned common sense.

The American people and the American government have near at home duties far more important than that of propping up artificially created nations in Europe. We are willing to go to the border line of safety in extending help to the poor and oppressed peoples of Europe. This has been demonstrated so often that such an assertion is not open to question by any reasonable person. Risking the peace and safety of this country by thrusting our nation into the maelstrom of European political intrigue, backed by bayonets and battleships, is quite another matter. We all have a right to be generous, but not with the interests and ideals of this republic of ours.

In the borders of this republic, in our island possessions, in Mexico, in Cuba, on the Isthmus of Panama, on the two continents of this hemisphere, are duties and responsibilities enough for the American people. Those who would lead this nation out of the old pathways and put its feet on the devious road of Old World politics, merely do not comprehend the mission of this republic. They are of the Old, and not of the New world. They are too much affected by European ideas, European ideals, European propaganda; too much influenced by the over-wrought sentimentalism carefully propagated by alien and domestic interests which have their own selfish ends to serve and are willing to make well meaning men and women their dupes in achieving these sinister purposes.

Let us stand by the Americanism of the founding fathers of this republic, and of the great line of American heroes and martyrs who have come after them,—who have fought and wrought that this nation might live in the fulfillment of the mission for which it was established. Let us serve the world by the upholding of an ideal and the power of a great example. Let us hold fast to the fundamentals of the faith of Washington and Lincoln and Roosevelt. Let us keep our America free from the entanglements of European politics, with its age-old hatreds and rivalries, its racial and dynastic conflicts, its clashing territorial and trade ambitions, which we are as powerless to compose as to stop with mere phrases the rolling flood of Niagara.

We stand at the turning of the highway of American destiny. Either we shall take the downward path, after a century and a half of upward climbing, to the old, dark, winding, bloody road we left behind with Washington, or we shall keep on forging toward the goal of good to all mankind the founders and preservers of this republic have constantly held as their objective.

Shutting our ears to the specious pleas of pretended and deluded humanitarianism, let us cling to the true internationalism our nation has exemplified from its earliest years, serving the world by upholding the ideals, the rights, the interests and the independence of that republic which is the world's last, best hope of ordered liberty: of Lincoln's

"Government of the people
"By the people, for the people."
—May 29, 1920.

Men, the hour is fast approaching on which the honor and the success of the army and the safety of our bleeding country will depend. Remember that you are free men, fighting for the blessings of liberty, that slavery will be your portion, and that of your children, if you do not acquit yourselves like men.—George Washington.

What flower is this that greets the morn,
Its hues from Heaven so freshly born?
With burning star and flaming band
It kindles all the sunset land:
Oh, tell us what its name may be—
Is this the Flower of Liberty?
    It is the banner of the free,
    The starry Flower of Liberty!

In savage Nature's far abode
Its tender seed our fathers sowed;
The storm-winds rocked its swelling bud,
Its opening leaves were streaked with blood,
Till lo! earth's tyrants shook to see
The full-blown Flower of Liberty!
    Then hail the banner of the free,
    The starry Flower of Liberty!

Behold its streaming rays unite,
One mingled flood of braided light—
The red that fires the Southern rose
With spotless white from Northern snows,
And, spangled o'er its azure, see
The sister Stars of Liberty!
    Then hail the banner of the free,
    The starry Flower of Liberty!

The blades of heroes fence it round,
Where'er it springs is holy ground;
From tower and dome its glories spread;
It waves where lonely sentries tread;
It makes the land as ocean free,
And plants an empire on the sea!
    Then hail the banner of the free,
    The starry Flower of Liberty!

Thy sacred leaves, fair Freedom's flower,
Shall ever float on dome and tower,
To all their heavenly colors true,
In blackening frost or crimson dew—
And God love us as we love thee,
Thrice holy Flower of Liberty!
    Then hail the banner of the free,
    The starry Flower of Liberty!
                —Oliver Wendell Holmes.

WHAT AMERICANISM MEANS,—
THE GENERAL WELFARE

Americanism means serving, through government, the general welfare, rather than the selfish aims and ends of groups, classes, elements or individuals.

The system of organizing groups and crowds and gangs of people and then forcing upon the people schemes hatched in the special interests of some one particular element, at the sacrifice of the general interests, is a violation of the fundamental principle of Americanism.

The man or woman to whom the general welfare is not more important than the attainment of the immediate selfish ends of the particular group to which he or she belongs, is not a good American, because not possessed by the true spirit of Americanism.

Government by bullyragging, government by threat, government by fear, as against the common good, has been the constantly increasing menace by which, now, the very life of this republic is threatened.

Class loyalty, group loyalty, gang loyalty, racial loyalty, loyalty to dynasties or persons rather than principles, as opposed to loyalty to government existing for the service of all, without regard to caste or class, is the curse of European civilization.

A larger fealty to the common good is what Americanism stands for. It is what Republicanism must stand for, if this nation is to be saved from that form of civil war which arises from the continuous battle of classes, within and without the law, for advantage attained at the sacrifice of the principles of equity in human relationship fundamental in a real republic.

Europe is a crazy quilt of warring tribes, races, tongues, each hating and ready to fight the others. Its age-old religious and racial antagonisms, its class and caste divisions, its commercial and dynastic jealousies and rivalries, are the things that have kept it and will keep it at war so long as they persist, regardless of scraps of papers or leagues of nations founded upon grandiloquent phrases.

Here in America we have a government whose national motto is "Out of many, one." Out of many races, religions, classes, groups, one people; one union, indivisible, now and forever.

To lose that ideal would be to lose America.

AMERICANISM

Yet many forces are at work seeking to destroy that for which this republic was founded and has to this time been maintained by the brave and the great who have fought and wrought that this nation might be born and live in the fulfillment of its mission.

There are those who would Europeanize America. They would involve it in the tangled web of European intrigue which we have no part in weaving and which would enmesh us only to our own destruction.

Then they would transplant here the same system of caste and class and warring groups that is keeping Europe face to face with civil as well as international war.

They are preaching here the gospel that every element, every occupation, every "class," should hate and fight and oppress the others; and that the purpose of every such class should be to seize the government and use it as a means of oppressing, undoing and even exterminating the others.

Those who preach, and those who accept, such a gospel, are traitors to representative republicanism in the true sense of that term, little understood anywhere in the world beyond the borders of the United States.

Now is a time for standing true to the real, underlying, fundamental and eternal truths of American republicanism and republican Americanism.

The Republican party must stand forth as the apostle of this historic conception of Americanism.

It must boldly fight for it if this nation is to be saved.

The perils of the time are not imaginary. We are face to face with them.

The nation will survive them. But only through the patriotic, the devoted, the consecrated service of men who comprehend and love and are willing, regardless of immediate consequences, to battle for true Americanism; the Americanism of Washington, of Lincoln, of Roosevelt and of the millions who have stood by and with them in all that they did to the great end that

"Government of the people,
"By the people, for the people,
"Shall not perish from the earth."

—June 19, 1920.

The states are represented by the starry flag, that their children have borne on so many fields of glory, the ever shining symbol of one nation and many states.—David Dudley Field.

Liberty is a slow fruit. It is never cheap; it is made difficult because freedom is the accomplishment and perfectness of man.—Emerson.

PRESERVE THE CONSTITUTION: AN OVERSHADOWING ISSUE

"The Republican party reaffirms its unyielding devotion to the Constitution of the United States. * * * It will resist all attempts to overthrow the foundations of the government, or to weaken the force of its controlling principles and ideals, whether these attempts be made in the form of international policy or of domestic agitation."

"We undertake to end executive autocracy and to restore to the people their constitutional government."

In these and other phrases the Republicans of the nation, in recent representative convention assembled, renewed their pledge of allegiance to the American Constitution.

Except for the unprecedented occurrences of the past few years, such a pledge of loyalty to the fundamental law of the republic would seem to be superfluous. Nothing is more apparent now, however, than that the preservation of the American Constitution, in letter and spirit, is one of the chief issues, if not the overshadowing issue, of the campaign.

The Constitution has been challenged, as the Republican national platform says, from within and without; from within by those who would change both the form and the spirit of our institutions; from without by those who would substitute for the American Constitution the constitution of a world government sacrificial of American rights, interests and ideals.

Gladstone said of the American Constitution that it was the greatest work ever struck off at a given moment by the brain and hand of man. It has been the chart and compass of American nationality from the inauguration of George Washington as President to the inauguration of Woodrow Wilson, who himself took an oath to support and protect the great plan of government it provides, under which the American nation has grown from a feeble band of petty states to the place of primacy in the world in national wealth and moral greatness.

That the charter of ordered liberty under which this nation has so far and so swiftly advanced, should be subjected to attack from within and without, and that these attacks should menace the perpetuity of our institutions as they were handed down to us by Washington and as they were preserved by Lincoln, seems incredible. Yet it is manifestly true that today, as never before in our history, the borers from within and the assailants from without have so far carried forward the work of undermining the foundations of American representative government, that the perpetuity of our institutions is at issue.

The American Constitution provides for a form of government without precedent in political history. It is a form of government which excludes all forms of autocracy,—the autocracy of the mob as well as the autocracy of the monarch. The American Constitution is built upon the theory that governments are made for the service of men, and not men for the service of governments. It has thrown about the citizen of the republic the protection of certain guarantees of person and property which no tyrant or body of tyrants may lawfully disregard. The theory of the American Constitution is that there is a sovereignty in the individual which even law making bodies and executives may not invade. Thus we have imbedded in the Constitution the guarantees of free speech, free press and the right of the individual to worship according to the dictates of his own conscience. Never until recently have the American people witnessed in high places a tendency to disregard some of the, fundamental rights of American citizenship.

Never until recent months have the American people confronted an attempt to consolidate the powers of at least two branches of government in one branch, and that branch representing only the will of a single individual. The Republican national platform makes an important promise to the American people when it pledges the end of executive usurpation and the restoration to the people of their constitutional government.

Never until recent months have the people of the United States witnessed an effort to nullify their Constitution through a proposed merging of American nationality into the world-wide sway of a super-state; the transference of powers hitherto exercised by representatives of the American people in legislative and executive authority, to a world council sitting on the other side of the Atlantic. That such a revolution could be seriously proposed would have startled not only the first President of the republic, but every chief executive of this nation from the beginning to the most recent years.

Demagogues and doctrinaires are filling the air with clamor in favor of the abandonment of the ancient landmarks of American constitutional government, and the launching of the ship of state upon the uncharted seas of internationalism and of "pure" democracy. What they propose has been warned against not only by the founders of this republic, but by the long line of national heroes and statesmen who have succeeded them as leaders and spokesmen of the thought of the American people. What has been secured to the American people at the sacrifice of so much labor and sacrifice, these demagogues and doctrinaires would risk in academic experiment, with no serious thought of the consequences of failure to this nation and to the world.

Well it is that the platform of national Republicanism should call upon the American people to rally to the support of their national Constitution. Well it will be if the people of this republic respond to that call in such emphatic and unmistakable fashion that never again within the experience of men and women now living will the controlling principles and ideals of this representative republic, as it was founded and as it has been preserved throughout a century and a third of national life, be seriously challenged by any political leader or any political party.
—July 3, 1920.

No cause is so bound up with religion as the cause of political liberty and the rights of man. Unless I have read history backwards,—unless Magna Charta is a mistake, and the Bill of Rights a sham, and the Declaration of Independence a contumacious falsehood,—unless the sages and heroes and martyrs, who have fought and bled, were impostors,—unless the sublimest transaction in modern history, on Tower Hill, in the Parliaments of London, on the sea-tossed Mayflower,—unless these are all deceitful, there is no cause so linked with religion as the cause of democratic liberty.

And, sir, not only are all the moral principles, which we can summon up, on the side of this great cause, but the physical movements of the age attend it and advance it. Nature is republican. The discoveries of science are republican. Sir, what are these new forces, steam and electricity, but powers that are leveling all factitious distinctions, and forcing the world on to a noble destiny? Have they not already propelled the nineteenth century a thousand years ahead? What are they but the servitors of the people, and not of a class? Does not the poor man of today ride in a car dragged by forces such as never waited on kings, or drove the wheels of triumphal chariots? Does he not yoke the lightning, and touch the magnetic nerves of the world? The steam-engine is a democrat. It is the popular heart that throbs in its iron pulses. And the electric telegraph writes upon the walls of despotism: "Mene, mene, tekel, upharsin!" There is a process going on in the moral and political world,—like that in the physical world,—crumbling the old Saurian forms of past ages, the heritage of the absurd and unjust feudal system, under which serfs labored and gentlemen spent their lives in fighting and feasting. It is time that this opprobrium of toil were done away. Ashamed to toil, art thou? ashamed of thy dingy workshop and dusty labor-field; of thy hard hand, scarred with service more honorable than that of war; of thy soiled and weather-stained garments, on which mother nature has embroidered, midst sun and rain, midst fire and steam, her own heraldic honors? Ashamed of these tokens and titles,

and envious of the flaunting robes of imbecile idleness and vanity?
It is treason to nature,—it is impiety to Heaven,—it is breaking
Heaven's great ordinance. Toil, I repeat, toil, either of the brain,
of the heart, or of the hand, is the only true manhood, the only
true nobility.—Edwin Hubbell Chapin.

Fair liberty, our soul's most darling prize,
A bleeding victim flits before our eyes;
Was it for this our great forefathers rode
O'er a vast ocean to this bleak abode!
When liberty was into contest brought,
And loss of life was but a second thought;
By pious violence rejected thence,
To try the utmost stretch of providence;
The deep, unconscious of the furrowing keel,
Essayed the tempest to rebuke their zeal;
The tawny natives and inclement sky
Put on their terrors, and command to fly;
They mock at danger; what can those appall
To whom fair liberty is all in all?
See the new world their purchase, blest domain,
Where lordly tyrants never forged the chain;
The prize of valor, and the gift of prayer,
Hear this and redden, each degenerate heir!
Is it for you their honor to betray,
And give the harvest of their blood away?
Look back with reverence, awed to just esteem,
Preserve the blessings handed down from them;
If not, look forward, look with deep despair,
And dread the curses of your beggared heir;
What bosom beats not, when such themes excite?
Be men, be gods, be stubborn in the right.
                                    —Benj. Church, 1765.

In our mighty development we have added to the perils of which
Washington warned. The danger has not been in party association, but in party appeal, or surrender, to faction.

Our growth, our diversification, our nation-wide communication,
our profit-bearing selfishness—these have filled the land with organized factions, not geographical as Washington so much feared,
but commercial, industrial, agricultural and professional, each
seeking to promote the interests of its own, not without justification at times, but often a menace in exacting privilege and favor
through the utterance of political threats. If popular government
is to survive it must grant exact justice to all men and fear none.
—Warren G. Harding.

THE INTERNATIONAL ISSUE BETWEEN
THE TWO PARTIES

The issue between the Democratic and Republican parties on international questions in this campaign may be summarized as follows:

The Democratic party stands for the perpetuation of the Wilson policy of one-man control in international affairs. It endorses President Wilson's course in treating the problem of American relations with the rest of the world as a mere personal affair of his own; his exclusion of all but his own partisans from participation in formulating the terms of peace and the construction of a plan of world government; his demand that a so-called covenant for a league of nations sacrificial in its original form of American rights, interests, ideals and even independence be adopted as a work of omniscience or inspiration, without alteration except in the direction of making clearer the obligations of this nation to the rest of the world under it.

The Republican party believes that treaties of peace should be formulated in accordance with American constitutional provisions, and in harmony with American precedents and traditions. Republicans believe that President Wilson violated the Constitution he swore to uphold when he constituted himself the legislative representative of the American people in the formulation of a world government and blocked a treaty of peace, first until he could link the league covenant with it for the announced purpose of preventing action upon it in the United States on its own merits rather than as a "rider" on the treaty of peace; and again until he could force it down the throat of an unwilling Senate and people. Still Republicans have demonstrated clearly enough that they have stood ready to accept whatever of good may have come out of the Paris peace conference and to make many concessions on matters of detail. There was never a time from the date of his return to the United States early last summer until the adjournment of Congress a year later when President Wilson might not have brought about the acceptance of a league covenant with Americanizing reservations Europe would have been willing to accept. He refused to accept the opportunity because he was more concerned in creating an issue for the 1920 campaign than in bringing about the establishment of a league of nations that would be something more than a monument to himself. .

AMERICANISM

The Republican party declares in its Chicago platform in favor of a league of justice for the preservation of the world's peace, rather than a league of force that would perpetuate every international injustice and thus make war perpetual. Its platform endorses the fight of the senators who stood for the Americanization of the treaty and pledges the next Republican national administration "to such agreements with other nations of the world as shall meet the full duty of America to civilization and humanity, in accordance with American ideals and without surrendering the right of the American people to exercise its judgment and its power in favor of justice and peace."

As a member of the Senate, Mr. Harding voted for the Lodge reservations, through which it was sought to make the treaty and covenant safe for America. In his speech of acceptance he clearly indicated that he was for no policy of aloofness in international relationships, and said: "We do not mean to shun a single responsibility of this republic to world civilization." He condemned the effort of President Wilson to force upon this country a covenant destructive of American rights, interests, sovereignty and ideals, and commended the battle waged for its Americanization. And Senator Harding makes this pledge for the future:

"Disposed as we are, the way is very simple. Let the failure attending assumption, obstinacy, impracticability and delay be recognized, and let us find the big, practical, unselfish way to do our part, neither covetous because of ambition nor hesitant through fear, but ready to serve ourselves, humanity and God. With a Senate advising as the Constitution contemplates, I would hopefully approach the nations of Europe and of the earth, proposing that understanding which makes us a willing participant in the consecration of nations to a new relationship, to commit the moral forces of the world, America included, to peace and international justice, still leaving America free, independent and self-reliant, but offering friendship to all the world.

"If men call for more specific details, I remind them that moral committals are broad and all inclusive, and we are contemplating peoples in the concord of humanity's advancement. From our own viewpoint the program is specifically American, and we mean to be Americans first, to all the world."

This is not to be interpreted as a repudiation of the position assumed by senators, including Mr. Harding himself, who voted for the league of nations covenant with Americanizing reservations. It shows that Senator Harding will approach the problem immediately after his inauguration with a view to working it out along the lines of the fundamental principles he states, in the light of conditions as they then exist.

It is of interest in this connection to recall the reservations proposed by Senator Lodge and supported in whole or in part not only by the Republican majority in the Senate but by some twenty-one members of the Democratic minority. In substance, they were as follows:

1. The United States shall be the sole judge of whether or not it has fulfilled all obligations essential to withdrawal under the first article. The Wilson-Cox position is that the council of the league should, by this power of determination, have the right to hold the United States in the league indefinitely, and regardless of any unfavorable development in its operations.

2. The United States assumes no obligations under Article X. for the employment of its military and naval forces without the consent of Congress. Opposition to this reservation by Wilson and Cox indicates that they object to permitting Congress to be the arbiter in this matter, and would leave with a council dominated by aliens in Geneva the right to order American boys to war anywhere in the world.

3. No mandate shall be accepted by the United States government except by approval of Congress. The Wilson-Cox opposition to this reservation indicates that they would give to an American President or representative in the league council the right to assume such responsibilities anywhere in the world on behalf of the United States.

4. The United States reserves the right to determine what questions are of a domestic character. The Wilson-Cox position, as shown by opposition to this reservation, is that a council of aliens should determine what matters of alleged domestic concern it may undertake to regulate even over our protest.

5. The United States will not submit to arbitration or inquiry questions depending upon or relating to the Monroe Doctrine. By opposing this reservation the Cox-Wilson Democracy indicates that it stands ready to reopen the Monroe Doctrine and let Europe determine what it does or does not mean.

6. The United States withholds its assent to the provisions of the treaty relative to Shantung. This provision of the treaty is the most infamous piece of international theft in history. It seizes the Chinese province of Shantung with 40,000,000 people and hands it over to the empire of Japan, although China was our ally in the World war and came into the struggle at our urgent invitation. The Cox-Wilson Democracy, and its supporters, stand for approval of the shame of Shantung.

7. The Congress of the United States will provide by law for the appointment of all representatives of the United States in the council and assembly of the league of nations and the various commissions. The Cox-Wilson Democracy objects to this reservation and would put the power to commit America to anything in the league council or assembly into the hands of the one man who happens to be the chief executive of the United States at the time.

8. The United States understands that the reparation commis-

sion will interfere with the trade of the United States with Germany only as the American Congress approves. The Cox-Wilson Democracy would turn over to a council composed of representatives of our great trade rivals the determination of what we may not do in Germany commercially. Already that power has been used to our disadvantage.

9. There is to be no obligation upon the United States for expenses of the league except upon the authorization of Congress. The Cox-Wilson Democracy objects to this, and would permit a congress of aliens to make any charges upon the United States Treasury it may like.

10. Whenever the United States is threatened with invasion the United States reserves the right to increase its armament. The Cox-Wilson Democracy would render the United States helpless to defend itself against invasion if forbidden to act by a council dominated by aliens, and possibly acting in the interests of our enemies.

11. The United States reserves the right to permit its individual citizens to maintain commercial relations with individuals in nations put under the international boycott by the league of nations. The Cox-Wilson position is that the council of the league of nations should be permitted to override Congress in this matter.

12. Nothing in Articles 296, 297 relating to debts and property rights shall be taken to sanction any illegal act or act in contravention of the rights of citizens of the United States. The Cox-Wilson Democracy would leave the decision of this matter to a council sitting in Geneva.

13. The United States withholds its assent to the labor provisions of the treaty, except in so far as Congress may hereafter provide for American representation in the organization to be established under terms of our own formulation. The Cox.Wilson Congress would turn over the control of American labor to a council of aliens, without permitting the American Congress to define the terms of our participation in what many liberal minded men think would develop into one of the most objectionable and oppressive institutions of the proposed world government.

14. The United States assumes no obligation to be bound by any decision of the league in which any member of the league with its dependencies casts more votes than the United States. The Cox-Wilson Democracy is in favor of the United States exercising one-sixth as much influence in the assembly of the league of nations as one other power represented.

After going over these reservations, which of them is objectionable to any real American? If they are not essential to the protection of American rights in the various matters covered, the worst that can be said of them is that they are superfluous. If they are essential for the protection of these rights, then what right reserved by them would you, as an American, whether Re-

publican or Democrat, sacrifice? Do you see any excuse for **making** the proposal of these reservations the basis of refusal **to** accept the league covenant and return it to Europe for approval? If **not,** then you stand with the Republican party, and against the Democratic party, on this great issue.
—August 21, 1920.

O Mother of a mighty race,
Yet lovely in thy youthful grace!
The elder dames, thy haughty peers,
Admire and hate thy blooming years.
  With words of shame
And taunts of scorn they join thy name.

For on thy cheeks the glow is spread
That tints thy morning hills with red;
Thy step—the wild-deer's rustling feet
Within thy woods are not more fleet;
  Thy hopeful eye
Is bright as thine own sunny sky.

Ay, let them rail—those haughty ones,
While safe thou dwellest with thy sons.
They do not know how loved thou art,
How many a fond and fearless heart
  Would rise to throw
Its life between thee and the foe.
   *   *   *   *   *
O fair young mother! on thy brow
Shall sit a nobler grace than now.
Deep in the brightness of the skies
The thronging years in glory rise,
  And, as they fleet,
Drop strength and riches at thy feet.

Thine eye, with every coming hour,
Shall brighten, and thy form shall tower;
And when thy sisters, elder born,
Would brand thy name with words of scorn,
  Before thine eye,
Upon their lips the taunt shall die.
     —William Cullen Bryant.

Patriotism, pure and undefiled, is the handmaid of religion. Love of country is twin to the love of God. The instinct of love **of** country, of patriotism, dwelling in every human breast, **is the abiding and** unchangeable source of every nation's strength **and**

179

safety and the inspiration of the most enlightened civilization has been the inspiration of all the people of the earth through all the ages: "Dulce et decorum est pro patria mori." Strong as love of country is instinctively, it can, by cultivation, be made stronger in each individual and thus become a source of greater national strength. It is a part of the education and experience of a true man and of the real business of life that he should be a patriot. The instinct of the love of country is as natural as the parental or filial love or as the attachment for home. As the bird returns to the nest, so every fiber of a well-educated and well-developed man swells in sympathy with associations of family, home, community, state or nation. No man liveth to himself and no man dieth to himself. There can be no well-rounded character in selfish individualism.—Chief Justice Hay Brown, of the Pennsylvania Supreme Court.

The vital lines of cleavage among our people do not correspond and indeed run at right angles to the lines of cleavage which divide occupation from occupation, which divide wage earners from capitalists, farmers from bankers, men of small means from men of large means, men who live in the towns from men who live in the country; for the vital line of cleavage is the line which divides the honest man who tries to do well by his neighbor from the dishonest man who does ill by his neighbor.

It is the man's moral quality, his attitude toward the great questions which concern all humanity, his cleanliness of life, his power to do his duty toward himself and toward others which really count; and if we substitute for the standard of personal judgment which treats each man according to his merits another standard in accordance with which men of one class are favored and all men of another class discriminated against we shall do irreparable damage to the body politic.

I believe our people are too sane, too self-respecting, too fit for self-government ever to adopt such an attitude. This government is not and never shall be government by a plutocracy. This government is not and never shall be government by a mob.—Theodore Roosevelt.

Those heroes are dead. They died for liberty—they died for us. They are at rest. They sleep in the land they made free, under the flag they rendered stainless, under the solemn pines, the sad hemlocks, the tearful willows and the embracing vines. They sleep beneath the shadows of the clouds, careless alike of sunshine or of storm, each in the windowless Palace of Rest. Earth may run red with other wars—they are at peace. In the midst of battle, in the roar of conflict, they found the serenity of death. I have one sentiment for soldiers, living and dead: Cheers for the living; tears for the dead.—Robert G. Ingersoll.

TRYING AN OLD SWINDLE IN A NEW WAY

The Republican party does not stand in this campaign for a selfish, isolated, unsympathetic nationalism, even invoked in behalf of such a republic as is ours. It is pledged to go as far in international cooperation for world justice and world peace as we can go without the sacrifice of American rights, interests, ideals and security. The man or the party that would go further is insufficiently American. The Bible says that the man who does not look after the welfare of his own household is worse than an infidel. The man who is willing to take chances on the welfare of his own country and his own countrymen merely in order that he may experiment with some theory of world government is less than a patriot and good citizen.

Any man has the right to make any sacrifice he wishes in behalf of others. That sort of sacrifice is noble, even when blindly or foolishly made. But the American citizen who is willing to sacrifice the safety of his country and countrymen in behalf of some preconceived theory of his own is not half so noble and self-sacrificing as he claims to be. He is a patriot after the pattern of Artemas Ward, "Determined to put down the rebellion even at the sacrifice of all his wife's relations." When some of the big talk that is heard in high places about being "unselfish" in our attitude toward the rest of the world is analyzed, we find it akin to that of the man who sits on the pier and talks eloquently to his wife about her duty to jump into the ocean and save a bystander who has fallen into the water.

Just as Republicans believed and said in 1916 that President Wilson's policies were not keeping us out but getting us into war, so they say now that the un-Americanized treaty and covenant, with Article X requiring the American people to send soldiers into every war that may begin anywhere in the world, is not a device to bring peace to this land, but to put it perpetually in the shadow of war. The league of nations as it was written at Paris is a combination of imperialism and communism. It represents imperialistic expansion and aggression by some of the powers, but so far as this country is concerned it represents sacrifice of our safety, our interests, our rights and our ideals.

The Republican party stands where Theodore Roosevelt stood in the matter of a league of nations. It stands for a league of justice as contrasted with this proposed league of force. It stands for the protection of the right of this nation to cling to its own institutions and ideals. Not a reservation was proposed by Republicans in the Senate giving to this nation the right of aggression against any other nation, the right to take from any other nation what belongs to it. The reservations adopted by the senate, and to which President Wilson was so much opposed that he killed the league and treaty rather than accept them, safeguard things that have been considered fundamental in Americanism from the days of the founding of this republic.

The Republican party is not responsible for the failure of a league of nations. For that, one wilful man is wholly responsible, because he insisted upon misrepresenting his country at Paris and then tried to coerce a coordinate branch of the national government into a betrayal of the duty it was sworn to perform. With him it was the Wilson league or nothing; he would not yield an inch to any plan for safeguarding America in the adoption of the covenant and treaty. Governor Cox says he is absolutely one with Mr. Wilson. This means that if Mr. Cox is elected there will be a resumption of the fight for the adoption of the un-Americanized covenant. The end of such a contest is certain because it is now sure that at least one-third of the membership of the next Senate will be opposed to any league scheme which puts America last, and in the destruction of what this nation stands for, would kill the world's last and best hope of the rule of justice throughout the world rather than the sway of force. This is the issue as it stands. Every man who wants to make the world safe for America must cast his ballot against those who think of this republic last, if ever, when they begin to develop their ambitious plans for the world's reconstruction.
—August 21, 1920.

Many of our citizens, including statesmen and soldiers who had been pre-eminent in achieving our independence, were bent that we should render to republican France some aid much more efficacious than sympathy. But there were others who looked into the very seeds of time. They remembered that the colonial system which they had lately overthrown was a vast and entangling foreign relation; that the tie which held it to the motherland was a tie that lacerated while it bound; that this country, by reason of that relation, had been invaded by enemies of the parent state. They saw that alliances with any European power, as to matters of European concern, were the same thing as their previous condition under another name, and that the consequences would be the same.

No one saw all this more clearly than Washington. In his farewell address—that political testament by which he bequeathed to posterity an imperishable legacy of wisdom—he determined our policy as to European nations by a few sentences which cannot be read too often, or reflected upon too deeply.—Cushman K. Davis.

SOME OF THE BULWARKS OF
AMERICAN FREEDOM

A scholarly New England publicist has written for a current magazine an attack upon the Senate for attempting to share with the President responsibility in the formulation of the peace treaty and league of nations covenant. In his criticism of the American Constitution for giving to the Senate such large power over treaty making, this able administration spokesman attacks as undemocratic the principle of state representation in the Senate. Why, he asks indignantly, should Nebraska have no more representation than Nevada in the Senate? Such constitutional inconsistencies, he intimates, prevent this country from having a genuinely popular government like that of England. In the United Kingdom, by the way, and in the European countries generally, public sentiment had about as much to do with the peace treaty's provisions as it has to do with elections in Mississippi or any other state where the Democratic oligarchy really runs things.

All this talk is in connection with an attack upon the Senate for failing to swallow whole the league of nations covenant as it was cooked up at Paris! And what does that covenant provide? That in the council of the league a few chosen powers constitute the entire governing body, excluding from the deliberations of a Senate undertaking to regulate the affairs of the world a vast majority of the people even of those nations which have subscribed to the covenant. Each power, according to the friends of the Wilson league, having the right to defeat the decisions of all the rest! It provides that in the assembly of the league the United States would have the same representation as Hayti, Santo Domingo, Colombia, Salvador or Costa Rica! Of course Franklin Roosevelt has explained this by saying that through the use of the bayonet we can control the votes of a half dozen of the little republics "represented" in the assembly! On the other hand, Great Britain is to have six votes in the assembly as against one for any other nation; one for India, for instance, where the people will have about as much to say about their representation as the negroes of South Carolina have to do with state government under their peculiar form of Wilsonian self-determination of peoples. Yet India is to have the same representation as the United States! If there is inequality in state representation in the Senate, denunciation of the injustice comes with poor grace from the defenders of the form of world government provided in the covenant of the league of nations.

Some of those whose admiration for European forms of government has weakened their appreciation of the American Constitution, ought to look to it that some of the superior virtues they perceive in parliamentary government should be embedded in the constitution of the super-state they are trying to shove over on the people of the United States. If the Senate is to be attacked for participating in treaty making, it ought to be shown that its interference is against, rather than in behalf, of the liberalization of the proposed super-government. Moreover, when the Senate is arraigned as misrepresentative of public sentiment, better evidence that it has defied public opinion in Americanizing the league of nations covenant should be produced than the mere bald assertion of the attacking special pleader. The election result of 1918, in the face of President Wilson's demand that he be given credentials as the sole representative of American sentiment at the peace conference, with its adverse plurality of a million votes, does not bear out the contention that Mr. Wilson is always old Vox Populi.

The real truth is that in the present emergency in the life of the republic the United States Senate has magnificently vindicated the belief of the founders of this republic, some of whom were almost as wise as their modern critics, that arbitrary power to determine the very destiny of the nation should not be lodged in the hands of one man, even one so much wiser and better than all his predecessors as the present inspired incumbent of the Presidency admits himself to be. The crisis has demonstrated that deliberation and debate are not out of place in a free government. The one legislative body in the world in which the peace treaty and covenant have been actually debated has been the United States Senate. The one nation in the world in which the people have discussed this question and in which popular sentiment has had anything to do with its determination, is the United States of America. Despite the overshadowing importance of the issue this is the one country in which the general public has studied and debated it.

The league of nations covenant was put through the assemblage of representatives of the victorious belligerents at Paris, without deliberation or debate, at the end of an hour's session during which even the asking of questions was shut off. It was not submitted to the legislative representatives, much loss to the people themselves, of any nation. It was thrust upon a world under the methods of a strong-arm ward caucus, with the order to "take it or let it alone." Here was a military council, convened without any authority to formulate a world government, "saving the world for democracy" by attempting final action upon a scheme of world government. It was as if George Washington and his generals had written a constitution for the United States at Yorktown, and told the several colonies that it was not their province to either initiate or amend, but only to accept in toto the scheme of government they had devised, otherwise the new government would bind them anyway and they would be treated as outcasts by their allies in the Revolutionary war!

It was because we had a Senate in this country that American public sentiment was brought to bear upon the treaty and covenant. It was the Senate that made it possible for the American people to inform themselves as to the provisions and implications of the treaty, without waiting for the rude awakening which has come to the rest of the world as to the real meaning of much of what was written into this most colossal failure in peace-making the world has ever witnessed. Possibly the treaty and covenant might have been rushed through a larger legislative body, like the House of Representatives, under the whip and spur of a few leaders and the five minute debate rule. But it is a fundamental safeguard of free government that the people should think first, and act afterward, rather than that, in such important matters, they should act in haste and repent at leisure.

Despite the assertions of those who contend that a European parliamentary election is the climax of democracy, and that the checks and balances of the republican form of government are handicaps to popular control of public affairs, the truth is that judging from the actual workings of the system rather than the theoretical imaginings of scholarly commentarians, we have the only government in the world guided by mass opinion. European governments are controlled today, not by mass opinion, but by certain group interests temporarily coalesced, each one of which is thinking, not of the general welfare, but of class or race advantage. This is the inevitable result of the parliamentary system of government as contrasted with representative republican government.

In this republic alone, of all the nations of the world, we repeat, there has been dissection and analysis and discussion of the proposed treaty and league covenant. Here, and nowhere else, the right and the wrong, for instance, of the Shantung decision, the greatest piece of political larceny in the world's history, has been talked of and understood by millions of people. Here, and nowhere else in the world, the great issues involved in the momentous decision involved in acceptance of the proposed world constitution, have been the subjects of discussion in the homes, the shops, on the farms, in the market places; just as the Constitution was discussed in the days of Washington, and again in the days of Marshall, of Webster and of Lincoln. And this great debate, with "the solemn referendum" of the present campaign, has proceeded over the protests of men and elements pretending devotion to democracy and professing to find in the insistence of the American

Senate upon the protection of American rights, interests and ideals in the terms of that covenant, only the machinations of an oligarchy!

Let every lover of human liberty thank God that, after all, there is one country in the world in which laws and institutions are not accepted from the hands of autocrats and super-men as if they were tablets from Mt. Sinai. Most of the world's wars have resulted from the failure of the people who fight and pay for the wars to subject the decisions of their diplomats to sufficient scrutiny and accounting. The professional workers in the secret council chambers of Europe, where diplomats gloss over selfish schemes of national and personal aggrandizement with the veneer of altruism, and divide up the world to the slow music of fine phrases, can put their stuff over on European peasantry all dressed up in the habiliments of a mock democracy they do not know how to use. But in this great reading, thinking land of America, where issues are fought out in the open forum of public opinion, it is necessary to support any project affecting the destiny of this nation and of the world with something more than high-sounding talk, even when backed up by the great world-wide instrumentalities of propaganda which the people of this country have learned, and the people of the rest of the world are learning, are only gigantic falsehood factories, operated in behalf of the concealed purposes of certain powers and international commercial and financial groups.

Yes, independence and freedom and popular government are something more than phrases here. Democracy is a reality and not a mere phrase with which to tickle the ears of the groundlings.

The founders of this republic built mighty bulwarks for the protection of free institutions when they created that trinity of republicanism,—the Congress, with its two chambers representing directly the people individually and in their collective capacity as states; the judiciary, to stand between the people and violation of their reserved personal and property rights by the power of government, and the executive, to take the initiative in foreign relations and to see to it that the laws be executed.

Whoever would tear down this fabric in any part is no true republican.

Whoever would subordinate this one real government of public opinion, this one actual, workable people's nation, to any super-state dominated by governments out of harmony in their purposes with the republic Washington established, Lincoln preserved and the Senate of the United States has saved, is lacking in comprehension of the fundamentals of Americanism, or has succumbed to the seductions of alien propaganda.

-–September 4, 1920.

THE DECISIVE BATTLE

The decisive battle in the last war for American independence will be fought five weeks from next Tuesday.

The LAST war, because if the decision by ballot is that which Americans have before effected by the bullet, the freedom of America to pursue her own way, untrammelled, in the achievement of her own destiny, free from European domination, will never again be challenged.

The American colonists revolted in 1775, and declared their national independence in 1776, because they objected to having their affairs directed from a political capital across the Atlantic, in an environment totally different from that which they had created here.

Our Revolutionary forefathers objected to furnishing men and money in wars, the result of European controversies, with which they had no natural concern. So long as the western hemisphere was a mere exploited area of European colonialism, it was involved in every European war. A family quarrel among European monarchs sent Virginia and Massachusetts soldiers upon forays into Canada, and set savages to scalping white settlers on the unprotected borders of the colonies.

It was to end the reign of Europeanism in the territory of the United Colonies that European soldiers were fired on at Lexington, and the war for independence thus begun was fought to its triumphant conclusion.

One of the objects of the Revolution was political, the other industrial, independence. In colonial days America was looked upon by her European masters as a legitimate object of commercial exploitation for the benefit, not of the colonists, but of Europe. In the repression of American industrial production, trade and shipping, our European masters went to unbelievable lengths. After the political independence of the United States had been achieved, the effort continued to keep America under the industrial domination of Europe. The United States was required to act as a subject nation on the oceans. To procure the freedom of the seas the War of 1812,—the second war for American independence, was fought, and while the immediate result was indecisive, the struggle strengthened the determination of Americans to be in fact, as in name, "free and independent states."

The men who wrote the Declaration and achieved American independence realized that Europeanism and Americanism could not live side by side, that the American continents could not remain "half slave and half free" in their relation to European imperialism. So, when the European yoke was being thrown off by Mexico, Central America and South America, the Monroe Doctrine was enunciated. This was notice served upon Europe that this hemisphere could not be made a field for European colonization, with the consequent transfer to the new world of the European system. The Monroe Doctrine was necessary to supplement American independence and the Washington-Jefferson doctrine of American non-entanglement in the age-old feuds of Europe.

The Wilson league of nations is a device for the sacrifice of American independence and the annullment of the Monroe Doctrine; for bringing the whole world under the domination of Europeanism. It is a plan for the transfer to the United States and to the whole western hemisphere of the European system which our forefathers poured out their blood and treasure to drive across the Atlantic. It was devised by European politicians who have never ceased to cast envious eyes upon the western hemisphere as an area for working out the purposes the European nations have invariably followed in Africa and Asia, where there has been no people strong enough to maintain continental self-determination. It has been accepted by American politicians of recent European origin, close European relationships and sympathies, who are lacking in comprehension of and faith in American fundamentals. Some of them are honestly mistaken, having succumbed to European "culture," and some are agents of Europeanism as surely so as were those a European power maintained in this country a century ago devising and applying means for throttling American commerce, stifling American industry and plotting American division and destruction.

The National Republican was perhaps the first paper of national circulation to begin warfare upon the Wilsonian scheme of sacrificing the identity of America in a world merger; of trading American control of American destiny for minority stock in a world political corporation. This paper deduced the purposes of President Wilson from his declarations during the European war, and the week the armistice was signed The National Republican gave warning that Mr. Wilson's object was to sacrifice American nationality to alienism and internationalism. From that day to this The National Republican has made uncompromising war against the plan to denationalize America, and to sacrifice American ideals, rights and interests to a paper scheme of world government dominated by influences out of sympathy with the fundamentals of Americanism, and during that period has stated many times the fundamental wrongs and errors of the Wilson covenant. But as this last battle for American independence approaches, it will not be out of place to review briefly the more important objections to the acceptance of the un-Americanized league.

AMERICANISM

The covenant of the league of nations was unconstitutionally framed. It represents usurpation of authority by a civil-military conference whose only proper function, under our form of government, was to write a peace treaty and settle the issues of the war. Failure to promptly do this duty has cost the world almost as much as the war itself. The covenant was interwoven in the peace treaty and thrust upon even the peace conference itself in arbitrary European fashion, without opportunity being given to most of those affected by it for either debate or decision. In the formulation of a world constitution President Wilson usurped legislative power not transferable to him under the American Constitution. It was as if Washington and his generals had undertaken to write a constitution for the colonies at Yorktown and to force it upon the American people. This does not fully suggest the odiousness of the usurpation, because in the case of Mr. Wilson he allowed representatives of alien powers to dictate, directly and indirectly, the provisions of this world constitution that was to bind this republic. When he brought it home it was a violation of every principle he had proclaimed as America's purpose during and subsequent to the war, as well as of the fundamentals of historic Americanism.

This usurpation abroad was followed by attempted usurpation at home when President Wilson sought to deny to the Senate a coordinate treaty making body, the right to consider his proposed world constitution, revolutionary in its influence upon American institutions and American destiny, apart from the peace treaty itself. This resulted in the continuance of a technical state of war, and of the unprecedented and in many respects unconstitutional war-time powers of the President. It resulted in vast injury to the interests of this nation and of the world in general.

Indeed, President Wilson carried his usurpation to the point of attempting to deny to the Senate its constitutional right of advising and consenting in the formulation of treaties. Refusing to yield an inch to the convictions of senators, bound under the Constitution they had sworn to uphold and protect, to see to it that their country was not sacrificed by any international convention, he and his followers have sought to coerce a Senate majority into action against its conscience and judgment. During all this time the physical and mental condition of the President has remained, through the course followed by his friends and followers, a subject of conjecture here and abroad.

The peace treaty itself sows the seeds of future war by parcelling out among certain victorious powers millions of square miles of territory and scores of millions of subject peoples, not to mention billions of dollars in indemnities. The treaty and the covenant provide the means of ensuring the permanency of these spoils of war, and make the United States, which has wanted and received no territory, trade advantage or indemnity, the principal, because

the richest and strongest, guarantor of these war gains. Under
the treaty as brought home by President Wilson this republic even
approves the substitution of a Japanese for a Prussian invader in
the richest province of the republic of China, a republic formed
in emulation of our own, which went into war at our instance in
the belief that this nation would continue to be the steadfast friend
of justice in the Orient. This vast acquisition of war gains, with
its underwriting not only by the powers which profit by them, but
by this country which asks and gets nothing material out of the
war, is the fundamental basis of the peace treaty, the commissions
created under it, and of the league of nations itself.

The league of nations covenant provides for the rule of the
world by force, through a world parliament of two chambers, in
which we have one vote out of seven in one body, and in the other
have as many votes as Hayti and Santo Domingo, Salvador and
Honduras, but one-sixth as many as the British Empire, which
has a smaller self-governing population than the United States.
It does not provide for disarmament, except of the central empires, or even provide the means whereby disarmament may be
brought about without the general consent which could effect it
tomorrow without the intervention of a league. No concealment
is made of the fact that while the chief military power of the world
has been destroyed, the chief naval power will maintain its mastery of the seas. This preparation for war recognizes the inev-
itability of war by the great nation which, with its world-wide
relationships, will necessarily be the dominating factor in the proposed world government.

Article X, which President Wilson has described as "the heart
of the covenant," binds this republic in language as clear as has
ever been used in a public document, to furnish men and money
to defend the boundaries of nations as defined in the peace treaty,
and to intervene by force in any war to which we are committed
by the league of nations. No amount of denial will change the
fact that this is the clear provision of the treaty. The objections
made to a declaration by the Senate in the form of a reservation,
that this country will not go into any war except by act of Congress, prove that the framers of the covenant know that the covenant binds us to participation in every war that may occur in the
world. Otherwise they would not object to the reservation.

Other provisions of the covenant, especially the labor clauses,
involve this country in a world-wide financial, industrial and labor
communism from which we could gain nothing and through which
we might be called upon to sacrifice much. In his famous Fourteen points, the chief proponent of the Wilson covenant declared
that one of his objects was to bring about universal free trade and
an equality of economic conditions among nations. These provisions of the covenant lead to the object of a world-wide leveling

of conditions. With some of the world it might mean leveling up; with us it would be leveling down.

The assumption of those who declare that the rest of the world wants peace and justice and good will among men, and is ready to disarm and dwell in brotherhood as one great happy family, is either an ignorant or an audacious denial of the most palpable facts. Such a theory in the present course of European and Asiatic powers encounters a thousand flat contradictions. The United States is the only powerful nation in the world that has up to this time developed an altruistic international policy. To go into a combination dominated by selfish, grasping powers, and their tools and pawns among the smaller nations, would be to sacrifice this nation's world-wide influence as an exemplar of free government and of fair treatment of other nations. It would involve us in the entanglements of European intrigue, with our own politics torn by constant conflict based upon the alien partisanship aroused in our polyglot politicians through the subordination of domestic to foreign issues.

Those who declare that Republican opposition to American subordination in a world league of force is based upon mere selfish nationalism either intentionally misrepresent the Republican attitude or are incapable of comprehending the fundamental American ideals upon which that opposition is based. When Governor Cox says that he sees no difference between the doctrine "America First" and that of "Deutschland Ueber Alles" he merely confesses that he cannot comprehend the difference between what America stands for and what imperial Germany stood for under the Kaiser. Republicans believe not in "America above all," but in "America before all" in the minds and hearts of Americans; and in this they think of America as an instrumentality of world-wide service to the cause of human liberty, as America has always been from the beginning. Republicans believe in a league of justice, a world court with its decisions based upon equity as defined in an amplified code of international law to which all nations shall pledge their allegiance; not a world government parallel with or superior to our own, with decisions by legislative representatives of the governments of the world, based upon interest rather than upon generally accepted basic principles of right.

Europeanism and Americanism are fundamentally at variance. Europeanism stands for that separateness in language, dialect, dress, race, religion and locality which has made Europe a crazy quilt geographically, and through religious, racial and dynastic antagonisms, the fruitage of centuries of circumstances beyond our influence or control, has kept that continent a bloody cockpit of nations for centuries. These conflicts have only been accentuated by the crowding process which has come with the improvement of means of transportation and communication. Internally these nations preserve the stratification of class and caste; their governments are dominated by groups and combinations of groups, composed of class conscious elements filled with a hatred that frequently blazes into conflict, because of which public order can be maintained only by force. Americanism stands for the blending of European races, classes, religions, nationalities, into one homogeneous whole, in accordance with our national motto: "Out of many, one." During the entire European war, with millions of people within our borders representing all the nations in conflict, there was no clash between Greeks and Bulgarians, Italians and Austrians, Turks and Serbians. Federation has solved in this republic problems which in Europe seem hopeless. We believe in America, too, that the general welfare should be the sole object of national legislation and administration. Those who seek to set up class government here, are agents of Europeanism incapable of comprehending American fundamentals. No man who seeks to place the selfish interests of a group or class or section above the general interests of the whole public, is a good American. He is tainted with Europeanism, and the sort of politics which is based upon group or class or caste demands is a European importation.

A few only of the important objections to American acceptance of the un-Americanized covenant have been mentioned. Are they not enough to prove that the United States should have the right to specify the terms upon which we will enter into a world-wide government? Should we commit ourselves, irrevocably, and without leaving an easy means of escape, to an experiment which hazards what Americans hold dear and which has been and is of so much value to the entire world,—independent American nationality, with its policy of disinterested friendship for all nations, alliance or combination with none?
—September 25, 1920.

The argument that the Monroe Doctrine can have no validity because it has never received legislative sanction, carries with it no weight. Many rules of international law impose an obligation derived from usage alone. The original declaration of Mr. Monroe is a precedent—acknowledged by the American people, and to a certain extent acquiesced in by European authorities. Hardly a President since Mr. Monroe has omitted to refer to it in language of approval. It has always been regarded as a question independent of party politics, save perhaps in its application to the Congress at Panama. It has been persistently asserted by the majority of American statesmen; and to declare that it cannot obtain as a universal obligation is practically to throw discredit upon Washington's farewell address, whose recommendations, though never embodied in statutes or approved by resolution of Congress, have frequently shaped the foreign and domestic policy of the government.—George F. Tucker, 1885.

PRESIDENT WILSON TO HIS "FELLOW-COUNTRYMEN"

A man may know the Bible by heart and still be an infidel. President Wilson's assertion, in his latest campaign letter, that he is better able to interpret Americanism than others are because he has spent his life in the study of American history, is not convincing.

A man may know all about American history and still be something less than a thoroughly indoctrinated American. President Wilson's study of American institutions has, confessedly, convinced him that some European forms of government, at least, are better than our own. Study of American and European authorities, admittedly, has Europeanized, not Americanized, him.

The most unlettered man in this republic, possessed by the spirit of Americanism, is a better exponent of American ideals than the most scholarly student of history and economics who has by that process become Europeanized. The man, illiterate or educated, who loves his own country better than he loves other nations, is a patriot. The man, illiterate or educated, who thinks it is a sign of narrowness to care more for his own land than he does for the world in general, is an internationalist.

There is poison as well as healing in mere learning. "Much learning hath made him mad," is a Biblical phrase as full of meaning today as when it was uttered. Unfortunately all our institutions of higher education have not been wellsprings of patriotism. Some of them have done much to undermine the faith of youth in the institutions of their country and to substitute alien for American ideals.

It may be said, therefore, that President Wilson has not settled the argument about the league of nations when he calls attention to the fact that he has studied American history more exhaustively than have most others, and therefore claims he is better qualified than are most others to say what Americanism is. It is not "audacious," as President Wilson claims, to suggest that George Washington, Thomas Jefferson, Andrew Jackson, James Monroe, Abraham Lincoln and Theodore Roosevelt were right in their views as to what constitutes real Americanism. If Woodrow Wilson is right, all these men were wrong, for what they established and preserved and maintained, Mr. Wilson, with his un-

Americanized league of nations covenant, would jeopardize and possibly destroy.

The men who established and preserved this republic were not Prussian in spirit, as President Wilson charges, because they believed, as they did, in the doctrine of America first. There is a world of difference between the Prussian doctrine of "Germany above all" and the traditional American motto of "America before all" in the minds and hearts of Americans. No one knows better than does President Wilson that the other nations with whose representatives he sat at the Paris peace conference were thinking of their own governments first. The terms of the treaty of peace prove that. Every man of common sense knows that these nations are still thinking first of themselves, and it is only here, in this one country which asked and got nothing material out of the war, where the doctrine is being preached that it is our duty to sacrifice national rights, interests and ideals in order to convince humanity in general that we are really as unselfish as we are supposed to be.

It is true, as President Wilson says, that the founding fathers thought of this nation as "the light of the world." But the men who cut this country loose from European domination, and sought to preserve it permanently from European entanglements, knew that this light would burn only in the untainted air of freedom. To carry the torch of Americanism across the Atlantic and expose it to the damps of European intrigue and conflict, without a change in the atmosphere, would be to extinguish the flame. A light house is of service only so long as it remains on its own foundations. To put it afloat at sea would be to destroy the beacon. "To set a responsible example to all the world of what free government is and can do for the maintenance of right standards" has indeed been the very mission which America has been performing all the way from George Washington to Woodrow Wilson. Now it is proposed by Mr. Wilson that we abandon this position as an exemplar of national righteousness, and go into political partnership, as minority stock holders, with all the rest of the world; to lose our identity in a super-state dominated by nations whose ideals are as far from those the history of our nation has exemplified, as Tokio is from Mt. Vernon. President Wilson says that failure to abandon the American tradition of independence—he calls it "isolation,"—would be to "relegate the United States to a subordinate role in the affairs of nations." Were we, as a nation, at the time Mr. Wilson came to the Presidency after a century and a third of the Washington policy, playing a subordinate role in the affairs of nations? In the opinion of President Wilson, of course, we were at least playing second fiddle,—but what did the war disclose as to the physical and moral power of America in the midst of a world crisis?

"Why should we be afraid of responsibilities which we are qualified to sustain?" inquires President Wilson. There are those who believe that it is not a sign of courage for any man to want to cause his country to abandon policies under which it has become the greatest nation in the world, and risk the very sovereignty of the republic through the national subordination involved in acceptance of the league of nations covenant as President Wilson brought it home with him. The American people are not "afraid" of their responsibilities; they were meeting them before President Wilson was born and they will be discharging them long after the Wilson league is dead and buried. The American people will "live up to the great expectations which they created by entering the war." They brought the war to a triumphant conclusion. Alone among all the victorious powers they asked nothing by way of reward. What other expectations were reasonably entertained of them? That they would remain in Europe for all time to police and finance the forty or fifty nations, little and big, which constitute Europe's political crazy quilt, as some slight recompense for having spent billions of dollars, raised millions of troops, and sacrificed scores of thousands of lives in the cause of European civilization?

There is a great deal of gabble like this about our "obligations" to Europe, but no one seems able to explain how the service and sacrifice involved in our thirty months of participation in the war made America the debtor of the allies, rather than the world the debtor of the United States, which did not ask for an inch of soil, a foot of shipping, or a dollar of indemnity while the other victorious powers divided up millions of square miles of land, fleets of ships, and billions of dollars. Of all the statements parroted in this country by mindless thinkers the claim that America owes Europe anything is by all odds the most asininely unpatriotic, because idiotically unjust to the United States.

"Surely we shall not fail to keep the promise sealed in the death and sacrifice of our incomparable soldiers, sailors and marines, who await our verdict beneath the soil of France." The reiterated claim that the soldiers, sailors and marines who died fighting on European soil under the American flag, fell for the Wilson league of nations is the grossest profanation. The Americans who died in France fell long before the league of nations was hatched in secret conclave at Paris. The vast majority of the men who fought and survived repudiate indignantly the suggestion that they fought for Wilsonism rather than Americanism: that they fought to involve their country in the meshes of European militarism and navalism, rather than to free their country from its menace.

"Those who do not care to tell you the truth about the league of nations tell you that Article X of the covenant of the league would make it possible for other nations to lead us into war whether we willed it by our own independent judgment or not," continues President Wilson, and adds: "This is absolutely false."

Article X will be judged by the American people not on the basis of what President Wilson thinks it says, but by what they know it says. Article X says that the members of the league are committed to participation in the military and naval measures necessary to the enforcement of the decisions of the league. Congress might, it is true, refuse to carry out our obligation, but only by the sacrifice of the plighted faith of the nation. President Wilson has described this as being "only a moral obligation." But a moral obligation means as much to a nation jealous of its honor as a legal obligation. If Article X does not commit the American government to contribute military force for the execution of the decrees of the league, why does President Wilson insist that a reservation setting forth clearly that this country will not be bound to do this except by the affirmative action of Congress, is a blow at the heart of the covenant? Why depend upon the mere verbal assurances of President Wilson that the covenant means this or that, while he so stoutly protests against a plain statement of the limitations of our obligations under the contract we are asked to sign?

President Wilson declares that the people "have been grossly misled with regard to the treaty, and particularly with regard to the proposed character of the league of nations, by those who have assumed the serious responsibility of opposing it." The advantages of publicity in connection with the league of nations covenant and the treaty have all been with President Wilson and his partisans. The President enjoys the peculiar privilege of having his every statement quoted by practically every newspaper in the United States. Since President Wilson returned from Europe and abandoned the policy of secrecy which surrounded every step in the formulation of the treaty and covenant, his contentions with reference to the meaning and implications of the treaty and covenant have been published so widely that every citizen of the country has had opportunity to read his side of the case. Millions upon millions of dollars of public money has been spent in propaganda in behalf of the unexpurgated treaty and covenant. Educational and religious agencies have been unsparingly used in the campaign to blot out the old standards of Americanism and substitute for them the tenets of Wilson internationalism. Great financial interests, having much to gain by the pooling of world interests and the underwriting of European obligations with all of America's wealth and man power, have brought heavy pressure to bear upon the business interests of the country. For a time this vast machinery of propaganda seemed about to accomplish its purpose. But here, and here alone among all the nations of the world, public questions are publicly debated and decided. Here, month after month, the tide of public protest has risen higher and higher as the people have better and better comprehended the true inwardness of what it has been sought to put over on them as a substitute for the old-fashioned Americanism that has maintained peace and prosperity in this free land while Europe and Asia have been suffering continuously the scourge of war, through deliberate failure and refusal to accept the ideals and institutions of which we have been, as President Wilson says, so long the exemplar.

Yes, the American people "want their country's honor vindicated." They do not recognize the vagaries of President Wilson, pressed upon the Paris peace conference by an executive fresh from repudiation by the American people under the "great and solemn referendum" of 1918, as in any sense binding upon them; they do not consider the rejection of his program under their constitutional rights, as a sacrifice of "their country's honor." They deny that there is any warrant for such a pretension.

"This election is to be a genuine national referendum." This statement of President Wilson's is fully warranted by the facts. The rumblings of that approaching referendum are already echoing. Georgia has spoken in the nomination, by the President's own party, of a bitter opponent of the Wilson brand of internationalism as a candidate for United States senator. Maine has spoken by an unprecedented Republican plurality. The rest of the country is ready to vote. For the first time there will be an expression on the commitments of the Wilson covenant by the one voice that is competent to bind the American people to any great national decision,—the voice of public opinion. The verdict will settle for all time, to the satisfaction of the world, the question of whether this is a government by one man or by a hundred million people. Even the author of President Wilson's campaign letter of 1920 will not be puzzled as to the meaning of the great referendum's result.

—October 9, 1920.

At what point shall we expect the approach of danger? By what means shall we fortify against it? Shall we expect some trans-Atlantic military giant to step the ocean and crush us at a blow? Never! All the armies of Europe, Asia and Africa combined with all the treasure of the earth (our own excepted) in their military chest, with a Bonaparte for a commander, could not by force take a drink from the Ohio or make a track in the Blue Ridge in a trial of a thousand years.

At what point, then, is the approach of danger to be expected? I answer, if it ever reach us it must spring up amongst us; it cannot come from abroad. If destruction be our lot we must ourselves be its author and finisher. As a nation of free men we must live through all time or die by suicide.

I hope I am over wary; but if I am not, there is even now something of evil omen amongst us. I mean the increasing disregard

AMERICANISM

for law which pervades the country—the growing disposition to substitute the wild and furious passions in lieu of the sober judgment of courts, and the worse than savage mobs for the executive ministers of justice. * * *

The answer is simple. Let every American, every lover of liberty, every well-wisher of his posterity, swear by the blood of the revolution never to violate in the least particular the laws of the country, and never to tolerate their violation by others. * * * Let reverence for the laws be breathed by every American mother to the lisping babe that prattles on her lap; let it be taught in the schools, in seminaries and in colleges; let it be written in primers, in spelling books and in almanacs; let it be preached from the pulpits, proclaimed in legislative halls and enforced in courts of justice. And, in short, let it become the political religion of the nation; and let the old and the young, the rich and the poor, the grave and the gay of all sexes and tongues and colors and conditions, sacrifice unceasingly upon its altars.—Abraham Lincoln.

We give thy natal day to hope,
  O Country of our love and prayer!
The way is down no fatal slope,
  But up to freer sun and air.

Tried as by furnace fires, and yet
  By God's grace only stronger made,
In future tasks before thee set
  Thou shalt not lack the old-time aid.

The fathers sleep, but men remain
  As wise, as true, and brave as they;
Why count the loss and not the gain?
  The best is that we have today.
          *   *   *   *   *
Great without seeking to be great
  By fraud or conquest, rich in gold,
But richer in the large estate
  Of virtue which thy children hold,

With peace that comes of purity
  And strength to simple justice due,
So runs our loyal dream of thee;
  God of our fathers! make it true.

O Land of lands; to thee we give
  Our prayers, our hopes, our service free;
For thee thy sons shall nobly live,
  And at thy need shall die for thee!
                    —John Greenleaf Whittier.

THE OLD GOSPEL OF AMERICANISM

There is no justification for the pretense of the Democratic press of the country that Senator Harding has, during the course of the campaign, modified his position on the league of nations.

The declarations of the Republican candidate have from the beginning squared with the Republican national platform declaration on the league of nations.

The notification speech, the speech on the league to the Indianapolis delegation, and the recent speech at Des Moines, are of exactly the same significance. They express unyielding opposition to certain outstanding features of both treaty and covenant as they were brought home from Paris by President Wilson, and voice a purpose to accept no international arrangement sacrificial, as these are, of the rights, ideals and interests of the American republic.

Candidate Cox, who at the very outset of the campaign journeyed to Washington to take the oath of allegiance to the Democratic sovereign and declare his complete at-oneness with the administration program of American denationalization, has been talking of his willingness to accept "clarifying resolutions." The Democratic national platform indicated willingness to accept reservations to the league of nations covenant which would "make clearer the obligations of the United States" under the league. There has been an effort to make the country believe that such declarations as these represent a spirit of compromise with those dubious of the treaty's obligations and implications. But what the supporters of the Lodge reservations demanded was not clarification, but rectification of the covenant. Their complaint was not and is not that the provisions of the contract are doubtful, but that they are clearly destructive of American sovereignty, peace and prosperity.

In his Des Moines speech Senator Harding in a few ringing sentences swept away all this fabric of false pretense. The evils of the covenant as proposed by President Wilson are not merely accidental and incidental; they are fundamental and fatal. The world must be made to understand that we will go into no arrangement for world regulation which leaves even a shadow of doubt as to the maintenance of our national independence or our continued adherance to the policies of Washington and Monroe. The differences between Governor Cox and Senator Harding on this issue are not mere matters of verbiage, but of principle. They involve

199

conflicting conceptions of the nature and mission and destiny of this nation. One of these candidates would Europeanize America and the other would make America more American than ever, believing that Europe is in more need of Americanization than America is of Europeanization.

The Des Moines declaration of complete disagreement with some of the fundamental provisions of the league of nations covenant represents no change of attitude on the part of Senator Harding or of the Republican party. The method of amending the league of nations covenant by the process of reservations was not intended to be a compromise of vital American principles and policies which the acceptance of the covenant as originally written would have destroyed. This method of amendment was adopted only because it seemed to be the process least destructive of the general idea of an association of nations for the preservation of the peace of the world, which the Republican party accepts. It was not intended to convey the idea that Republican leadership accepted the general policy of erecting a super-government sacrificial of American sovereignty, rights and ideals. Because these reservations involved a declaration of such non-acceptance they were termed "destructive" by President Wilson. His conception of a reservation, and the conception accepted by Governor Cox when he embraced the Wilson program, is that there should be even more clearly written into the covenant the doctrine that this nation takes upon itself responsibility for forever feeding, financing and fighting the world as occasion may demand under the terms of the pact. And so Senator Harding said at Des Moines:

"My position, I think, has been made perfectly plain; but whether it has or not, his (Governor Cox's) position is beyond cavil, and that is that we shall go into the Paris league without modification or substantial qualification.

"To such a betrayal of my countrymen I will never consent. To those who desire to incur the hazard of intrusting any of the powers of the republic to the direction of a super-government, or, if you prefer, to a council of foreign powers, whether the obligation to follow the council's direction be one of legal or of moral compulsion, I frankly say: 'Vote the Democratic ticket and pray God to protect you from the consequences of your folly.' "

Again Senator Harding said:

"I oppose the proposed league not because I fail to understand what a former member of the Democratic administration has said 'we are being let in for,' but because I believe I understand precisely what we are being let in for. I do not want to clarify these obligations: I want to turn my back on them. It is not interpretation, but rejection, that I am seeking. My position is that the proposed league strikes a deadly blow at our constitutional integrity and surrenders to a dangerous extent our independence of action."

AMERICANISM

These declarations are exactly in line with the Republican national platform and with the prior pronouncements of Senator Harding. The real complaint against them is not that they lack clearness, but that they are entirely too clear to suit those who either openly or by stealth would alienate the blood-bought rights and liberties of the American people. In his Des Moines speech Senator Harding does not, as is falsely asserted, reject the general plan of international cooperation for the preservation of world peace in so far as this may be done without incurring obligations which, while they might help to guarantee for the time being the peace of other continents by making us the world's policeman and almoner, would perpetually menace the peace of our own republic because of the obligation to keep the quarrelsome powers of older continents from one another's throats. Senator Harding declared in his Des Moines speech that "to formulate a plan of international cooperation which will contribute to the security and peace of the world without sacrificing or dangerously diluting our power to direct our own actions is a task of no small difficulty." He therefore does not arrogantly assume to say, without regard to the opinions of others it is proper for him to consult in formulating plans on behalf of the nation, just what the program will be when responsibility comes to the new administration, but:

"I am in favor of America meeting her every righteous obligation in this respect. But I shall never present to the Senate any compact by which we shall in any degree surrender or leave in doubt the sovereign power of the United States to determine, without the compulsion or restraint of any extra-constitutional body, how and when and to what extent our duty in that respect shall be discharged.

"As soon as possible after my election I shall advise with the best minds in the United States, and especially I shall consult in advance with the Senate, with whom, by the terms of the Constitution, I shall indeed be bound to counsel and without whose consent no such international association can be formed. I shall do this to the end that we shall have an association of nations for the promotion of international peace, but one which shall so definitely safeguard our sovereignty and recognize our ultimate and unmortgaged freedom of action that it will have back of it, not a divided and distracted sentiment, but the united support of the American people. Without such united support no plan can be made fully or permanently successful."

Is there anything ambiguous, or objectionable to any genuine American, holding to American rather than to alien ideals, in this declaration of principles or in this program? In view of the fact that in any association of nations for the preservation of the peace of the world, this republic must contribute the influence of the one great power that has no selfish interest to serve either in the treaty of peace or the league of nations compact, why should not the United States say upon what terms it will enter such an **asso-ciation**, rather than accept a hand-me-down, made in Europe world constitution framed by Europeans on the European model? And if the rest of the world is unwilling to accept a league which imposes obligations upon the United States without honestly meeting the conditions essential to our consistent entry into it, why should the American republic feel the slightest obligation to enter the arrangement at all? Why should any American who thinks of the interests and ideals and security of his own country before he thinks of the selfish interests of other nations, want to involve this country in a world organization to which we contribute assets and from which we contract only liabilities? Why should the blood and treasure of this country be pledged to the rest of the world except on terms acceptable to the people of this country, and why should any man or set of men undertake to commit the American people to any arrangement in the perfection of which they have not been consulted, as Senator Harding proposes to consult them?

The lines of battle have not changed in this campaign from the day of the adoption of the Republican national platform. Senator Harding has stood squarely upon that platform. He has proved himself a candidate who fits that platform. He has expounded it with a thoughtfulness, eloquence and patriotism which has commanded, increasingly from day to day, the admiration and respect and confidence of the American people. The claim that the Des Moines speech or any other speech from the notification address on down, has represented a shift of position, expresses either a failure to comprehend the plain meaning of the English language, a failure to read the speeches, or an unfair partisan desire to misrepresent them.

Senator Harding stands for any plan of international association for the restoration and maintenance of world peace that will not sacrifice the American people's own hope of security, progress and fulfillment of national destiny. He is against the bogus, made-in-Europe, scheme of super-government which mentions, but does not provide disarmament, which speaks of, but does not arrange for that justice in international relationships upon which alone peace may securely be established, which, while breathing sentiments of international altruism, is linked with a treaty conveying more of the spoils of war than were ever before transferred by a conqueror's terms of peace and under which more wars are raging today than were ever in progress at any one time in world history prior to the outbreak of the very war this treaty and covenant were written to terminate!

The meaning of all this may not be clear to Governor Cox, his running mate, Mr. Roosevelt, and the Democratic press and politicians; but it is sufficiently plain to the American people in general. With a unanimity unprecedented in American history

since the second election of James Monroe, they will **go to the** polls on November 2nd and there give notice to **the** world that the doctrine preached in this campaign by Warren G. Harding **is** the **undefiled** gospel of Americanism as we inherited it from **our** fathers, and as we will transmit it, please God, to our **children and** our children's children.
—October **16, 1920.**

Flag of the heroes who left us their glory,
  Borne through their battlefields' thunder and flame,
Blazoned in song and illumined in story,
  Wave o'er us all who inherit their fame!
    Up with our banner bright,
    Sprinkled with starry light,
Spread its fair emblems from mountain to shore,
    While through the sounding sky
    Loud rings the Nation's cry—
Union and Liberty! One Evermore!

Light of our firmament, guide of our Nation,
  Pride of her children, and honored afar,
Let the wide beams of thy full constellation
  Scatter each cloud that would darken a star!

Empire unsceptred! what foe shall assail thee,
  Bearing the standard of Liberty's van?
Think not the God of thy fathers shall fail **thee,**
  Striving with men for the birthright of **man!**

Lord of **the** Universe! shield us and guide us,
  Trusting Thee always, through shadow and **sun!**
Thou hast united us, who shall divide us?
  Keep us, oh, keep us the Many in One!
    Up with our banner bright,
    Sprinkled with starry light,
Spread its fair emblems from mountain to shore,
    While through the sounding sky
    Loud rings the Nation's cry—
Union and Liberty! One Evermore!
                    —Oliver Wendell Holmes.

America, in the assembly of nations, since her admission among them, has invariably, though often fruitlessly, held forth to them the hand of honest friendship, of equal freedom, of generous reciprocity. She has uniformly spoken among them though often **to** heedless and often disdainful ears, the language of equal liberty, equal justice and equal rights. She has in the lapse of nearly half

203

a century without a single exception respected the independence of other nations, while asserting and maintaining her own. She has abstained from interference in the concerns of others even where the conflict has been for principles to which she clings as to the last vital drop that visits the heart. She has seen that probably for centuries to come all the contests of that Acceldama, the European world, will be contests between inveterate power and emerging right. Wherever the standard of freedom and independence has been or shall be unfurled, there will be her heart, her benediction and her prayers. But she goes not abroad in search of monsters to destroy. She is the well wisher to the freedom and independence of all. She is the champion and vindicator only of her own. She will recommend the general cause by the countenance of her voice and the benignant sympathy of her example. She well knows that by once enlisting under other banners than her own, were they even the banners of foreign independence she would involve herself beyond the power of extrication in all the wars of interest and intrigue, of individual avarice, envy and ambition which assume the colors and usurp the standard of freedom. The fundamental maxims of her policy would insensibly change from liberty to force. The frontlet upon her brows would no longer beam with splendor of freedom and independence but in its stead would soon be substituted an imperial diadem flashing in false and tarnished lustre, the murky radiance of dominion and power. She might become the dictatress of the world: she would no longer be the ruler of her own spirit.—John Quincy Adams.

Give me white paper!
This which you use is black and rough with smears
Of sweat and grime and fraud and blood and tears,
Crossed with the story of men's sins and fears,
Of battle and of famine all these years,
    When all God's children had forgot their birth,
    And drudged and fought and died like beasts of earth.

"Give me white paper!"
One storm-trained seaman listened to the word;
What no man saw he saw; he heard what no man heard.
    In answer he compelled the sea
    To eager man to tell
    The secret she had kept so well!
Left blood and guilt and tyranny behind—
Sailing still west the hidden shore to find;
    For all mankind that unstained scroll unfurled,
    Where God might write anew the story of the World.
                  —Edward Everett Hale.

LAST CALL TO SERVICE

We are in the closing days of a national campaign. The next issue of The National Republican will record the result.

If you have not been stirred by the issues of this campaign, there is something the matter with you, as an American citizen. For these issues have been fundamental. They affect for better or worse the status of every citizen of this republic, now and henceforth. The effect of the great decision of November 2nd will be felt to the last generation of Americans. In a vital way it will determine the destiny of this republic.

There are those who affect a pose of indifference to politics. They scoff at interest and activity in politics. They profess to be too wise, too impartial, too judicious, to take seriously the debates and the organization activities of a campaign. Whether such an attitude be the result of ignorance, of indifference, or of selfishness, the effect is the same. A republic having for its support and direction the suffrages only of such people as these would be a nation adrift upon the rocks.

No one is foolish enough to imagine that any business enterprise is destined to success if its affairs be indifferently conducted. Thoughtful direction is necessary to the progress and prosperity of any human undertaking. A government like ours, in which sovereignty is vested in citizenship, will go to wreck unless the people study and help to solve by active participation in the settlement of public questions, the problems which confront the nation.

Every national election determines national destiny. As between the alternatives presented in each national campaign the choice of the people cannot lead to identical results. Either choice cannot be equally wise. This year the issues are more clearly defined than usual. The differences between the two great political parties, in their platforms and in their candidates, are so distinct that no one not dull witted or thoughtless could contend for a moment that conditions in this country four years, ten years, fifty years hence, will be the same regardless of which ticket is successful.

Looking back over the history of this republic from the very beginning we know that every election result has been important in its permanent influence upon national history. This is not the same country it would have been if Douglas had beaten Lincoln, if Seymour had defeated Grant, if Harrison had been re-elected, if Bryan had defeated McKinley or Parker, Roosevelt. Who knows

205

what the history of this country would have been during the past few years if a united Republican party had elected a President in 1912, or if Hughes, instead of Wilson, had been chosen President in 1916?

How closely a national election result may touch any given home no member of that household may be certain. It may put its hand upon some boy and send him to die in Siberia or Italy. It may bring unemployment to the head of the household and consequent deprivation to every dweller in the home. It may cheapen or heighten the cost of daily living; it may broaden or narrow opportunity for a new generation; it may lighten or make heavier the burden of taxation; it may increase or decrease educational or economic opportunity; it may make more secure or insecure the guarantees of free citizenship. In some degree every national election decision is certain to do some of these things.

But, some cynics argue, all political parties are "rotten,"—all are therefore unworthy of confidence. Political parties are "rotten" just in proportion as the millions who go to make them up are "rotten" or indifferent to rottenness themselves; no more so; no less so. Political parties may be the playthings of politicians having in mind only the spoils of office, and the advantages of power; or they may be noble instrumentalities of public service. What they are depends upon the people themselves, and those who argue against general participation in politics contribute thereby to the very end they suggest as an argument against participation in party affairs.

But political parties are not rotten. Sometimes they have wrong headed and even corrupt leadership. It is safe to assume that the overwhelming majority of the members of all political parties have the same object in view,—and that their country's good. But good intentions do not of themselves produce good results. Some of the most harmful men and movements in history have been inspired by good purposes. What the citizen must study and decide is whether the record of a given political leadership in power, and whether the measures it proposes in the country's interests, lead to the conclusion that this leadership will in fact help or harm the republic. Here arises the necessity of public discussion of public issues, that they may be decided intelligently as well as patriotically.

This is the one government in the world under which general public opinion is determinative of public questions. Here alone public questions are the subject of universal popular discussion. Alien and domestic critics may ridicule the excitement of a national campaign, but it is the manifestation of the public intelligence and the public conscience engaged in arriving at those fateful decisions at the ballot box that represent the exercise of the only sovereignty to which we as Americans yield allegiance.

Does your government, your nation, your republic, mean anything to you? Have you caught something of the spirit of the men who gave it being, and who at the cost of such toil and sacrifice have made it and kept it that you and yours might live within the shelter of a flag that is the symbol of orderly freedom; the banner of the freest, mightiest, happiest land beneath the sun? Are you grateful for your national heritage as an American; are you thoughtful of the national heritage you and others of this, your generation, will hand down to your children and your children's children?

If the pride and sense of responsibility and power of American citizenship dwells within you, apologize to no one for the interest you take in politics, for politics in a republic is the determination of public questions by public opinion. Apologize to no one for having the courage and the enthusiasm of your convictions,—which is no more nor less than partisanship in behalf of the fundamentals of your own creed of patriotism. Feel sorry for, but do not be influenced by any critic of politics or political interest or political partisanship who is too selfish or careless to do the duties of free citizenship manfully, or too bloodless to feel the thrill of participation in a great national decision such as that we are now about to make.

And you who read these lines,—if you believe the cause of Republicanism this year to be, in effect, the cause of your country; if you feel that Republican victory in the election of a Republican President and Congress, is essential to the highest and best interests of your nation; if you feel that by Republican failure the prosperity, the security and even the sovereignty of your republic may be menaced,—why stop with casting your ballot for this cause on November 2nd? Why not arouse your indifferent neighbor to a sense of his responsibility? Why not present your views to your doubting friend? Why not bear a hand in bringing to the polls every possible Republican vote on Tuesday next?

Election day should be a sacred day in the calendar of patriotism. It is a day that every man and woman who can afford to do so should be willing to give to his country. As the evening shadows fall on Tuesday next the fate of this republic, not merely for four years, but for all time, will have been determined. Between now and that time why not do something for your party,—for your country? Not because mere party victory is worth while in itself, but because you, as a Republican, believe that such victory will open to your party the opportunity to bring order out of chaos, to restore the foundations of constitutional government, to throw up once more the coast defenses of American interests and ideals against injurious alien invasion, and to put in the hand of America once more, instead of the club of a world policeman, the blazing torch of Liberty enlightening the world.
—October 30, 1920.

AMERICANISM

In a chariot of light from the regions of day,
  The Goddess of Liberty came;
Ten thousand celestials directed the way,
  And hither conducted the dame.
A fair budding branch from the gardens above,
  Where millions with millions agree,
She brought in her hand as a pledge of her love,
  And the plant she named Liberty Tree.

The celestial exotic struck deep in the ground,
  Like a native it flourished and bore;
The fame of its fruit drew the nations around,
  To seek out this peaceable shore.
Unmindful of names or distinctions they came,
  For freemen like brothers agree;
With one spirit endued, they one friendship pursued,
  And their temple was Liberty Tree.

Beneath this fair tree, like the patriarchs of old,
  Their bread in contentment they ate
Unvexed with the troubles of silver and gold,
  The cares of the grand and the great.
With timber and tar they Old England supplied,
  And supported her power on the sea;
Her battles they fought, without getting a groat,
  For the honor of Liberty Tree.

But hear; O ye swains, 'tis a tale most profane,
  How all the tyrannical powers,
Kings, Commons and Lords, are uniting amain,
  To cut down this guardian of ours;
From the east to the west blow the trumpet to arms,
  Through the land let the sound of it flee,
Let the far and the near, all unite with a cheer,
  In defence of our Liberty Tree.
                              —Thomas Paine.

America is more than fertile fields, more than bursting banks, more than waving flags. The America in which one must believe, and for which he must sacrifice, is constitutional liberty and justice according to law, guaranteed and administered by three coordinate branches of government. Just in proportion as we weaken the energy of the system through changes in the Constitution—which Washington so earnestly warned against—we undermine what thus far no one has succeeded in overthrowing.—Leslie M. Shaw.

THE MEANING OF TUESDAY'S TRIUMPH

By majorities which stagger the imagination, the Republican party has been swept into power on the crest of the most tremendous tidal wave that ever bore one political party to triumph and engulfed another in disaster. The most sanguine expectations of the prophets of Republican success have been exceeded in the unprecedented magnitude of Republican triumph. Every state in the Union where elections represent a real expression of public opinion has broken all records in the size of its Republican majorities. City and country, east, north and west, have joined in rendering a common verdict; in setting the seal of condemnation upon the party in power and in calling the Republican party to the great task of national restoration.

In all the history of this republic there has not been a more impressive manifestation of the power of public opinion. Millions have yielded up their traditional party predilections, and have joined in a vote of protest against the record of the present national administration in both domestic and foreign affairs. These same millions have selected the Republican party as the instrumentality through which the republic is to be led from chaos to order; through which the fundamentals of constitutional government are to be re-established; through which this nation is again to be governed by a leadership frankly and fearlessly pro-American in its spirit and its policies.

* * * * *

How remarkable this manifestation of what we call public opinion; of the essential homogeneity of the millions who, scattered over a continental domain, go to make up the American republic! The same facts, the same arguments, the same thoughts, the same ideals, which made New England overwhelmingly Republican on Tuesday last, brought a similar result equally decisive in the states on the Pacific slope, in the Rocky Mountain regions, in the prairie, Mississippi Valley and Middle West states. In this great decision there was no sectionalism, except in that portion of the republic where a partisan Democratic oligarchy has put the "mock" in democracy and made elections of no significance whatever as expressions of opinion and conviction upon national questions.

How truly national this verdict in behalf of the preservation of American nationality! With what finality it serves notice on the world that the American people are highly resolved that no man, or set of men, shall barter away the ideals, rights and interests of the American republic; that no man or set of men, indeed, shall ever be accepted abroad as having the right to pledge the faith of this nation to any compact in the formulation of which this self-governing people has not been consulted, and to which our assent has not been secured.

Here, indeed, is the one nation in the world, in which this problem of the proposed super-government of force was submitted to the people, discussed by them in their shops, homes, fields, mines as well as in the halls of legislation; where any serious effort was made by the masses of the people to reach a conclusion as to the merits of the proposals of the Paris peace conference for world government, and where the people were privileged, after consideration of the great questions involved, to register their decision. Every other nation which has subscribed to the unamended league covenant, has been committed to it not by the will of the people, but by the mere decision of officialism.

It has, indeed, been a great and solemn referendum; here we have seen, in this matter of vital moment to the whole world, the one instance of government of, by and for the people in the decision of a matter vital in its bearing upon the destiny of the people involved. We are told that some forty nations have accepted the covenant of the league of nations; what we have not been told is that in our country alone among all the great powers of earth there has been a deliberate decision of the matter based upon months of discussion and deliberation.

* * * * *

To attribute this tremendous groundswell of public sentiment to any one cause would be to ignore a dozen important elements which have contributed to Republican victory and Democratic defeat. It would be a waste of space to recount and to discuss them here. They have been fully discussed in the columns of this paper during the historic campaign just closed. The people were wearied with Wilsonism and all it represents. They were tired of autocracy, of usurpation, of inefficiency, of insincerity, of fine phrases unaccompanied by deeds which bore them out, of the concentration of the powers of government in the hands of an executive who felt himself above taking counsel with the representatives of the people in matters of public concern, of carelessness of the public interests as manifested in extravagance and waste. They were out of patience with breakers of pledges and betrayers of public trust; of government by a leadership capable of sacrificing public interests to personal and partisan ends.

Disgusted as the people were with the hopeless incompetency of the leadership in power, they were repelled even more by the administration's disavowal of a duty to represent and to serve the American people as against any other people or combination of people on earth. Visionaries may cry that the disposition of the great mass of the American people to think of their own republic first is a manifestation of national selfishness, but the average American knows that despite all this hypocritical profession of altruism, the man who does not think first of his own country does so because he is lacking in the loyalty to this republic that characterizes every true patriot. The average American knows that we have made great sacrifices in behalf of the rest of the world during the past few years and that these sacrifices, unaccompanied by any demand for material gain, have failed to earn for us the gratitude or even the respect of nations which have been busily engaged during the past two years in trying to grab every inch of soil, every dollar of money, every prospect of trade and every foot of shipping of which a fallen adversary could be despoiled.

* * * * *

The champions of the un-Americanized covenant of the league of nations may take whatever satisfaction they like out of the claim that the people repudiated the unexpurgated world constitution because they did not understand it. The truth is that we are the only people in the world who made any effort to understand it; who did not take it hand-me-down from its makers, thanking them for the privilege of rubber stamping our signatures upon it. The American people do not propose to have America Europeanized either by the conscious or unconscious agents of alien powers or by theoretical idealists who have lost the fundamental doctrines and ideals of Americanism through too much absorption of European "culture."

July 4, 1776, stands forth in American history as the day upon which the American colonies declared their freedom from European domination, and proclaimed themselves "free and independent states." November 2, 1920, will go down in American history as our second Independence day, when the American people served notice on the world that this national independence, so dearly bought and so long maintained, would never be surrendered, and that America proposes to maintain forever unimpaired, her sovereignty, her security and her ideals.

America is not now, has never been and never will be a hermit nation, careless of the welfare of the rest of the world. No nation in history has written so glorious a record of altruism in international relationships. Willingness to cooperate for the maintenance of the world's peace, prosperity and happiness does not mean, however, readiness to enter into political partnership with all the rest of the world without thought of the influence upon the destiny of this republic and of the world, of the surrender of America's right of independent decision upon the problems which affect the future of this one nation where public questions are actually thought out, and fought out in the great forum of public opinion.

AMERICANISM

But with the great triumph of Tuesday the task of Republicanism is not completed. It is only begun. As President-elect Harding has said, this is not the time for exultation, but, as Lincoln said, for "dedication to the great task remaining before us." Republican leadership faces the greatest task that has been committed to it since the inauguration of the first Republican President. Upon the ability of Republicanism to meet the new duties of this new occasion depends not merely the fate of the Republican party, but, in no small measure the destiny, even the safety, of the republic itself. The people have given expression to their bitter disappointment over Democratic failure. The failure of Republicanism would put millions of Americans in a frame of mind where they would say: "A plague on both your houses;" where they would lose confidence in party government and in representative republican government itself.

In the nature of things it will be impossible for Republicanism to satisfy all the elements which joined in Tuesday's vote of protest; for with many it was only a vote of protest, and not a vote of confidence in the Republican party. In the nature of things the next four years will witness greater activity on the part of revolutionary radicalism than has ever been known in this country before. This spirit is abroad in the world; the United States will not escape its dangers. The new administration will be subjected not only to reasonable, but to unfair criticism. The battle is on in this country between fundamental Americanism and European revolutionary radicalism; it will be the duty of those who believe in American institutions to rally to their defense during the next few years as never before, for now the necessity will be greater than ever before.

The Republican national platform of 1920 declared that too much must not be expected quickly in the restoration of satisfactory national conditions. The job, after eight years of Wilsonism, is one for a wrecking crew. The first task is to clear away the debris. Too much must not be expected from the development of elaborate "programs" of legislation. When a house is on fire, the first step toward reconstruction is to put out the fire. The first great task of the Republican party will be to stop many things that have been going on destructive of the general welfare. To restore efficiency in the administration of the public business; to put an end to criminal waste and extravagance; to reduce the operations of the national government to a business basis; this in itself is a giant task which must be accomplished before the work of building anew can be much advanced.

* * * * *

The National Republican has unbounded faith in the power for good in public affairs of common honesty and common sense. It has not the faith felt by many in the power of mere legislation to create social, economic or political perfection. The outstanding

lesson óf our recent national experience is the power of governmental authority, misused by misguided or ill-intentioned officialism, to inflict harm upon the people; to wreak havoc and spread
ruin. The country is suffering at this time from over-government.
Fundamentally the greatest harm done by the present national
administration has been the attempt to substitute in this country
the socialistic state under which the citizen is the slave and tool
of government, for the American conception of a government
which is the servant and the instrument of citizenship. This is
only another phase of the Europeanism which has held sway in
Washington as an attempted substitute for traditional Americanism. We have found that through this continual extension of the
power of government, this concentration of public power in the
hands of a few, and its exercise without regard to the basic principles of historic Americanism, great wrongs and abuses may be
created, and the people may be led to look upon the government
as an engine of compulsion and coercion rather than of service.

In such a crisis in national affairs, with its clear call for return
to the highway upon which our forefathers set the feet of this
republic in the days of Washington, no leader better fitted for the
tremendous tasks ahead could have been chosen than Warren G.
Harding. Comparatively unknown to the American people at the
beginning of the campaign which has resulted in his triumphant
election, the people have come to believe that in him they have
found one who will enter upon the work of national restoration
with the humility, the wisdom, the courage, the patriotism, the
common sense requisite to the mighty task committed to his
hands.

The people believe that President-elect Harding will bring to
the highest post of responsibility in the world, the courage, the
vision, the loyalty, the wisdom, above all the spirit of consecration to duty, which will enable the Republican party, and the American people, under his leadership, to meet and solve the great
problems which now confront the nation. The American people
have responded to the call of Republicanism for a Congress in
harmony with the purposes of the new administration. We are
assured of the team-work at Washington essential to the har-
monious functioning of the two branches of government which
must cooperate in the development of a national program.

We are to enter again, in national affairs, upon an era of government by common counsel. The newly elected President has
announced his intention of calling to larger participation in government the Vice President of the United States. In Governor
Coolidge the American people have chosen a Vice President competent to restore the second office in the republic to that larger
place in the national economy contemplated by Senator Harding.
Senator Harding will be found consulting the Vice President; he
will choose a cabinet, not of puppets and rubber stamps, but of

men of demonstrated capacity, and he will consult his cabinet; he will consult the representatives of the people in the Congress; he will confer with representative men and women in private life; he will consult with Democrats as well as Republicans. The day of White House isolation, of personal government, is over; the windows are to be thrown open. The business of the American people is to be transacted within their view and with their help, by a President who enters upon his duties with no delusion that he is a super-man, or an inspired prophet, but only with the thought of serving well the people who have committed to his hands the national leadership, the world leadership, involved in election to the Presidency of the United States.

* * * * *

But the responsibility does not belong alone to the new President or to the new Congress. The rank and file of Republicanism has its part to play in the new era upon which we are about to enter. It must stand behind, and support and uphold Republican leadership in all that it may undertake for the country's good. It must insist upon cooperation of all elements of Republicanism at Washington. It must demand that every man entrusted with a commission to public service through the favor of Republicanism, must subordinate personal and factional ends to the common welfare of the party and the country. The people have not elected individuals to office. They have chosen the Republican party for leadership. We must have a restoration of party responsibility and of party government, using that term in no narrow or proscriptive sense, but in the sense that Republican leadership must counsel together in the formulation of policies, and then loyally cooperate in their execution.
—November 8, 1920.

We are in the war and we can come out of it only as conquerors or conquered, victorious or dishonored: as an independent or a subject nation. Our lives, our homes, our institutions, all that Washington fought for and Lincoln died for, are at stake. Our only way out now is to fight it out for the simple cause of America and Americans. We must, as John Hancock said, "hang together or hang separately." The man who in public or private life subordinates this cause to any other consideration, no matter what, or who fails in the full, devoted and efficient performance of his duty to the nation, is a traitor to himself, his family, the republic and the right.—An editorial printed in The National Republican every week during American participation in the World war.

I speak as one who is old-fashioned enough to believe that the government of the United States of America is good enough for me.—Warren G. Harding.

A LEAGUE OF JUSTICE vs. A LEAGUE OF FORCE

Much of the discussion in the public press of the probable attitude of the next national administration on the league of nations issue, is a mixture of speculation and propaganda entitled to little more consideration than the serious discussion by the same journalists of the "drift to Cox" during the last three or four weeks of the recent campaign.

There is no ground for doubt as to the attitude of the new administration toward the Wilson league of nations, or any other league or association or scheme of super-sovereignty which involves the sacrifice of American independence, rights, interests or ideals. It was made clear in many public utterances by Senator Harding. The election result was a repudiation of the whole plan of sacrificing America for the sake of Europe, in whose behalf America has already sacrificed so much, without the hope or desire for recompense. The American people said with an emphasis never to be forgotten that they were not in favor of guaranteeing European peace at the sacrifice of American safety; that they were not in favor of stabilizing European finance at the sacrifice of American prosperity; that they were not in favor of risking American ideals in order that certain more or less definite and tangible world ideas might be put to the test of experiment, until, at least, we had better evidence than was at hand of the sincerity of European profession of a willingness to adopt a system of international ethics of which their own recent conduct has constituted an almost continuous repudiation.

Unquestionably the whole league idea, even as modified by Americanizing reservations, has been endangered by the stubbornness of its chief American exponent in refusing to accept modifications of the covenant as he brought it home from Europe. The more the American people have talked about and thought about the plan of involving the United States in the affairs of Europe, the more they have become awakened to the dangers of our unguarded participation in world politics. Presumably President Wilson thought, when he welcomed the plan to submit the covenant to a "great and solemn" referendum, that he, in his position, represented American public opinion. Possibly he has suffered no awakening as the result of the election verdict of November 2nd, —for with some people voices in the air are truer indices of public sentiment than a popular decision itself, however overwhelming in its character. Presumably there were other people similarly deluded. Yet upon the issue the Wilsonian candidate was unable to carry a single state of the Union in which there is a free, untrammelled expression of genuine public sentiment on public questions at the polls, losing the country by a vote approaching a two to one proportion.

* * * * *

This paper long ago called attention to the fundamental weakness of the proposed world constitution, in that its very formulation was by methods alien to the spirit of American constitutional government or representative republican government of any sort. We are not accustomed in this country to have constitutions and laws handed down to us from on high. It has always been the theory of our form of government that legislation was the function of representatives of the people deliberately chosen for that purpose. But in the case of this proposed world constitution the most undemocratic, the most unrepublican methods, were employed in its preparation. Those who wrote it were not chosen for the task by the peoples, or even the governments, they supposedly represented. They were ambassadors to a peace council, created for the purpose of settling the immediate issues of a great war. They chose, without the slightest semblance of authority for so doing, to resolve themselves into a constitutional convention for the formulation of the fundamental law of a world government.

It is not usually true that you can get right results by wrong methods. The whole league plan began with flagrant usurpation by its sponsors. It was developed in an atmosphere of secrecy and intrigue entirely inconsistent with the ideals professed by the authors of the scheme. There was an exclusion of public opinion not only in the nations directly concerned in the formulation of the covenant, but in the neutral nations and generally throughout the world, which made it impossible that anything actually representative of the desires of the people of the world should be evolved. This is the only nation in the world in which the people, after thorough debate and deliberation, passed judgment upon the scheme and the manner of its evolution. But for the wise provision of the American Constitution that the American people, through their legislative representatives, must be consulted in international decisions affecting themselves, the unamended covenant would have been shoved over on them just as successfully as it has been upon the peoples of other nations not accustomed to deciding questions of this kind for themselves.

* * * * *

The people of the United States are willing to commit themselves to the determination of international questions by equity, but not to their decision by political processes in which we would play a subordinate part, and in which we might become the victims of alien alliances and combinations of interest.

We believe the American people would be willing to choose representatives to a world congress assembled for the purpose of formulating a complete code of international law, erecting a world court chosen to act in a legal rather than a representative capacity, in the determination of all future subjects of international dispute, subject to such reservations as that no power in either hemisphere shall seek to extend further its territory in the other hemisphere, the doctrine which with America is a better guarantee against becoming involved in the complications of European politics than any league of nations could be. We believe the American people could agree with the rest of the world upon the question of what international problems are justiciable, and which are fundamentally domestic and therefore not properly subject to decision by extraneous authority. Such a question, undoubtedly, is that of every nation to determine upon what conditions, and to what extent, aliens may enter, live and transact business in it. America would not leave to any court the question of whether an unlimited number of orientals may come into the country, nor would any other civilized nation menaced by possible inundation from that quarter. America would not leave to any court the question of our right to protect and foster our own industries to the end that our own standard of wages and living and rewards for enterprise may be maintained, nor would any friendly nation seriously ask that we should do this.

We believe the American people would gladly consent to a mutual plan of world disarmament, requiring that nations should abolish conscription for military service and maintain only such armies and navies as may be necessary to police their own territories. Nothing of that sort, be it remembered, is provided for except in a few indefinite phrases in the covenant of the league of nations. We believe they would gladly agree to cooperation with the rest of the world in agreeing to treat as a pariah any nation which refused to observe good faith, give to all nationals residing within their borders the equal protection of their laws as to person and property, and respect the decisions of the world court.

It has been argued that The Hague tribunal failed to prevent the World war, and that any mere judicial arrangement would have the same weakness. The Hague tribunal and the whole plan of international arbitration failed for the simple reason that the great powers of Europe were not inspired by the purposes and ideals which before the World war made peaceable determination of international disputes possible. Until they are controlled by such purposes and ideals, any plan for international cooperation will fail. That statement applies more forcibly to the league of nations as proposed in the Paris covenant than to any other scheme yet suggested.

The World war has not whetted the taste for war throughout the world. Rather it has sickened the people of the world with war as never before. The people are ready for peace. Only the diplomats, the professional politicians of the Old World, only the masters of the present Russian despotism, anxious to ravage and loot the world, only certain survivals of mediaeval militarism in the Orient, stand in the way. Not for the next generation would any government dare reject the decision of a great judicial tribunal, solemnly rendered after a full hearing of the cause; no government would dare go to war with the subjects of dispute pending before such a tribunal. And if there should remain such a nation, the object lesson of ruined Germany will long linger in the minds of men to deter governmental leaders from flying in the face of world opinion.

* * * * *

The world's peace will be best preserved not by the creation of a political world machine, not by setting up somewhere in Europe a world Congress to become the center of world intrigue, where nation will be played against nation by the skilled masters of diplomacy, but by the creation of a code of law and procedure, based upon equity, to which all nations will mutually agree to yield respect and obedience, within those limitations necessary for the preservation of national self-respect and independence.

The historic error of President Wilson in yielding to the idea of a world government, rather than standing sponsor for world jurisprudence and a world court, may be retrieved by President Harding in requesting the nations of the world to choose representatives to a world assembly, to meet in Washington, the capital of the one great power which is not trying to put anything over in world politics, and there to agree upon a code of international law covering every possible phase of future dispute, and the creation of a world supreme court, composed of representatives of the highest judicial tribunals of the great powers; each of the chief powers to select one representative, perhaps, the remainder of the court to be chosen of representatives of the smaller powers serving alternately. There might be added to the supreme court, indeed, a secondary chamber corresponding to the league assembly, composed of legal representatives of all the associated nations, to which might be given the power, by a two-thirds vote, to return for modification decrees of the supreme body.

This is the form of internationalism which would be desired by any nation which is actually seeking justice rather than advantage, in arrangements ostensibly perfected for preserving the world's peace. Lasting peace can be based only upon justice. Justice can be based only upon fundamental principles of right and wrong. The trouble with the arrangement perfected at Paris was that those chiefly interested in its formulation did not honestly desire the rule of justice throughout the world. Their thought was only to advance their own interests. The nations of the world should be given an opportunity to prove their good faith in present protestations of a purpose to bring about the reign of peace and of

justice throughout the world. By the proposal of a world agreement upon the fundamental principles of international law and
relationship, and the creation of a court acting in a legal rather
than a political capacity to interpret and apply these principles;
by the further proposal of a definite agreement of decreases of
armament; by an agreement to support the decisions of the world
tribunal by every economic weapon at the command of the associated nations; by these and similar proposals the test of good
faith would be applied to the great powers and the smaller nations
of the world.

As to whether or not we should become parties to the treaty of
Paris is not a matter of great concern to Americans. Its indemnities and territorial dispositions do not affect us. Self interest
does not prompt our participation, and for the injustices of the
treaty, many of which are clear enough, we have no reason to
share responsibility. With Germany and Austria disarmed and
crippled beyond the possibility of early recovery, we need no guarantee against the aggressions of our former foes. Nor is there
any apparent necessity for our participation in the enforcement
of provisions of the treaty which the beneficiary nations may be
depended upon to execute. Our separate peace with the central
powers long ago became an actuality.

* * * * *

No motive of self interest prompts this nation to desire membership in any world government so constituted as to involve the
danger of American complication in the combinations and collisions
of European politics. No one but a madman or a theorist drunk
with his own impractical ideas would wish to make American
peace contingent, for all time to come, on European peace. For
Americans know that the soil of Europe, with its crazy quilt of
jarring nationalities, is sown thick with the seed of age-old rivalries, hatreds and conflicting ambitions; racial, religious, territorial
and dynastic. Americans who understand the theory of their own
government and the merit of its institutions, know that the obstacles to peace are greater now than ever, since Europe's further
departure from the American idea of federation and international
admixture toward the war-breeding plan of "self determination of
peoples." We have shown the whole world by our great experiment that under a government which exists for public service,
rather than for oppression and exploitation, peoples and states
which might otherwise be at war may be united in loyalty to one
flag. Our representatives at Paris should have sought a more
united, and not a more divided Europe. With sixteen new nations
sixteen more causes of war have been created. Yet it is seriously
proposed that we shall take pot luck with humanity in the matter
of peace, economic stability and financial integrity, which, otherwise stated, means that we shall assume a contract to feed, fight
and finance the world.

AMERICANISM

Justice and peace are the need of the world. There can be peace only through justice. Justice is attainable through equity, and not through force. America should lead the world to peace through justice.
—November 20, 1920.

Our foreign policy is always at last determined by the processes of popular opinion. For this reason, it is the duty of citizens to know as much as possible of the questions which they themselves must decide, of the history of our principal international events and of the diplomatic policy of our country.

The diplomacy of the United States had its origin with the Revolution, by which our liberties were secured. Its principal representatives in Europe were Benjamin Franklin and John Adams. They were great men; but the latter was by disposition singularly unfit for a diplomatic position. Dogmatic, suspicious, turbulent, domineering, bluntly and inflexibly honest, burning with a love of country which sometimes set fire to and consumed the objects of his noblest efforts, Adams left little trace of his exertions upon our foreign relations except the traits of his character.

Franklin went to France as our envoy in 1776. He was then seventy years of age. In less than two years he had negotiated a treaty by which the most absolute monarch in Europe, excepting the sultan and the czar, agreed to make common cause against England, with a republic which was itself a protest against his royal tenure by Divine right, and "to guaranty to the United States their liberty, sovereignty and independence absolute and unlimited, with all their present possessions, or which they should have at the conclusion of the war."

This is the most momentous event in our diplomatic history. It made our independence unquestionably secure. It is more than doubtful whether our ancestors could have succeeded without it. It was also momentous for Europe in its consequences. The soldiers of France saw in the United States a religion without an established church, a free press, a government by the people. When they returned, they set up their examples before the French people, whose thoughts had been liberalized, whose devoutness had been impaired, whose sense of allegiance had been weakened by the encyclopaedists and their propagandists. The French Revolution came within ten years, and it is sad to read in its annals, as passing under the knife of the guillotine many a noble head which was crested with exaltation in the fleet of De Grasse, and in the army of Rochambeau, when Cornwallis surrendered at Yorktown.

Franklin was a born diplomatist, and he was much more. His genius for negotiation was but one face of his many-sided character.

This old man appeared in the gayest and most conventional

court in Europe, in the midst of the most elaborately artificial society ever known to civilization, in plain coat, white hose, spectacles on nose, and wearing a soft white hat. And that court and society were at once charmed and subdued by his majestic and simple presence.

It is impossible to read the accounts of his transactions in Europe without realizing his patience, his method, his foresight, his knowledge of all kinds of human nature, his finesse, his righteous dissimulation, his impregnability to be overreached by anybody, his capacity to get the better of everybody who attempted to outwit him, his firmness, his integrity, his proud humility. All these are manifest throughout his entire career in Europe, and they are particularly plain in the negotiations of the treaty by which Great Britain recognized our independence.

He formed the model upon which American diplomacy has ever since generally been shaped,—plain dealing, plain speaking, simple dignity, adequate, but not superfluous, ceremonial and unswerving fidelity to the interests of his country alone.—Cushman K. Davis.

Columbia, Columbia, to glory arise,
The queen of the world, and child of the skies!
Thy genius commands thee; with rapture behold,
While ages on ages thy splendors unfold,
Thy reign is the last, and the noblest of time,
Most fruitful thy soil, most inviting thy clime;
Let the crimes of the east ne'er crimson thy name,
Be freedom, and science, and virtue, thy fame.

To conquest, and slaughter, let Europe aspire;
Whelm nations in blood, and wrap cities in fire:
Thy heroes the rights of mankind shall defend,
And triumph pursue them, and glory attend.
A world is thy realm; for a world be thy laws,
Enlarg'd as thine empire, and just as thy cause;
On Freedom's broad basis, that empire shall rise,
Extend with the main, and dissolve with the skies.
—Timothy Dwight.

This (Monroe) doctrine, so profound of import, was not, we apprehend, the sudden creation of individual thought, but the result rather of slow processes in our public mind, which had been constantly intent upon problems of self-government, and intensely observant of our continental surroundings; though carried forward, no doubt, like other ideas in the colonial epoch, by the energy and clearer conviction of statesmen who could foresee and link conceptions into a logical chain. Neutrality as to European affairs, freedom from all entangling alliances with the Old World, was the legacy of experience which Washington bequeathed to his successors. This might have seemed at first to discourage all external influence, and remit our union to the selfish and isolated pursuit of its own interests. But the annexation of Louisiana proved that the union itself was destined to expand over an uncertain area of this continent. And, when, inspired by our example, the Spanish colonies of the American continent were seen one after another to shake off the yoke of the parent country, and spontaneously assert their independence, the philanthropic leaders—and none among them so quickly or so persistently as Jefferson—began to predict the fraternal cooperation in the future of these free republics, all modelled alike, in a common scheme for self-preservation which should shut out Europe, its rulers and its systems of monarchy forever from this hemisphere; for by such means only could the germ of self-government expand, and the luxuriant growth of this hardy plant make it impossible that the monarchical idea should ever strike a deep root in American soil. * * * When liberty struggled in America we were not—we could not be—neutral. The time of announcement and the choice of expression, nevertheless, awaited events. * * * It was the courage of a great people personified in a firm chief magistrate that put the fire into those few momentous though moderate sentences, and made them glow like the writing at Belshazzar's feast. * * *— James Schouler, 1885.

The years that are before us are a virgin page. We can inscribe them as we will. The future of our country rests upon us. The happiness of posterity depends on us. The fate of humanity may be in our hands. That pleading voice, choked with the sobs of ages, which has so often spoken to deaf ears, is lifted up to us. It asks us to be brave, benevolent, consistent, true to the teachings of our history, proving "Divine descent by worth divine." It asks us to be virtuous, building up public virtue upon private worth; seeking that righteousness that exalteth nations. It asks us to be patriotic, loving our country before all other things, making her happiness our happiness, her honors ours, her fame our own. It asks us in the name of charity, in the name of freedom, in the name of God!—Henry Armitt Brown.

The Monroe Doctrine is a simple and plain statement that the people of the United States oppose the creation of European dominion on American soil; that they oppose the transfer of the political sovereignty of American soil to European powers; and that any attempt to do these things will be regarded as "dangerous to our peace and safety." What the remedy should be for such interposition by European powers the doctrine does not pretend to state. But this much is certain; that when the people of the United States consider anything "dangerous to their peace and safety" they will do as other nations do, and, if necessary, defend their peace and safety with force of arms.

The doctrine does not contemplate forcible intervention by the United States in any legitimate contest, but it will not permit any such contest to result in the increase of European power or influence on this continent nor in the overthrow of an existing government, nor in the establishment of a protectorate over them, nor in the exercise of any direct control over their policy or institutions. Further than this the doctrine does not go.—John Bach McMaster, 1897.

Ye sons of Columbia, who bravely have fought
  For those rights, which unstained from your sires have de-
            scended,
May you long taste the blessings your valor has bought,
  And your sons tread the soil which their fathers defended.
      'Mid the reign of mild peace,
      May your nation increase,
With the glory of Rome, and the wisdom of Greece;
  And ne'er shall the sons of Columbia be slaves,
  While the earth bears a plant, or the sea rolls its waves.

Our mountains are crowned with imperial oak,
  Whose roots, like our liberties, ages have nourished,
But long ere our nation submits to the yoke,
  Not a tree shall be left on the field where it flourished.
      Should invasion impend,
      Every grove would descend
From the hill-tops they shaded, our shores to defend.

Let our patriots destroy Anarch's pestilent worm,
  Lest our liberty's growth should be checked by corrosion;
Then let clouds thicken round us; we heed not the storm;
  Our realm fears no shock, but the earth's own explosion;
      Foes assail us in vain,
      Though their fleets bridge the main,
For our altars and laws, with our lives, we'll maintain.
                  —Robert Treat Paine, Jr.

Fellow Citizens: Clouds and darkness are 'round about Him. His pavilion is dark waters and thick clouds of the sky. Justice and judgment are the establishment of His throne. Mercy and truth shall go before His face. Fellow Citizens: God reigns, and the government at Washington still lives.—James A. Garfield.

THE NATIONAL REPUBLICAN

WASHINGTON, D. C.

Following is the prospectus and platform of The National Republican issued upon the removal of the publication to the national capital in January, 1918. It will be noted that the policy laid down for the publication at that time has been followed unswervingly in the editorial utterances of the succeeding three years as quoted in the pages of this volume.

A national, weekly, condensed review of public affairs, published from the center of national events.

A mouthpiece of traditional, constructive principles and policies which have secured to this republic economic independence, material wealth and moral greatness.

A foe of that revolutionary, unreasoning radicalism, which would abandon the landmarks of representative government, and risk in academic experiment the perpetuity of the great constitutional system under which this nation has enjoyed a century and a third of orderly, progressive government, safeguarding those rights of person and property for the preservation of which, as essential to human happiness, governments are instituted among men. It stands for the perfecting, rather than the destruction, of that system.

An enemy of socialism, anarchism and bolshevism, whether open or covert, in public or private life.

An advocate of industrial peace, through justice to all elements of American citizenship, and the overthrow of demagogism, with its appeals to class prejudice and hatred; to envy and cupidity, to laziness and disloyalty, to indifference and inefficiency.

A preacher of the duties as well as the rights of American citizenship; its obligations, as well as its opportunities.

An antidote for that vast volume of socialistic and anarchistic agitation which is flooding the country, polluting public sentiment, undermining the faith of the people in the historic fundamentals of Americanism, destroying the industrial and political efficiency of the American people, and tending to establish in this country, in place of just and judicious government, that irresponsible usurpation of power by class-conscious groups which has hurled Russia from the extreme of autocracy to that of anarchy and wiped it from the map of the world as a power.

A champion of a stalwart, unwavering Americanism, which at all times and everywhere throughout the world stands for the protection of lives and rights of American citizens, on sea or land, on this and other continents; which is for America first, last and all the time, and would sacrifice no just interest of the American people in behalf of any visionary scheme of internationalism; which will devote itself in domestic legislation and administration, and in its diplomacy, to the welfare of America and Americans, backing its words with deeds, and commanding respect for itself in both hemispheres by deserving, firmly demanding and promptly enforcing that respect where it is not voluntarily yielded.

A propagandist of preparedness for war in time of peace, and for peace in time of war; for the protection of the American people against the invasion of arms and the invasion of foreign competitors armed with the weapon of a cheapness attained through the sacrifice of human values.

A foe of sectionalism, of political division based upon class or occupational self-interest, of corruption and intimidation, of the use of great government agencies having the power of life and death over industry, for personal and partisan purposes.

An advocate of the doing, by parties, party leaders and individuals, in all matters affecting the public interest, of that which is morally and intellectually safe and right, rather than the merely expedient thing.

A believer in the Republican party as the natural conservator and administrator of the fundamental traditions and doctrines of historic Americanism, laboring, as the organ of no feud, faction or individual, for the upbuilding of that party, from without and within, as an essential instrumentality for the preservation and progress of the republic in whose history it has written so many splendid pages, and, if true to its traditions, will write many more.

CPSIA information can be obtained
at www.ICGtesting.com
Printed in the USA
LVHW020725241118
598014LV00009B/202